GRACIE FIELDS

A BIOGRAPHY

JOAN MOULES

SUMMERSDALE

Copyright © Joan Moules 1997

Summersdale Publishers Ltd
46 West Street
Chichester
West Sussex
PO19 1RP UK

A CIP catalogue record for this book is available from the British Library.

ISBN 1 84024 001 6

**Printed and bound in Great Britain
by Creative Print and Design Wales, Ebbw Vale**

For my grandchildren

CARA, ANGHARAD,
REBECCA and DANIEL

with love

Acknowledgements

Boris Alperovici, Clifford Ashton, Lillian Aza, Will Ayling, BBC Written Archives, BBC Tape Unit, BBC Sound Recording, BBC Copyright, Bernard Braden, Irene Bevan, Broadfield School, Stanley Clements, Russ Conway, Mary & Leon Davey, Florence Desmond, Sir Anton Dolin, EMI Records, Norman Empire, Harold Fielding, Joy & Frank Foster, Cecil Gilmour, Nat Gonella, Alan Goode, Larry Grayson, Edna and Bill Grime, Doris Hare, Hilda Harris, Margaret Hazell, Teddy Holmes, John Graven Hughes, Norman Jackson, Mr Jefferson, George F. Letts, Dennis Lowndes, Geoff Love, Evelyn Lucas, *Manchester Evening News*, Lord Bernard Miles, Dorothy Mitchell (Doris Paul), Lady Morrison, Mona Newman, Grace Orbell, Tony Parry, J.B. Priestley, David Pluckrose, Hazel Provost, Ray Rastall, Red Funnel Group, Rochdale Library, Rochdale Museum, *Rochdale Observer*, Mr Rushworth, Gertie Sammon, Semprini, Fred Shepherd, Donald Sinden, Bill Sowerbutts, Cyril Smith, May Snowdon, Rosalind and Neil Somerville, Michael Stansfield, Annette Stansfield, Tommy Stansfield, Patience Strong, John Taylor, Roy Taylor, Dame Eva Turner, Derek Warman, Bob Watts, Mary Whipp, Nell Whitwell, Paul Ward, Mr Wilde, Maurice Warburton, Debbie Walker (Rochdale Museum Service).

I also thank the many newspapers for permission to use reviews and *Lancashire Life* for its article.

Thanks also to the Associated Newspapers Group and to the publishers of the following books: *I Had To Be Wee* by Georgie Wood (Hutchinson), *Me and the Mediterranean* by Naomi Jacob (Hutchinson), *Sing As We Go* by Gracie Fields (Frederick Muller), *The Greasepaint War* by John Graven Hughes (New English Library), *Our Gracie* by Bert Aza (Pitkins).

To my husband, Leon Moules, for the many journeys initially to talk to and record the views of people who knew or met Gracie in several different aspects of her life.

Most of all to Gracie herself for being such a warm, lovely person who brightened our world for so many years.

Contents

Prologue

It was bitterly cold in the bedroom above the fish and chip shop in Molesworth Street, Rochdale, but nineteen year old Jenny Stansfield was sweating. She was in labour with her first child, and on 9th January 1898 her daughter, Grace, was born.

In 1979 that daughter became Dame Gracie Fields, arguably the most loved and revered British entertainer of modern times.

She reached the top of the show business tree after years of touring to become not simply a star, but a national figure. Singer, dancer, actress, comedienne - in the thirties the police put out the same traffic controls for three people: the King, the Queen, and Gracie Fields.

She became a legend during her eighty-one years on earth, and legends are notoriously difficult to live with or write about. They shouldn't be, for they start and finish life the same as anyone else. Gracie always realised this and, whatever other faults she had, her size in hats stayed the same.

When the house where she was born was demolished to make way for a new factory, one of her fans took the latch from the door and sent it to her in Capri. He knew she would understand why he had done this. For although so much of her heart was in the Mediterranean island where she lived for over forty years, a part of it never left Rochdale in Lancashire, and all of it stayed in England and with her own folk.

Known affectionately as Our Gracie, she was honoured many times, both in her own country and abroad, for wartime exploits, for services to all branches of entertainment, for her work for hospitals - and Italy even made her an Official Knight of the Republic for her services to tourism.

In her fifties she had records in the hit parade, was the subject of two *Desert Island Disc* programmes (1951 & 1961) and a *This Is Your Life* (1960).

Every entertainer is a private person as well, and in her life Gracie knew tragedy and triumph, happiness and heartbreak. She married three times but an operation for a cancerous growth resulted in a hysterectomy and denied her the chance of children of her own. So she opened and supported an orphanage for the children of actors and actresses. 'The best investment I ever made,' she called it.

Although she became rich and famous she never lost touch with reality. Her confidence offstage was a frail thing which she covered well but which often left her lonely. Gracie was a communicator, who got through to people of all ages and in all walks of life. Some of her songs have become part of our heritage, and her memory lingers in the hearts of her legions of friends and fans of all ages, an inspiration for all.

The loving salute she gave her audiences became her trademark, along with a scarf which transformed her into anything she wanted to be, from housewife to duchess.

She went from mill town to millionaire island. She was usually talked of as an ex-mill girl, which she was, yet she spent little time in the mill itself. She was rich for longer than she was poor, but poverty often leaves the deeper impression, and she never forgot, nor wanted to forget, the destitute days. She did good by stealth as well as publicly; no one will ever know how much money she gave to needy causes, both public and private, during her lifetime, but it was a vast amount. All the private documents I have seen verify this.

She lived through two world wars, entertaining the troops both times, and saw tremendous changes in the way of life of working class people - her kind of people. She had a roguish wit and a huge personality. Her magnificent voice never let her down, something she attributed to it being 'a gift from God which I kept clean and true with work and practice.'

Her love for Italian-born Monty Banks, whom she married early in 1940, brought her the greatest conflict with her public. It involved two of the most poignant emotions anyone can face, love and duty, for three months after their marriage her husband faced internment as 'an enemy alien'. His death, a decade later, devastated her.

Her indomitable willpower and the love of her audiences got her through that dark period eventually. Of that love, from stage to auditorium and back, she said, 'It's like an invisible silver thread between us.'

She was a multi-talented lady, ambitious, and tremendously professional, but anybody who can win a nation's love - a world's love - and keep it for over fifty years, in spite of vast differences of opinion because of personal choices, must have something extra. Circumstances, character, temperament, talent: they all count, but there is a spark in every one of us that can make us the person we want to be. We all have the power within us to turn that spark into a flame. Dame Gracie made it blaze.

Joan Moules

1. The Early Years

Gracie Fields was in America when the 1979 New Year Honours List was published. 'Dame Gracie' ran the headlines, just one week before her eighty-first birthday.

She came over in February to receive her award from the Queen Mother. Crowds of fans were waiting outside Buckingham Palace for her. It was a cold day, but Gracie, well wrapped in an apricot mink, waved happily to the people outside the Palace. She was nervous: 'It was like a first night', she said.

As her car drove through the Palace gates, the cameras clicked. Gracie wound the window of the car down so the fans could get their pictures. It was almost second nature with her to make it as easy as possible. Over the years a wonderful rapport grew between Gracie and her fans - a tangible feeling, strong and honest; as they waved, and she waved back, you could feel the gaiety in the air. It was like a party, the fact that Gracie was going to receive the highest accolade, official recognition at last. Many of her admirers felt that she should have had it twenty or more years earlier, but the delight in the crowds outside the Palace was evident then.

The band played, television cameras rolled, people talked, reporters roamed amongst the crowd recording interviews; and all the while the excitement mounted.

After a time, cars began to return. Air Force, police, then, after a long while, the Queen Mother drove through, beautiful and gracious as ever. The people waved, and still the crowds stayed. The Victoria Memorial was crawling with life - people clung on and watched, waiting for the car that would bring Dame Gracie through the gold-tipped gates.

She came at last, and she waved and smiled, but it wasn't enough for everyone. On this day of days they wanted to see more of her, and suddenly, like a huge wave that had got out of control, the great crowd surged across the road and into the path of Gracie's car. The driver stopped as people lay across the bonnet, peered into the windows, trying for a glimpse of their idol. All traffic was held up (not for the first time - Gracie was always a traffic-stopper). The driver did not dare to move for fear of hurting the people surrounding the car.

Looking rather nervous, but with a courage she had displayed so often in her life, Gracie stepped from the car. And there, outside Buckingham Palace, with traffic squeezing by where it could, she talked to her fans.

There was a party that evening and those present toasted Dame Gracie. 'I'm still the same cup of tea I've always been,' she said, 'I haven't changed colour or anything.'

Grace Stansfield was the first of Jenny and Fred Stansfield's four children. She was born on January 9th 1898, in the bedroom above her grandmother's fish and chip shop in Molesworth Street, Rochdale, Lancashire. Grandmother Sarah couldn't read or write - she never had the chance to learn because she started work in the coalpits at six years old. Her job was to open and close the heavy iron doors between each shaft to let through the pit ponies pulling the coal trucks. She worked twelve hours a day. Later she went into service - where she eventually met Fred's father.

His family were mill owners and he was an alcoholic. Young Sarah refused to marry him in spite of pressure from her family. Fred never knew him, and in fact he died quite young.

By the time Fred was out to work, Sarah had married Jim Leighton. She took in lodgers, saved every penny she could, and eventually bought a barbers shop for £15. She sold the stock and refurbished it as a fish and chip shop. Sarah was a bit of a character around Rochdale. She once took a lodger because she was sorry for him, he had nowhere to go; then after a few weeks she had four of them. It built her savings up, but she gave them all notice in the end because she couldn't get near her own fireplace. She wasn't afraid of hard work and became known as Chip Sarah.

Gracie's mother, Jenny, born in 1879, was baptized Sarah Jane Bamford. Orphaned at ten, she went to live with an aunt in Rochdale and, like many children then, worked in a cotton mill. Her aunt sent her to Sunday School twice a day on the sabbath, and to the Band of Hope several evenings a week. Jenny used to play truant whenever she could and go to the music hall instead. When she was fourteen she left her aunts and went to live with two friends from the mill. Her evenings at the music hall seemed magical and gave her a lifelong ambition to go on the stage.

Blond, curly haired Fred Stansfield became an engineer on a cargo boat, and worked his passage to America to work for his uncle in Massachusetts. When he was twenty-one he returned, having bought high heeled boots and a huge stetson hat that he wore around town to impress the girls. It impressed Jenny, who thought with a hat like that he must surely be an actor. When he spoke to her in a Lancashire accent she was initially disappointed, but he soon won her over and after a short courtship they married in Rochdale parish church.

Fred went to work for Robinsons Engineering Works, and they lived with his mother, Chip Sarah. A year later, in the bedroom above the chip shop, Grace first tried out her lungs, those lungs that were later to be described by reviewers as 'leather lungs with a silver lining.'

Within a few years Betty and Edith arrived. As the eldest, Grace often had to help with her sisters, and later with her brother, who was born when she was ten.

Whenever Fred had a rise they moved. This was the pattern of Gracie's childhood - each time there was sixpence a week more wages, it meant another house - always in Rochdale, but 'We're going oop in the world', Jenny told them all.

Rochdale then, in the early 1900s, was a busy mill town. There were few motor cars: only the very rich could afford them, and in any case many fought shy of this noisy, modern monster. Mostly it was horse and carriage for the mill owners, and the tram or Shanks's pony for the rest. The trams ran through the centre of the town, and for the thrill of it young Grace Stansfield used to hang onto the back of a tram when it started and run with it until it went too fast to hold on to.

They had few toys: Grace had a 'bogie', a handmade truck that she used to pile her sisters and brother into and pull round the streets. Rochdale is very hilly, and they often used the bogie as a sledge, whizzing down the hills to the danger of anyone walking by. 'Mostly though it was quiet in the daytime', Gracie recalled. 'When the mills were working there were few people on the streets.'

She also had a hoop, 'and we all played hopscotch, jacks and dabbers. Cowboys and Indians was a favourite game, though I was too good an Indian, no one could ever find me!' She went paddling in the canal, and learnt to swim in the canal too, against parental rules, but right from a small child she loved the water.

Grace Stansfield knew from an early age that she would go on the stage, because her mother told her so - knew also that if she wasn't talented enough, or professional enough, she would finish in the mill.

The mills dominated the skyline of Rochdale, their chimneys standing tall and proud above the town. They manufactured cotton, wool and rayon, and sent their products all over the world. Barry Cockcroft, writing in 1956 (when Rochdale still had forty mills working) said about Gracie's voice, 'The high note on the second "Sally" is the one the mill girl has to hit if she's to make herself heard in the next line of the noisy doubling department. It has a quality peculiar to the cotton mill.'

The Pennines circled the town, giving escape from the noise and grime of industry. A short walk or a penny tramride and there were the hills, the fresh air, and the freedom of green, green space.

In each house they lived in, Grace and her sisters slept together, all three in one large bed. Each place looked the same - flagstone floor in the kitchen, steel fender with a bright ragged rug in front, and on the mantelpiece two shiny brass candlesticks. A wooden kitchen table and chairs, and light from a gas lamp.

The parlour, used for high days, holidays and funerals, had cream lace curtains and rose patterned wallpaper. A carpet square in the centre of the room, over lineoleum, and a grandfather clock that had lost its chime. The sofa and matching chairs, stiff and shiny, were ranged round a marble-styled fireplace.

The heart of the house, whichever house in whichever street, was always the kitchen, where in winter a fire blazed cheerfully and the gas lamps shone on the pictures Jenny bought with the Mazawattee tea coupons: 'Rock of Ages', showing a storm tossed sea and a girl clinging to a sturdy cross-shaped rock, and, Jenny's favourite, 'Driven From Home', depicting a woman clasping her baby and being driven from the house by an angry and shocked father.

Betty, three years younger than Grace, and known in the family as Our Lizzie, had fiery red curls. Edith's hair, also curly, was dark, and she was very pretty with sherry coloured eyes and a gentle nature. Gracie's hair was blonde with a hint of ginger like Betty's, but there the resemblance stopped, for hers was totally straight. Strangely, she wasn't the most mischievous of the family - that title went to Betty. I say strangely because from the public figure most of us know it would be easy to imagine her as the leader of the gang; but as a child, Grace, as she was known then, was very shy and seldom spoke up for herself.

When she was seven she went into hospital in Manchester for three weeks with a rupture. She came home with leather straps bound tightly round her thighs to keep her still for several more weeks. It was always difficult for her to stay still for long and, a few months later, completely healed, she took part in a time-honoured custom.

Each street had its maypole, and she was all set to join hers when her mother said, 'Nay, lass, tha'll have thy own pole.' The three Stansfield girls and Gracie's best friend at school, Ruby Rylands, helped to decorate a broomstick with brightly coloured ribbons and paper flowers. Gracie's sense of showmanship was evident even then, for she knew a girl who 'looked classy', she said later, and, with the promise of being allowed to hold the 'Maypole' and given the title of 'May

Queen', the child put on her best silk frock and went with them.

Gracie held the box and led the singing, and at the end of that day they had 530d (old coinage) which works out to £2.25 - not much today, but more than a family's weekly wage then. Gracie sang all the songs she knew, sang them at the top of her voice, and the others followed her lead as she rattled her collecting box and roamed the town. 'I led them outside every pub,' she said years later, with a twinkle in her voice, 'and I knew plenty because I used to go with my Dad to his allotment, and we often stopped off on the way.'

There were three theatres in Rochdale at that time, the Hippodrome (which used to be the Old Circus), the Theatre Royal (originally the Prince of Wales) and the Empire (eventually showing silent films with a 'turn' in between). Jenny not only worked in the mill and in the kitchens of some of the big houses, she also got a job in the Rochdale Hippodrome. This was to scrub the stage every Sunday, and she took her eldest daughter with her.

'For that day we were both in Wonderland', Gracie said later, 'and Mumma's ambitions for me had full rein as we moved around the theatre when we had finished.' Jenny's next venture was taking in theatrical washing; again it was Grace who helped her do it. They hung it in the kitchen at night and took it down early next morning because neighbours were likely to come in at any time during the day.

'They'd see if you needed anything if they were going to shop, bring in a bit of stew if you hadn't been well - you all helped each other in those days', Gracie said later. 'So the theatre washing had to be a secret. Jenny had her pride.'

When the washing was ready to be returned, they ironed it between them, then packed it up and walked down to the Hippodrome. They timed it so they could stand in the wings and watch the show. 'Three times a week,' Gracie said, 'once to collect and twice to deliver. Jenny thought it wouldn't hurt to take in an extra performance. When we reached home I had to mimic everything I'd seen for the others.'

Jenny gave concerts to the neighbours too. They were known as her 'Lavatory Concerts', because the audience used to sit 'in the stalls' on the well-scrubbed lavatory seats to listen. The communal lavatories, eight in a row to serve twenty-five houses, became a theatre once a week while the children were at school or in the mill. Taking the large key from its hook in the kitchen, Jenny would collect eight neighbours, settle them comfortably and go through her latest repertoire. She changed the programme every week, but favoured serious songs, which she delivered in an excellent contralto voice. Years later she was to say, 'I can't abide it when Grace mucks up a beautiful song.'

These lavatories featured in Gracie's life too, for once a week she used to clean them out. She did six at a halfpenny each, and she sang while she was doing them. Her mother encouraged her to sing loudly, and she had a powerful voice even then. One day after school, as she was scrubbing away and belting out the songs she had heard the night before at the Hippodrome, a woman popped her head round the door. 'I've been listening to you. You've got a wonderful voice. Where do you live?' Gracie told her and the woman said, 'Let's go and see your mother. I think you should go in for the singing competition if she'll let you.'

The woman was a music hall singer called Rose Bush, who used the name Lily Turner on stage, and she was lodging along the road. Gracie was seven years old, and it was a blow when the family discovered that no one under eleven was allowed to enter. Not for long though. Gracie was tall for her age, so Jenny simply made her look older with a more sophisticated hairstyle, a purple velvet blouse and long skirt. When she was ready, Lily Turner gave her the only singing lesson of her life. She taught her the song *What Makes Me Love You As I Do?* and she tried to get her to sing the 'h' in 'what' - without success, for Gracie sang 'wot', and after many frustrating attempts, she managed 'quat'. She tied for first place and won 10/6 (53p).

After that she took part in many local charity concerts, earning herself a tuppenny pork pie or two by the end of the evening, and her first title of 'The Benefit Queen'. When Lily Turner next had work, she took Grace Stansfield with her. To get to the theatre in time they had to catch a bus or train before school finished, and her dad wrote a note for the teacher that day to say she was sick. This became the pattern whenever they were appearing a few miles away, to enable them to leave in time.

At first Gracie sat in the gallery, and when Lily had sung the verse 'The time will surely come some day', and one chorus of her song, Gracie stood up and dramatically sang the chorus back to her, 'Give up the life, give up the life...'

People didn't always realise this was part of the act, and one day a woman sitting next to Grace thought she was trying to interrupt the performance, and hit her on the head with her umbrella. After that Lily, had her protegée on the stage with her. When Lily Turner left the stage to get married, Grace auditioned for a place with 'Clara Coverdale's Boys and Girls'.

There were a lot of juvenile troupes in the theatre in those days - most of Clara Coverdale's troupe were between fourteen and sixteen, and although Grace fitted in for height, she was only ten years old. The others resented having such a young child with them, and, on the pretext of teaching her some of the acrobatic dancing that she would have to do, they made certain she wasn't in a fit state to appear the following day.

'They strained the ligaments of my legs and arms', Gracie said later, 'and bruised my bones. I was in agony and simply wanted to go home. But I knew I had to stick it out - you didn't give in at the first setback, not if you were going to be an actress you didn't.' Aching, and crying as silently as she could with the pain, Grace sat on the edge of the bed while the three culprits she shared the room with slept. The swellings and stiffness grew worse as the week progressed, and she was sent home without once setting foot on the stage.

Grace's father was for sending her into the mill and forgetting about 'all this theatre nonsense', but her mother won the day.

She had dreamed of a stage career practically since she was born, first for herself and then, when that hadn't materialised, for her family. Grace was the eldest and she had talent; you didn't need to be her mother and possibly a bit biased to see that. Someday her Grace would be a star.

Jenny Stansfield was a very determined woman. Like her mother-in-law, she wasn't afraid of hard work either, and she did it all willingly, sure that at least one of her children would make it; possibly they all would, but there was time enough for the others after she had Grace launched.

The next troupe was called 'Haley's Garden of Girls' and these too were much older - between fourteen and eighteen. Grace still hadn't had her eleventh birthday. Being the youngest, she was the only one who had to go to school each day, a different one in each town they played - and before she could become used to the routine, they moved on and she was fitted in somewhere else. It was a lonely life for a little girl, with no time to make friends of her own age at school, and considered too young to be included in the theatre group outside working hours.

Because of their extra years the others sent young Grace on all the errands for them. One day, when she took a jug of hot water upstairs to the bedroom, she found the landlady's son in bed with one of the girls. Embarrassed she turned to go, but, fearful she would talk and get them into trouble, the girl leapt from the bed and pounced on her.

'Here,' she shouted to the boy, 'come on, I'll hold her.'

'Somehow', Gracie says in her book, *Sing As We Go*, 'I scratched and fought myself free and ran in silent terror to my bedroom where I shoved a huge chest of drawers that only my panic gave me the strength to move, in front of the door. I wouldn't let anybody in all night.' The following morning Mrs Haley got someone to break the door down. Grace was a twitching bundle of nerves with St Vitus' Dance.*

---

* St Vitus' Dance (Chorea): A disorder of the central nervous system characterised by uncontrollable, irregular, brief jerky movements. Often brought on by shock.

Imagine what that night must have been like! Ten years old, and terrified almost out of her mind, completely alone in an alien place with the horror of what nearly happened... They took her to Rochdale Children's Convalescent Home at St Annes on Sea, and slowly she recovered. When she returned home she went as a halftimer - mornings in the mill and afternoons at school one week, and vice versa the next.

She didn't like school much. 'Mumma used to do my hair up very tightly in paper or rag curlers if I was appearing anywhere that evening, and this used to infuriate the teachers, who made me take them out. Then I'd worry about how I'd look that night, because although my sisters had nice curly hair, mine was dead straight.'

In the mill Grace was a cotton winder, but often the other girls minded her frames so she could entertain them. Above the noise of the factory she sang her heart out, and when the overseer was on the way round they warned her and she went back to work.

On morning shifts she had to be at the mill at six, which meant rising just after five when Old Amy, the knocker-up, came tapping at all the bedroom windows in the street with her long pole. Next a cup of tea - all her life Gracie enjoyed her cup of tea - then out into the street, wearing clogs because they were sensible footwear on the cobbles and cheaper than boots, a shawl over her head and shoulders against the early morning cold, and carrying two tin cans, one containing bread and the other tea, for breakfast at eight o'clock. After three months Grace got the sack. 'My work was being neglected', she said.

In between local concerts Grace worked in a papermill, as an errand girl, and behind the counter of a local drapers. She joined the 'Nine Dainty Dots' for a while, and everyone who remembers her from those days says, 'She was always singing and clowning.' She used to sing, whistle and turn cartwheels at Bob Brierley's cloggers on Milnrow Road and usually had her clogs mended free; she did her impressions of George Formby (senior) and Gertie Gitana (her idol) for old Fred when she came in from school or mill.

Old Fred was like the man who came to dinner and stayed to tea and supper too. Originally he came to them for a week while waiting for his relatives to take him to live with them when he could no longer look after himself properly, and he never left. He thought the world of Grace and encouraged her a great deal.

It was old Fred who heard that singer Jessie Merrileas, who was comedian Jack Pleasant's wife, was sick and unable to appear at the Hippodrome one night. Jenny went down to the theatre with Grace and they booked her as a substitute. A hastily printed poster went up on the billboard: 'Tonight - Young Grace Stansfield, Rochdale's Own Girl Vocalist.' She was paid 35 shillings for that week, 7/6 more than her dad was earning at Robinsons, and she was booked for the following one.

That was when Jenny insisted on Grace staying at home and looking after the family, while she went to the mill. 'That way you're free to take any theatre work that comes along', she said. Grace was now thirteen, and the rest of the family consisted of Betty, Edie, three year old Tommy, their father and old Fred.

Not many jobs came up. It was a time of great wealth and equally great poverty in Britain. King Edward VII had died the year before, after a lifetime of waiting for his nine years on the throne, and his son George V reigned with the beautiful, naturally-regal Queen Mary.

A census taken in 1911 showed there were 9,171 actresses in the country. What chances against those figures would there be for a skinny thirteen year old with no previous theatrical background?

Gracie mothered her family, wrote for auditions, sent her one professionally posed photograph to an agent. It was returned two weeks later, cracked through the centre where someone had folded it in half, and scrawled across the bottom were the words, 'Hardly suitable'.

2. The Touring Years

When Gracie was fourteen she was offered four shillings a week with 'Charburn's Young Stars'. This was another juvenile troupe and she had to get to Blackpool to join them. The fare was four shillings - she would be paid when she had worked a week and they simply did not have the money.

'Dad refused to pay', Gracie said later. 'He hoped I'd finished with "all that nonsense"... "Get a job in mill where tha'll get regular wage."'

Old Fred came to the rescue. He had no money in his pocket either, but he had read in the paper details of a singing competition in Middleton that evening. Her friend's aunt went with her and paid both their bus fares.

The first prize was five shillings and Gracie won, but the audience would have none of it. 'She's not a Middleton girl,' they shouted. The judge gave her the second prize of two and six. 'No, she's from Rochdale.' He made another effort with the third prize of a shilling, but to no avail; the few miles between the towns were an insurmountable boundary.

'It was hard not to cry,' Gracie said later, 'but I wasn't going to let them have the satisfaction of seeing that.' On the way out the judge caught them up and, diving his hand into his pocket, gave Gracie five shillings. 'You should have had the first prize - you *won* it, Middleton girl or not', he said.

That is when Grace Stansfield became Gracie Fields. Many people claimed the idea as their own, but Gracie said it was on the advice of a theatrical manager who said her real name was too long. Her mother played around with several possibilities, eventually settling for Gracie Fields.

She stayed with the Charburn troupe for almost two years, 'I used to clown around backstage, but the first time an audience laughed at me I cried because I thought I was acting. It was a duet, and the boy singing it with me whispered, "Come on, give it everything." I did. The song was *Coax Me, Come On And Coax Me*. I was really upset when they laughed.'

She danced, sang, took part in the sketches and enjoyed her time with them. The four shillings a week were increased to eight, most of which she sent home to her mother along with the notices from each town they played. As Gracie had a good mention in every one, Jenny decided that the time had come for her to branch out on her own.

She found work where she could, but it was sparse. She filled in with errand girl jobs, anything which would bring in a few more pennies, and Jenny argued fiercely against her going back to the mill whenever it was mentioned, which was often, as more months went by without her finding regular theatre work.

Then Mr Ernest Dotteridge at the Palace in Oldham booked her for a week. She was fine until the last night, when she had a different song to sing. She forgot to tell the band, who played the old one while she sang the new. Anyone who has heard Gracie do this routine since will know how funny it can be when she argues with the conductor, finishing by saying, 'I'll win, you'll see,' and overriding, almost drowning the band with her powerful voice. But that first time wasn't a routine - it was real, and the manager dropped the curtain on her. Ernest Dotteridge was generous. He wrote, saying, 'We must not condemn a good week for one bad performance. I can offer you a season with "Cousin Freddy's Pierrot Concert Party" at St Anne's on Sea.'

Gracie was reluctant to accept because she had set herself a target of £5 a week, and this was £3. Also she had indulged in some childish showing-off when she was at St Anne's in the convalescent home a few years before - telling the staff how big she was going to be once she returned to work. Jenny looked aghast when Gracie questioned it. 'We need the money, £3 is better than nowt,' she said, 'you'll go to Concert Party.' It was valuable training for Gracie because that was really where she discovered how good she was as a comedienne, and how to enjoy it.

Fred Hutchins was the man who developed her burgeoning comic talent. Gracie said he taught her three important lessons. Not to *mind* being laughed at; to be a generous performer; and timing. In the first show she did with him, she had to ad lib until he touched her with his 'magic' wand, when she had to freeze and become like a statue. She was so good with the ad libbing that he let her carry on, and never used his 'magic' wand at all. She had one season with Freddy and his Pierrots, then she was back home and looking for work again.

At pantomime time she landed a small part. It wasn't a happy show, and when she had an enormous success with one of the songs, the principal boy objected and it was taken out. Fred Stansfield had an accident at work and was in hospital and Gracie knew she had to stick it out and send home what money she could. There was a show on Boxing Day, so Jenny sent Betty to spend Christmas with Gracie as they could not all be together.

'It was a terrible Christmas,' Gracie remembered years afterwards.

> Dad was very ill, mum desperately worried over everything, but determined we should all carry on. I was homesick, miserable with the pantomime, hurt by the jealousy that abounded each time I had a song, then to put the finishing touches Betty and I bought two oranges as a special treat for Christmas afternoon - we picked out two of the largest ones we could find - and they were as bitter and sour as the rest of that horrible Christmas. They turned out to be not oranges at all but grapefruit.

When the pantomime finished, Gracie was out of work again. Her father was still in hospital, and even old Fred was poorly. They broke up boxes the greengrocer gave them for firewood, and huddled round the warmth in the evenings, longing for the warmer weather, but more than anything praying for something to turn up. Nothing did, and Gracie resigned herself to going back to the mill, if she could get 'set on'.

Then old Fred was taken bad and had to go to hospital. He had pneumonia and died a few days later. In an envelope with Jenny's name on was his will. He'd left her £100, his insurance money. 'Tha knows best how to spend it', he'd written on the accompanying note. When she had paid for the funeral, settled the debts and stocked up the larder, Jenny took Gracie to a Manchester studio to learn extra tap-dancing steps. 'Step dancing we called it in the north in those days', Gracie said. The instructor was Corlette, and his fee was 2/6 for thirty minutes. Gracie had six weeks, and in that time she learnt the basis of all the dancing and acrobatics she was to do later in her films. She did the rounds of agents again - a week's booking here, another there, still nothing regular. By now Gracie herself was mesmerised by the theatre and determined to succeed. Deep within herself she knew she could.

From time to time, if they had room, her mother's younger brother, Joe, lived with the family. He too was a good singer, but said the stage was out as a career for him because he had a deformed nose and a stammer. He also had a terrific sense of humour and Jenny, who didn't regard comedy as a great talent, tried, unsuccessfully, to get his nose put straight so he could enter the theatre as a singer (he didn't stammer when he sang). When the extended family were together they had enough talent and material to put on their own variety show. Jenny would have liked one of them to have been an opera singer, and she worked on Grace every day, trying to strengthen those already powerful vocal cords.

From the beginning of the First World War in 1914, Gracie sang to the troops, the wounded in hospitals in the area, and the refugees who were housed in some of the larger places nearby. She saw lads she knew go out to France, many never to return, and, tremulously at first, she sang to those who did come back. She went with a group, and often had to turn her face away as they went home, so the others wouldn't see the tears that threatened. Gracie fought the 'soft' side of herself all her life.

Her father came out of hospital and then Mr Percy Hall, a Manchester agent, offered her a six week engagement, with an option for ten years at no less than £5 a week, and if she earned more, the balance to be divided between them.

Comedian Sandy Powell recalled the occasion. 'It was at a little cinema at West Houghton, near Bolton. Gracie was nearly sixteen and I was thirteen. I remember that there was great excitement one night because word got round that an agent was out front. It was Percy Hall, and he came round afterwards and booked Gracie...'

The Stansfields were living in Whatmough Street by then. They were still moving around. 'I reckon I lived in nearly every street in the town during those early years', Gracie said later. Each different house had something more, an extra room, or a larger one, a cellar, a hall or a tiny patch of garden.

Sister Betty remembered the day the piano was delivered. 'It cost £20, with as many years to pay for it. It was never fully paid for. Weeks when we couldn't afford it Mumma had us all hiding under the table and behind the door when the collector came!'

All the children learnt to play. Gracie had a few lessons but found she could play by ear best. 'Playing scales was too slow and monotonous and I could usually pick out a tune if I heard it once. Waste of money to send me for lessons.'

When she was working regularly, Gracie fulfilled one of her ambitions and bought a travelling basket. She was very proud of this. It was kept in the hall and was always neat and tidy. It was a habit she never lost - folding her clothes and keeping everything orderly.

She was full of energy and enthusiasm for the theatre and taught Edie and her young brother Tommy the latest song and dance routines. They were still at school, but, with a borrowed straw hat and walking stick for a cane, Gracie had them doing, *Tell Me, Pretty Maiden, Are There Any More At Home Like You...* She was very severe, making them practise until they had it exactly right.

When Percy Hall procured her an audition for a revue, *Yes, I Think So*, Gracie was overjoyed. She was accepted - regular work at last, or it would be if the show did well.

The revue's comedian was Archie Pitt. Gracie didn't think he was funny on stage, and off stage she felt in awe of him. He was bossy, and although she didn't *have* to take notice of what he thought and said about her act, it was difficult not to listen because he was so absolutely engrossed in the mechanics of the theatre.

While *Yes, I Think So* was touring the Manchester area, Jenny had arranged for Gracie to lodge with people she knew through mutual friends. They were cheap digs, but they were three miles from the theatre and Gracie walked each way to save money on tram fares. Archie persisted in questioning her as to why she was staying so far out and never believed her answers that she was with friends.

'It's false economy to try to save on cheap lodgings,' he told her, 'I'll fix you in with me when we move to Preston.'

Even though she was away from home quite a lot touring, Gracie was still very much under her mother's influence. She went home most weekends, unless she was working too far away, and Jenny would make her impersonate the stars she had been working with - this time for the neighbours to hear. Imitations came easily to her, and she was amazed to find that people she had been on the bill with two years previously hadn't changed. 'They paused for breath in exactly the same place, never altered their phrasing...' She decided that when she became a star she would change it. 'If somebody was mimicking me, I'd do something else. I wouldn't be stuck - would never give exactly the same rendering...'

Yes, I Think So toured for eighteen months. Gracie celebrated her sixteenth birthday with the show and tasted champagne for the first time in her life. Archie bought it for the party he gave to the cast, and Gracie asked everyone present to sign her autograph book. Archie wrote, 'To Gracie Fields; one day you are going to be a big star.'

Her name on the posters and billboards was in very small print, but she did well in the show - so well with her songs that there was jealousy among some of the others, and the manager would take away any song that proved too successful and give her a new one to work on. 'It was good experience', Gracie said later. 'It taught me how to turn a mediocre song into a good one with vocal acrobatics, although at the time I didn't think of it in that way.'

When the tour ended, Percy Hall had another revue lined up for Gracie Fields, but Archie wanted her to join the company he was about to launch. Jenny thought this would be a good idea too. She never found Archie a great comedian, and she told him so, but she recognized his flair for managing. Gracie, the least keen of all, produced her trump card - her contract with Mr Hall - but Archie wasn't worried over that.

'I can deal with him,' he said. He bought Gracie's contract for £12, which at that time he didn't even have in hard cash. He made an agreement to pay the money in instalments once he had his own show on the road. If he could be as persuasive as that with an agent, what chance did seventeen year old Gracie stand? Especially as her mother, who was the other dominant force in her life then, approved wholeheartedly.

Jenny and Archie didn't like each other much, but they had one strong ambition in common - getting Gracie to the top. That she had the talent to reach the highest rung of the theatrical ladder neither doubted, and they knew also that she would work; what they had to chance were the breaks every performer needs.

'Right,' Archie told Gracie, 'it's fixed. Your mother approves, and I've got your contract from Hall; we're in this new show together now.'

Gracie held out her hand, 'It's a bargain', she said, and that was the only business contract they had. No papers were signed, there were no rules or conditions. A handshake sealed their partnership for a show as then only half written.

'That's what we'll call it,' Archie said triumphantly, *'It's A Bargain.'* Archie's brothers joined them in this show. There were three of them - Bert, Pat and Edgar - and although their name was Selinger, Archie had changed his to Pitt and the other three to Aza, which was the trade name of a manufacturer whose cloth they advertised in their stage suits. They started off in *It's A Bargain* as 'The Three Aza Brothers', doing a comedy act, but this was altered fairly soon afterwards to two. Bert Aza became the company's manager and later went on to manage Gracie's professional life until he died in 1953, when his wife, Lillian, took over. Edgar, who died in 1970, left the show when he met the woman he wanted to marry, and they eventually bought and ran a garage. Pat, who was the junior lead then, lived well into his nineties.

Mona Frewer, who had been in *Yes, I Think So* with them, had helped to write the new show and came into it as leading lady, with Gracie as second lead. It was Mona who, watching Gracie from the wings as she mimicked Charlie Chaplin, went for her when she came off to thunderous applause. 'Any monkey can do imitations, that's just stealing other people's material.'

Shocked and hurt at the vehemence of the words, Gracie gave up doing her impressions on stage from that night.

Gracie liked Mona Frewer. 'I understood how she felt. I'd have felt the same in her shoes, because Archie had cut her number to let me do the Chaplin impression. I'd worked hard to get it right, but I never did it again, not on stage anyway.' In later years, off stage, Gracie was a great imitator and could probably have earned her living in a one-woman Mike Yarwood-type show.

It's A Bargain ran for two and a half years, and both Gracie's sisters joined the show as they became old enough. Betty, nervous at first, but an extrovert at heart and the most confident of them all, and shy, gentle Edie, who was an especially good dancer. They were a talented family and had been brought up with the idea of show business as a career. Jenny was ambitious to better them all - with her own theatrical dreams and her family's undoubted talent, she never needed to look elsewhere for a different career for them.

It's A Bargain went into theatres and halls all over the country. It tested the dedication of its performers to the utmost. Often Bert Aza went ahead to the next town they were playing to get an advance on their salary to enable them to pay the company's fares to their destination. In his book *Our Gracie*, he tells of the 'deathtrap theatres, draughty ill lit and insanitary dressing rooms, fire buckets for washbasins, interminable Sunday journeys, scratch meals and dingy lodgings', and of halls without pianos, let alone bands, and houses with twenty people in front. Gracie learnt her craft touring with these shows. Bert Aza says in his book, 'Gracie was superb in these romps, and her natural flair for burlesque had plenty of scope.'

In a letter written in 1917 to Doris Paul, who had left the show the year before to be married, Gracie said, 'We are working such terrible places, they make one feel very miserable. Thank goodness we have better work coming in.' It was at this period that Gracie began wearing clothes with a Scottish flavour, a fashion she loved for the rest of her life.

'We have been out shopping all day', she reveals in a letter to Doris. 'I'm going in for Scotch outdoor things, looks good - nice Tammy and socks, and a nice Scotch coat...'

Mona Frewer left the cast through ill health, and Gracie, who had often taken Mona's part as well as her own on days when Mona was too ill to play, became the leading lady. Halfway through the run Annie Lipman joined the show as a chorus girl. She was really a musician, but as they didn't have an orchestra to conduct at that time - all taking turns at playing the piano when they were not on stage - she turned her hand to anything that needed doing. One of her greatest assets was her enthusiasm. They all needed this, especially on the bad days. She and Gracie became friends, and Gracie took her when she visited her own pals around the north.

Archie and his brothers were Jewish, born to German parents who had become British subjects. He had tried several careers, as a shop assistant, a commercial traveller, then he began entertaining in the pubs in London, going on to working mens clubs up north. Realising he would not make a fortune in that line, he became interested in the theatre. He recognised talent in the raw, and in Gracie he saw the beginnings of something very big, and had the courage to foster it.

Clarkson Rose, that inimitable man of the theatre, and great pantomime Dame, says in his book *With A Twinkle In My Eye*:

> Mr Archie Pitt observed many of the old-world courtesies. If he went to a show and saw an artiste that he would like to book, he would not communicate with the artiste until he had first contacted the artiste's employer. In several instances he booked artistes from Twinkle, and always paid me this courtesy. In management he had high ideals. He studied the welfare of his people quite outside the ordinary managerial spheres. He had a savings scheme for his companies in which he encouraged thrift, and made tangible contributions to that thrift himself. His companies were run with discipline and law and order that was refreshing.

In later years Gracie's view of Archie was obviously and naturally coloured by their unhappy marriage, but she always acknowledged that he had channelled her talent in the right direction. He pushed her forward, often bypassing others in the show, to give her room to grow professionally.

'He took over where my mother left off,' she said, 'and he did it with her full approval. I was young, pliable, and very used to doing as I was told at that time.'

When *It's A Bargain* finished, another revue written by Archie, called *Mr Tower of London*, began.

3. Family Affair

Mr Tower of London was an incredible show. Gracie said that in the beginning it was poor but they all worked on it. It ran for nine years, and was the one that eventually took Gracie into the West End. In 1918, when it started, the Great War was almost over, but there was no money about and the country was still in a state of depression. The 'land fit for heroes', which never quite materialised, was talked about with optimism by the politicians and scepticism by the people.

The show's name was a result of a visit to the Tower of London. Originally it was to be called *Mr Bank of England*, but the Tower of London seemed a brighter title for a revue. There was already *Miss Relish of Yorkshire* and *Miss Sauce of Worcester*, so keeping in the same trend, *Mr Tower of London* it became.

Mr Tower started life at the Coliseum, Long Eaton, Nottingham, on 28th October 1918. It toured the country, playing in whatever theatre or hall would book it. The company travelled thousands of miles with that show, and it was estimated that seven million people saw it.

Gracie was the star, and the revue had most of the Pitt and Fields families in its cast. Archie was the boss, 'the guvnor' they all called him later, but during the *It's A Bargain* and *Mr Tower* days it was 'Daddy Pitts'. He signed photographs to the cast as this, and referred to the girls as his daughters. Bert was the business manager, and he and Archie were the ideas men, but it was Gracie who carried them out, often with Annie Lipman's help. She did most of the training for the show, drilling the chorus girls and getting the whole thing shipshape.

They introduced new sketches and scenes every so often, and one of these was 'The Dolly Sisters'. Dressed in crinolines and white wigs, Betty and Edie rehearsed until Gracie was satisfied that they were professional enough to appear. Betty said, 'Grace would stand in the wings and yell at us to keep in tune. I usually burst out laughing and this would set Edie off too. Grace would be going frantic which made me laugh even more.' The number didn't stay long in the show, 'It was no good', Betty said, 'night after night the same thing happened, so she withdrew it.'

Gracie sang a lot of songs, and took part in numerous sketches. In one of these she had on a short frilly apron. Gracie was quite a tall lady, and while she was laying the table and singing she was also doing crazy acrobatics with her legs, hoisting them in and out, putting one behind her then suddenly giving a funny little kick with it. Her long thin legs were sometimes a source of embarrassment to her, so she turned them to her advantage in the sketches by using them to make people chuckle. The audience rolled about laughing at her antics.

One sketch involved Gracie and company being locked in the Chamber of Horrors at the waxworks. Another took place on top of a bus, with Gracie often ad libbing to keep it fresh and the others on their toes. Yet another sketch took place in a courtroom. Archie was the judge, and one night, when he asked the name of the prisoner, she said, 'Tom Whitwell' (this was her friend Nell's father) and the cast had to follow through with this name to keep it sounding right. She often did this, bringing her local friends into the act, and sometimes she would mimic Nell on the stage, especially about how she was at getting up in the mornings when she was not feeling her brightest. Gracie knew about this because, before the touring days, when she was still living in Rochdale, she had often stayed at Nell's house after the theatre, and they slept in Nell's bedroom and talked until the small hours. She had great reserves of dynamic energy - after a matinee and two shows a night, Gracie would come in and leap right across the bedposts - she seldom got into bed by the normal method. Gracie said she inherited her vitality from her mother, and anyway she 'couldn't ever do nowt.'

Certainly she was always working, and as the show began to make money, she bought black silk material in the market very cheaply and made underwear for herself and the chorus girls. She used to embroider red roses onto the panties and slips to make them beautiful and more exotic-looking, and the girls loved them. She liked dressmaking and sometimes said that if she hadn't been on the stage she would have enjoyed being a dress designer. (Many years later she did design the stage clothes for some of her tours.) When *Mr Tower* eventually went into the West End, it was Gracie and her sisters who made new dresses and hats for the show (under the collective name of Madame Roberts) because she thought theirs were too shabby for the Alhambra after all the touring years.

'They were wonderful days', she said later. 'We would rehearse in the mornings, then back to the digs for lunch, which we had already bought and taken in to the landlady to cook. The afternoon was free. Most of the girls went to the pictures, but I nearly always used to go on the tram as far as it would take me. Usually the trams ran into the country and I loved it. I'd breathe in all the lovely fresh air, then back on the tram and get ready for the show in the evening.

Her sister Betty used to mimic some of the theatrical landladies, and this provided a great deal of entertainment and material for the show. Most of the landladies kept visitors books and you were expected to write something in at the end of the week. A lot of the remarks were written in code to warn the following week's intake. 'Thank you, Mrs Smith. Nuff said.' 'This is home from home, with home comforts.' This told the men that the landlady and her daughter were very kind indeed. Sometimes, if you were that way the following year, the landlady would be nursing a child or grandchild!

Young brother Tommy, joined the company when he was thirteen, and one of his tasks was to sell Gracie's photograph to the audience for a penny a copy. In many of these photographs she has her hair styled in 'earphones', which were very fashionable during that period. She bought Tommy his first pair of long trousers when he joined *Mr Tower of London*. They were playing in Bolton and she took him to a tailor and had him try on top hat, tails, the whole outfit.

'You look really smart,' she said, 'like Fred Astaire.' Tommy worked with Gracie many times, long after Betty and Edie had given up show business and were concentrating on their own families. They toured the British Isles. 'All the geography I never learnt at school I caught up with during that show', Gracie said. When they were in Ireland, so many people could not buy tickets that they started hammering on the door to get in. On hearing the pandemonium from her dressing room, Gracie opened the window to see what it was about. When she knew she said, 'Don't worry, I'll give an extra show on Saturday afternoon. Listen, when this house goes in you can book for it. Just tell the management you want tickets for a matinee on Saturday and I'll be there.' Already she knew it was *her* audience.

When they were touring and had to make the often long train journeys from one town to another each Sunday, they met other companies: all of them dressed up to the nines to let each other see how well they were doing. The men wore long black overcoats which often covered a shabby suit, and in the cold weather the overcoats doubled as blankets. Often they would settle down in the carriage and play cards. Gracie knew only one game - pontoon - and she always won.

'She was terribly lucky with cards,' her brother Tommy said, 'she'd start to play, then take over the bank and win all the way. When she had taken everyone's money she used to lay it all over the table and say, "I've had enough now, share it amongst you, I'm going to have a rest."'

Mr Tower of London moved from Selby in Yorkshire to the Queen's Theatre in Poplar, London, during the railway strike of 1919, so the company travelled with all their props on the back of a lorry. It was cold and foggy, and it became colder and foggier as the day wore on. The driver lost his way more than once. They hadn't been able to travel on the Sunday for the simple reason they could not obtain transport until early Monday morning, or they would not have cut it so fine.

It was past five o'clock in the evening when they finally arrived, cold, tired but triumphant - to find that the manager of the Queen's had engaged another revue because he thought they weren't going to make it! However, they *had* made it, after a particularly gruelling journey. An argument ensued.

'We are here in time and we shall go on. You booked us,' Archie said. The other company left, tea and sandwiches appeared, the scenery was brought in and set up and the curtain went up on time. Archie gave them all a pep talk about this being their chance to make it in the capital, and the adrenalin began working. The audience was small and unenthusiastic. Gracie did some songs in Lancashire dialect, which didn't go down well, and she felt very depressed and anxious afterwards.

They were booked for the week and the following night they made several significant changes in their material. Word got around that it was a good show and by the end of the week the applause had pushed the memory of the nightmare two hundred mile foggy ride and the first night's reception into the background for them.

Other bookings followed and night after night, as Gracie had them rolling in the aisles with her comedy and brushing tears from their eyes with her songs, managers and agents came along to see this girl who had caught the public's imagination with her work. One of them, Archie Parnell (his brother Val Parnell later became manager of the London Palladium and a good friend of Gracie's), offered her £100 a week, then £200 - she was earning about £28 a week at that time because all the profits were being ploughed back into the business. But it was only her he wanted, not the entire show.

'It was tempting,' Gracie said later, 'but there were the others to think about. It was a family show really, we were all in it, Edie, Betty, Tommy, Bert, Archie, Annie Lipman... anyway I wasn't sure if after all these years being with the company, I'd be any good on my own again.'

The show went on and on and on... It made money - after all the struggling years when Bert and Archie had accepted bookings in the worst theatres in town (and in those days there were a lot of very rough ones) on a percentage of the profits. They had worked unceasingly and believed completely in the ultimate success of the company, and they were proved right. But it was Gracie the people wanted to see and hear. It was that liquid voice which soared so effortlessly up and up and up, taking you with it until you were floating somewhere above ordinary life, somewhere among the gold and silver of the universe.

In those days Gracie's ambition was to have £200 in the bank for her mother, then get married, have a family and settle down to a home life of her own. In her autobiography (published in 1960), Gracie says of her marriage to Archie, '*Mr Tower of London* was in its fourth year of touring. In its fifth year I married Archie Pitt. Archie insisted.'

It is a sad little statement. Although those two words, 'Archie insisted', may sound incredible, they are not surprising when you remember that for nine years, since she was sixteen, Gracie had been used to doing as Archie told her. She said no at first, because she didn't love him, and she knew he didn't love her. She went on saying no for many months. She met few men outside her work. There had been a brief romance with the brother of a friend, but mostly life had been all theatre since she was a child, or very nearly so, and she was used to Archie. Sometimes a little afraid of him, but used to him. Ever since that attempted rape when she was ten years old, Gracie had felt wary of men, and to a certain extent Archie was the known quantity.

He told her he was afraid she would marry someone quite unsuitable and ruin all they had both worked for. Her mother was pleased; her father said, 'It's up to you, lass.' Years later she told Florence Desmond, 'I wasn't in love with Archie, but he was the boss and I was afraid if I didn't marry him he'd give me the sack, and I had all the family to keep.'

Gracie was a strong character, but she didn't like fights. It went even further than that - sometimes she simply could not bear fights. Lillian Aza has said that she considers Gracie always let the men in her life dictate to her, and she knew Gracie for over sixty years. Gracie herself, when talking of that marriage, compared it to 'a black existence, the whole thing is like a black hole.'

When asked outright in an interview why she married Archie Pitt, she said, 'Because I didn't know anything else. Perhaps I'm a bit sloppy. It sounds silly to say it, especially to everybody who seems so able to stand on their own feet. My mother could, yet I can't bear anybody arguing over anything. They all said,

"It's perfect, wonderful." It was just one of those things that happened. My mother didn't tell me to do it, we all have free will, but it turned out badly for both of us.'

Although she was twenty-five, Gracie was fairly naive. Life was mostly work, and the goal towards which everyone seemed to be pushing her was stardom. She wanted this herself but she wanted other things too, and a home and family of her own were high on the list.

'When you've been working together every day for six years, travelling round England together, often in the same digs, when you've weathered the same financial storms, been broke together and been in funds together, then it is easy to drift into marriage', she said.

Whatever did finally induce Gracie to marry Archie, neither of them ever pretended that it was the love match of the century. The ceremony took place at Wandsworth Registry Office on 21st April 1923. Archie was forty-three, eighteen years older than his bride. After the wedding they went to Paris for a few days' honeymoon.

Life went on much the same after they were married as it had before. Gracie still drilled the girls, and now that they were making more money she often hired a coach and took them all out into the country for a picnic. She bought cricket sets and footballs and packed several hampers with food. After rehearsing they settled down to enjoy the rest of the day in the fresh air, and Gracie's voice rang out across the fields as she practised her high notes and continued the 'training' her mother had begun, to strengthen her voice. For although she had exchanged a mother's control for a husband's, she wasn't free from higher domination.

Her sister Betty said she worked hard on her voice, listening to gramophone records, especially Galli-Curci's (her favourite singer at that time), and producing some remarkable notes.

Irene, Archie's daughter by his first marriage to May Deitchman, was about seven then. 'When my father told me he was going to marry again, I said, "Are you marrying Auntie Grace?"' Irene was pleased. She spent holidays from school touring with the company, and a few years later, when she was old enough, she appeared with them.

Eighteen months after Gracie and Archie's marriage, Sir Oswald Stoll came to see the show, liked what he saw and booked *Mr Tower of London* for the Alhambra Theatre, Leicester Square, to fill in a spare week. The Alhambra stood (it was demolished in 1936) where the Odeon Cinema is now. In 1925 it was one of the leading theatres in London and had seen George Robey and Violet Loraine in *The Bing Boys Are Here* and *The Bing Boys On Broadway*, and had staged ballets, variety, revue and opera. In 1925 and 1926 it was also the theatre chosen for the Royal Command Performance.

To the *Mr Tower of London* company, a booking for the Alhambra seemed like heaven. Practical Gracie looked at the vast stage, then at their ten chorus girls, and decided they needed more. 'We can only afford two more', Archie told her grudgingly.

'All right, two more, and we'll spread 'em out a bit', she agreed. It was for this West End début that she re-costumed the show, bribing the cast with oranges, which they all loved, to help her sew the new dresses she was determined to have for this production.

The week before the Alhambra début they were in Halifax, and as usual Gracie, this time with her sister Betty, went on a tram to the edge of the town, and then for a walk. Gracie was nervous about the preformance and when they saw a couple of donkeys in a field with a notice 'Donkey Rides 4d', Betty said, 'Come on, let's have a ride, it will take our minds off our worries.'

They mounted and coaxed the donkeys round and round the field, then Gracie burst out laughing. 'What a situation,' she said, 'to think we'll be making our West End début next week, and now we're just two crazy girls having fun.'

They were all nervous on the first night of the Alhambra opening. Gracie tried to keep them calm, but it wasn't easy. When Evelyn Laye sent her a good luck telegram she said it nearly finished her: 'After all, Evelyn Laye was a big star.' All her life Gracie thought there were brighter stars than herself - this wasn't a put-on act for she knew her own worth, yet found it difficult to accept. 'I always knew I had more, much more than most', she said once in an interview with the BBC when asked if she had known she would go so far.

On that night in 1925 she came down a stairway on the stage of the Alhambra behind a huge white fan, opened her mouth and poured forth notes that sent shivers along the spines of those present. The reviews in the following day's papers confirmed what the provinces had known - as Gracie humorously said many years later, 'They proclaimed me a star!'

The cash really started to roll in then, and Archie launched several companies which he sent out on tour. One with Betty Fields, who was a tremendously talented artiste too, but who later left the stage and did excellent sculpturing work and also patented many of her own inventions; one with Edie and comedian Duggie Wakefield, the man Edie had married; and yet another with Tommy. Gracie topped the bill in London.

Jenny and Fred Stansfield had moved to Middleton Square, Islington a few months before, when Fred was offered a job with Gillets Engineering. He had been reluctant to accept, but Jenny encouraged him. 'After all they are all working more that way now than up north. It will be a good base for the family', she said. Fred missed the north. Up there he had had his allotment to escape to when the house became too noisy or overcrowded. Not that he grew many vegetables, but he had two wooden cabins there: one to house his racing pigeons and one as a sort of clubroom for him and his pals.

Jenny loved London. Especially the theatres. She saw every show, usually sitting high up in the 'gods'. Then she would return home to cook for the family. For although Gracie and Archie were married, they had no home of their own - they lodged with the rest of the company on tour, as they always had done, and the Stansfield's house was still home to them all, wherever it was.

4. The Hectic Years

Reviewer James Agate said of *Mr Tower of London* at the Alhambra, 'If some impresario doesn't snap her up quickly, Miss Gracie Fields will go back to the provinces where they know her worth, and London will be the loser.'

Life changed rapidly. There was still hard work, but now it was earning very substantial cash for the Fields and Pitt families. Gracie's Auntie Margaret, her mother's cousin, came to be her dresser. Everyone, it seemed, wanted to meet Gracie Fields.

Archie loved the fame, but Gracie was frightened. She had worked for this since she was a child entering the competition at the Rochdale Hippodrome; for years she and her family had dreamed of the day when they would play the top theatres in the land. What came next? Every night the audience, wherever she was appearing, clapped and cheered, and she was terrified in case she could not live up to their expectations. Yet the moment she walked onto the stage, *any* stage, she knew she could. It was off stage she was scared.

'I've never done a show when I haven't been a bundle of nerves and a bunch of butterflies', she said later. 'I somehow think I put as much nervous energy into the bit before the show as I do when I'm out there in front.'

Her husband had no such qualms. He was supremely certain they could keep this up. Now that she was more in the public eye than ever before, Gracie became nervous of doing the wrong thing. Archie took it all in his stride, but she needed longer to adjust to such a different lifestyle. When, on Archie's orders, she had a chauffeur-driven car to take her to the theatre, she sent the driver home afterwards because she didn't like to spoil his evening.

Gracie said there were four beings of tremendous importance in her childhood. 'God, the King and Queen, and the Mayor of

Rochdale, in that order.' When Sir Gerald du Maurier sent an engraved calling card to her dressing room with a request to see her, she wasn't sure of his ranking. Not that she ever treated people differently from each other - she gave her attention to dustmen and dukes, chars and countesses - but she did like to create the right impression and get it neat and tidy in her mind.

Sir Gerald asked her if she would play Lady Weir in *S.O.S*, his next play to be put on at the St James Theatre. She told him she would need to think about it, she was a music hall artiste and, tempting as the offer was, she didn't feel sure.

He sent her the part to read, and she said yes. Archie, Bert, her mother - they were all worried - here she was, one of the biggest names now in music hall, accepting a part in a straight play. But it worked. Whatever reason Sir Gerald du Maurier had for asking Gracie Fields to play opposite him (and some said it was a gimmick), she did him proud. It wasn't a long part - in fact her character died in the first act - but Gracie proved herself as a straight actress.

Her fans went to see the play because of her, many leaving after the first act and following her to her next venues. This, while being both complimentary and embarrassing to Gracie ('It's a bit rude', she said), also made it more difficult to judge the audience's reaction to her as an actress.

Gerald du Maurier, one of the last of the actor-managers, was fifty-five then but still had the image of a matinee idol. He usually fell in love with his leading lady, and Gracie was no exception. The first time he kissed her, after she had dined with him and his family at Cannon Hall in Hampstead, she said, 'Don't be soft, lad, you're older than me dad.'

'He got used to me,' she said later, 'but I didn't understand then how sensitive he was about the loss of youth - and anyway, even if I had, it didn't seem right when I'd accepted the hospitality of the family.'

Gerald du Maurier took Gracie out to lunch every week and bought her flowers and little gifts, and they became very fond of each other. She understood that his attentions to other women never detracted from his love for his wife, and she enjoyed the romance of being entertained by a man whom half of London were falling over themselves to meet.

He was so very different from most of the men she had met until then. Suave, debonair, and yet with a devastating passion for practical jokes that belied his image. He played one on her: suddenly throwing onto the table a box from a very well known jeweller, 'Wear it for me,' he said, and as she opened it, 'It only cost £700...' Without looking further, Gracie slapped him round the face. It says much for both their senses of humour that, when she realized that it was a fake - a mock-up diamond ring costing less than a pound - she laughed with him, and they stayed good friends.

Because she was on stage only during the first act of *S.O.S*, Gracie went on to play the second house music hall at the Alhambra, and then a late night cabaret at the Café Royal. She was paid £100 for *S.O.S*, £200 for her Alhambra appearance and £300 for the Café Royal show. A fortune in those days.

At the Café Royal she met Noel Coward (he told her to get rid of the 'kiss curl' in her hairstyle), Beatrice Lillie (forty years on, she, along with Cilla Black, persuaded Gracie to accept a booking at Batley when she was seventy) and writers and artists - including Augustus John, whose studio in St Johns Wood she eventually bought.

Although everything Gracie touched in the theatre now seemed to succeed beyond everyone's wildest dreams, her private life was unhappy. She and Archie, never madly in love, had less in common now - success had driven them further apart.

'We reacted to it in such different ways', Gracie said. 'Archie lapped it up like a kitten with a saucer of cream. He was at home with it and I wasn't. That was the great difference between us. If we had been happy together maybe we could have ironed it all out, but we weren't, and never had been. We shouldn't have married really, we were totally wrong for each other.'

Archie bought a plot of land in Bishops Avenue, Hampstead, and had a house built there. He called it The Towers, after the show which had been the turning point for them professionally.

It had twenty-eight rooms, a bathroom for every bedroom, a huge ballroom, a lift and a staircase fit for a palace. Archie loved it and Gracie hated it. 'The only place then that seemed like home was the middle of a stage', she said.

Archie had a passion for monkeys, always having one about the place wherever he lived; it had the run of the house, sat to table and ate with them. In The Towers Archie had several, which had the freedom of the large garden too, and he also had his parrot, Mac, who had been part of the household for years.

Annie Lipman moved into The Towers with them, and although it was Gracie who posed with Archie for the publicity photographs, it was Annie who shared his life. Now the Musical Director for Pitt Productions, Annie was small, dark-haired and as hard a worker as any of them. She enjoyed the opulence of The Towers and wasn't overawed by any of it. Gracie was. All her life she did things for herself. She had been brought up with the idea that you should always make yourself useful and not cause extra work, and habit dies hard. If an ashtray needed emptying, she did it; if something needed making, putting away, scrubbing out, and she was there, she got on with the job. The servants who shooed her out of the kitchen, the butler who hovered over her, the housekeeper who said she was really a Russian princess, terrified Gracie. 'I feel a bit like a real life Cinderella', she said.

Amid all the splendour she turned her sitting room into a small retreat with furnishings which reflected her love for homely, comfortable surroundings and bright cheery colours. *Home Chat*, one of the leading magazines of the day, ran a feature on Gracie's new house. 'The last thing The Towers reminds me of is a home', Gracie said privately. Two paragraphs seem significant in that account now. First, the description of Gracie's bedroom:

> Really adorable it was, a tiny room (compared to most of the others) furnished in a French style of the Pompadour period. Green and gold taffeta curtains and bedspread, beautifully embroidered in pastel shades. Then a truly feminine dressing

table painted in gold with a triple mirror to match. Softly shaded silk lamp shades in shell pink completed this pretty picture.

The other telling paragraph is this: 'When I asked Gracie Fields how she liked her new house, she said, "Of course I love it. It's beautiful", and then, her inimitable humour sparkled and she added, "but the sad thing is, after all you can only live in one room at a time!"'

Was she remembering all the little houses of her childhood, the three to a bed and the cosy kitchen where you were all together? She didn't want to live like that again, but this was too far in the other direction. Yet she was trapped - trapped in marriage to a man she didn't love, and trapped with an 'image', a word she disliked, which was only one aspect of her many-sided character. She needed people - all her life Gracie needed human contact. Sometimes she had to get away before it overwhelmed her, but never for long. *People Who Need People* was a song she often sang later in her career, and it was true for Gracie.

Sometimes she returned from the theatre at night and went into the staff sitting room to perch on the arm of a chair and chat. The ostentatiousness of the The Towers was too much for her to accept when she was so unhappy, but she could unwind after the show with folk who were in tune with her, whether they were rich or poor, beautiful or ugly, just as long as they cared.

Right from the start Gracie had a tremendous affinity with the human race. Most of us have our own small circle but she reached millions. Possibly the part of her that did this would have done so even if she had not been in show business. She said once, half jokingly, half seriously, 'I used to think I'd be a missionary...'

She wanted to help people, but without intruding, and because of her singing she was able to do this. During the thirties she topped the bill at every leading theatre in the country. She laid foundation stones, opened theatres, stores and cinemas, and people flocked to watch. In her professional life it seemed she simply could not go wrong. She brought her own happy-go-lucky style to these ceremonies, kneeling to lay foundation stones and smooth them in properly, pretending to lick the cement from the trowel ice-cream fashion, 'Got to make a good job of it' - climbing the scaffolding with the workmen and singing to the huge crowds who always gathered where she was. Extra police were drafted into the area when Gracie Fields was there officially, to control the usually good natured crowds who waited hours for a glimpse of her. People *expected* her to play the fool, and, as she often said, 'You can't disappoint the customers.' She was a natural, but in that period of her life she probably felt less like being funny than at any other.

'Because it was of my own making you see. I had all this wealth, all this glory, yet I was so very unhappy; and that seemed wrong when there were so many folk who had much greater cause to be than I did.' So she carried on clowning and singing and found in her work the solace of a job well done, the warmth of a relationship with not one but thousands of people at a time - her audiences.

1928 was a year for firsts; first straight part, first commercial record cut (she had made some in 1923, but they were not released) and her first Royal Variety Show. The Royal Variety Show was in March at the London Coliseum, and from that often hard to please audience she received a heart-warming ovation.

The record was *My Blue Heaven*, and on the flip side was *Because I Love You*, which she burlesqued. This was the pattern for future recordings - not all, but many of Gracie's records have a serious song on one side and a comic one on the other.

'When I first started making records I used my stage style with a great number of starts and stops, acted my head off in fact, and had to learn the totally different technique of singing for recording.'

She began her recording career with HMV and during the next fifty years recorded on every important label in the

business. The early records cost a shilling, and millions were
sold throughout the world.

In 1898, the year of her birth, the record industry, although
twenty-one years old, was still in its infancy commercially.
Improvements in the technique of cutting a disc were swift
during the following decade, and during the 1920s electrical
recording was introduced. By the 1930s, when Gracie was
recording abundantly, the gramophone and radiogram were
important features in many homes.

Gracie's sister, Betty, had married scenic artist Roy Parry and
now they had a baby son. Betty hadn't been well and went to
stay with Archie's mother in Brighton, and one day she took a
bus ride along the coast road out of Brighton. When she returned
she wrote to Gracie about a place called Peacehaven.

This development began just after the First World War but
was still lacking most amenities. However, the entire family
went down to look, and Gracie and Archie bought a bungalow,
'Telford', there for her mum and dad. It was in Dorothy
Avenue, nestling snugly beneath the South Downs, and about
a mile from the main road. There was no gas or electricity at
first, and the dirt roads became quagmires when the weather
was bad.

Gracie tried to get down there every Saturday after her show.
Archie seldom went with her.

In 1928 a show called *Topsy and Eva* (the musical version of
Uncle Tom's Cabin) came to the Gaiety Theatre in the Strand.
It starred two American girls, the 'Duncan Sisters', Vivian and
Rosetta. One week after the opening, Rosetta was taken ill and
rushed to hospital. Gracie, who was rehearsing for *The Show's
The Thing*, stepped in at the last moment to keep *Topsy and Eva*
open. She had met Vivian and Rosetta and liked them, so when
Vivian called into Bert Aza's office to ask Gracie if she could
possibly help, Gracie never hesitated. With a single-mindedness
which many envied her, she learnt the part in twenty-four hours
and proved a huge success as black-faced Topsy.

Crowds waited outside the famous Gaiety stage door for her and chaired her down the Strand, alternately singing and cheering. She stayed in the show for two weeks, playing to packed houses every night, took not a penny for doing so and, when Rosetta left the hospital, returned to her own rehearsals.

Her sister Betty had introduced her to an artist and a writer some months before, and these two were to greatly influence Gracie's life. The artist was John Flanagan, whom Betty's husband Roy had met in France during the war when they were both infantry soldiers, and the writer was Henry Savage.

On the first night they met, at the Café Royal after her cabaret act, they talked for a while, and suddenly John Flanagan said, 'I should like to paint you.'

Gracie was embarrassed. She thought artists only painted beautiful people, and she didn't think she was beautiful. Years before, her mother had put her hair in rags to make it curly, but Gracie never thought she succeeded, either in making her hair curly or in making her beautiful. Her features were strong and, when she grew older, gentle. In the late twenties they didn't have that gentleness. Mostly, in the publicity pictures, she had 'character'. A strong chin, high cheekbones, vigorous hair, a high forehead, a singer's long, slender throat, and good legs and ankles - those long legs that had been an embarrassment to her in her teens, that she hadn't known what to do with, were now an asset.

She met John Flanagan again and agreed to let him paint her portrait. He was Irish, and Gracie said he had one of the saddest faces she had ever seen. 'Big brown eyes, dark hair, and a wistfulness in his expression that sometimes caught you unawares.' Gracie and John fell in love. She and Archie Pitt were still together, but a few days before *The Show's The Thing* opened in 1929, they had another row.

'It was terrible,' she said, 'and the tension of it all drove me to do something I'd never have contemplated under normal circumstances. I packed a bag and left.'

She went to Victoria Station and boarded the boat train for France, where John and Henry were on holiday. On that long journey on her own, each mile taking her further from her homeland and nearer to the man she loved, she had plenty of time to think, and she knew she could not do it that way. Without leaving the station she telephoned her family from Paris. 'It's all right, I'm coming back', she said, 'the show will open on time.'

Then she phoned her husband. 'I never asked you to leave in the first place', was Archie's comment.

'I cried a lot on that return journey,' Gracie said, 'everything seemed such a muddle and I was desperately unhappy, but I knew by then that I had to go back and sort it out properly. I couldn't just walk out and let everyone down.'

The Show's The Thing opened at the Victoria Palace, and people flocked to see it. From the career point of view, Gracie's skies could not have been bluer, but for the 'inner person', life was painted in dark colours, except for the splashes of warmth and brightness of those audiences; they didn't know about the turmoil of her feelings - on stage with her audience everything else was forgotten, and there was only that deep and instant rapport between them. Afterwards she was alone again inside herself.

The Show's The Thing ('an apt title', Gracie said later), ran for eighteen months, and when it finished she moved out of The Towers, acknowledging that her marriage had irretrievably broken down. 'We never loved each other,' she said much later, 'yet I had hoped it would work out. Somehow it didn't seem right to mess things up.'

There was no legal separation - they just ceased to live together. The Towers was offered for sale, and Archie and Annie Lipman set up house together, while Gracie moved into a studio near John Flanagan's, in St John's Wood. She also bought a caravan to use when she was on tour, preferring a place where she could brew a cup of tea herself to an hotel.

In the climate of the early thirties a divorce would not have been good for her spiralling career, although in retrospect she was so adored by the people that it might not have made any difference. In any case she did divorce Archie in 1939, and it wasn't her divorce that sent her flying from the top of the pedestal but the nationality of the man she subsequently married...

After *The Show's The Thing* finished, Gracie took the train again to France, where Henry and John were both working and 'absorbing atmosphere' but she never had any intention of staying there, because she had been reading Norman Douglas's book *South Wind* and had developed a great yearning to see for herself the island it featured.

She had read a lot since the time she discovered the great joy to be found in books, which was not until she was in her teens. (Almost every photograph of Gracie as she boarded a ship, plane or train shows her with a book, a scarf and either a box of chocolates or a bouquet of flowers in her hands.) While John and Henry were in the south of France, Gracie had been reading books about islands.

'They all fascinated me', she said. 'Maybe I needed the seclusion of an island at that time, I don't know, but I found myself longing to have a place somewhere away from the crowds, away from the pressures and stress of too many people. For a while, after reading Somerset Maugham, I fancied Tahiti, then I thought maybe it was too far from all I loved; but Capri, which was called Nepenthe in Norman Douglas's book, was only in Italy - with the money I was earning now I could get home quickly from there if I needed to.'

Gracie arrived in the French village where John and Henry were living, but, instead of staying there and enjoying it with them, she wanted to whisk them both off to Capri.

'Neither of them were keen,' she said, 'but sometimes I can be a bit of a bully, and anyway John was so glad that I was finding my feet, so to speak, because by then he knew, more than most, how difficult life had been, and so they agreed to come.'

In spite of the fact that Gracie and John loved each other, she wasn't free, and John, although he was selling pictures, wasn't making anything like the sort of money she was. They went to

Capri, and at first glance it simply seemed a very beautiful island. They explored it from the harbour up to Anacapri, and, on the day they planned to leave, the driver of the carriage taking them to the boat asked if they had seen 'the little seashore' - 'la piccola spiaggia.'

When they told him they hadn't, he took them there. It was the most uninhabited part, and when she saw it, Gracie knew she had found her Shangri-La. Here was the beauty and peace, the feeling she had sensed before she set out. They stayed for ten days in the place that some time later Gracie bought, eventually added to and made her home. It was owned by an Italian, Marchese Patrizi, who lived there with his wife and sixteen year old son.

During that idyllic holiday - the first real one Gracie had ever had (unless you count her weeks recovering in the St Annes convalescent home) - Henry wrote, mostly about cats, which were his speciality, John painted and Gracie relaxed and dreamed. Deeply in love for the first time in her life, Gracie was happy and fulfilled.

Capri in those days was a little known island, even the now famous song about it hadn't been written. Travel was usually by horse-drawn carriage, or on foot along the steep, winding paths, bordered by oleander and bougainvillea; past the perfect bay of Marina Piccola and the Faraglioni Rocks, looking like a jumbo sized version of the Needles off the Isle of Wight. The island, which is a vast limestone rock, is four miles square - Mount Tiberius (1,100 feet) and Mount Solaro, the hightest point at 1,700 feet, affording a marvellous view of the whole.

Gracie, already in love with John, went on to fall in love with Capri. Some years later she was to write to a friend about it, 'It's the most wonderful spot in the world, almost unbelievable. God was good to me when He guided me there.'

Back in England John was welcomed at the Peacehaven bungalow, where he stayed for a fortnight to paint Fred's picture. They got on well. 'I work for two hours each morning,' he told Gracie when she arrived after her show on Saturday, 'then your dad and I cycle to the Dewdrop Inn until lunchtime. His portrait's coming on well.'

The place where they had stayed in Capri came up for sale, and Gracie began negotiations which resulted in her buying the area of cliff and beach which included what she described as 'the long, low, shanty like shack', where she had been happy.

Between her shows they went to Ireland, and it was there, in Donegal in 1932, they made a documentary called *Riders To The Sea*. John produced it, Henry directed it, and Gracie financed it.

John Flanagan was a good artist who loved his work, which was included in several exhibitions at The Royal Academy. He loved Gracie too, but had seen the adulation she inspired and could visualise a little of what life might be like married to someone who could, and did, command such intensity from others.

Their romance didn't work out and years later she talked about her bittersweet memories of that time. 'I was desperately unhappy when he left, yet, in retrospect, I can see why. I was rich and famous, and although it didn't matter to me which of us brought in the money, it did to him. He didn't want to be tied down and didn't want the burden of money, either. I had worked hard and I loved my work and my audiences too much to give them up.'

After they parted in the thirties - and at the time the world knew nothing of their romance - a friendship remained, and when John needed money for a nightclub he wanted to open in Knightsbridge, it was Gracie who financed the project.

5. The Film Years

Gracie's film career began in 1931 with *Sally In Our Alley*, and it was in this film that her signature tune was born. Gracie disliked filming. She felt claustrophobic when the heavy doors were closed and locked before shooting, and she missed the immediate reaction of a live audience, but *Sally In Our Alley*, which was adapted for the screen from the stage play *The Likes Of 'Er*, by Miles Malleson, was a huge success, and she went on to make fourteen more films. Most of them disappointed her as representative of her talent. 'They always wanted me to sing', she said, which of course wasn't surprising, but Gracie would have liked to have acted more in her film life.

She fought her family and managers when she was offered the lead in *Holy Matrimony*. She admitted to being easily swayed. 'Sheer laziness sometimes,' she said, 'but I was always glad I stuck to my guns over that film. I adored it, the words were rich, it was a real story. Some of my films were built around a few songs, and although they were successful they weren't good, not what I'd really call good.'

They were also hard work. She had to be at the studio at six in the morning and often did not leave until eleven o'clock at night. 'And it was doing the same thing over and over and over again', she said.

Ideally she liked doing things once. Lillian Aza said, 'We called her "one take Joe", but she used to say about some of the others, "There's twenty take Charlie and thirty take Fred - it drives you mad."'

Sally In Our Alley was a hit with the public, and many people feel that it was the best film Gracie made. It had all the ingredients for appeal - laughter, sadness and drama. It had Gracie singing - *Sally* was the song on everyone's lips when the film was released, and became the one associated with her forever after.

Sally was written by Will Haines, Harry Leon and Leo Towers and almost did not get into the film at all. It started life as *Gypsy Sweetheart*, the music written by Harry and Leo, and Will Haines (who was usually called Bill) started the lyric as 'Mary, Mary', which he discarded in favour of 'Sally, Sally'. While he was writing it, someone came into his office, he looked up and said, 'What rhymes with smiling?'

'Beguiling,' came the reply.

When they took it round to Gracie in her dressing room at the Metropolitan Theatre in Edgeware Road, she turned it down. 'I think it's more the sort for a man to sing', she said, then suddenly remembered that the title of the film she was doing was *Sally In Our Alley*. 'Tell you what, show it to Archie - I'm doing a film and it might fit in.'

Archie didn't care for the last line, so they all played about with it until Annie Lipman came up with 'You're more than the whole world to me.'

Sally became so much a part of Gracie Fields that letters were often addressed to her as Sally, London, England, and they were delivered without delay. Gracie says in her book *Sing As We Go*:

I have sung *Sally* all over the world, in peace and war, triumph and disaster, but never in such nightmare conditions as that first time, in the film studio. I was supposed to be in a coffee house when I was singing it, and to get what they called 'the right smoky atmosphere' they decided to burn brown paper. The fumes made the technicians sneeze, and each time one of their muffled sneezes was picked up on the sound track we had to scrap that recording and start all over again. I can't remember how many times we had to do it before it was recorded properly, but I can remember standing there, my eyes streaming with the smoke from the burning paper and the glare from the baking kleig lights, and all the camera, sound, and lighting crews going red in the face and working like mad to get it all in the can before they either coughed or choked.

It became one of the most famous signature tunes of all time. Every orchestra worth its name knew it, errand boys whistled it, and if Gracie appeared anywhere in public where there was anything from a piano to a full scale band, they struck up with *Sally*. Gracie grew tired of the song, but, as she said more than once, 'It appeals to so many. We have all said, or wanted to say to someone we love, "Don't go away, you're everything to me", and *Sally* says it for us most beautifully.'

In 1962 Harry Leon, one of the three involved in *Sally*, was playing the piano in a pub for a living. He was earning about £5 a week from some of his old songs, but had sold *Sally* to a publisher for £30. 'The craziest thing I ever did,' he said, 'because up to then it had earned more than £250,000 in royalties.'

All Gracie's early films were made in England, most of them at Ealing Studios, and whatever she may have felt about the lack of storyline in them, there is no doubt about their cheering-up qualities.

Gracie's art flourished in an impoverished time, when so many were out of work and really 'on the breadline', when the word 'poverty' meant exactly that in its stark reality. It was the days of the means test (introduced in 1931) when, if you applied for unemployment money, it was refused while you still had more than a table, chairs, a bed and a cooking stove. The piano, a feature in so many homes then, was often the first thing to go - it had no practical use; but if people had 6d left at the end of the week, they went to see Gracie, either in person at one of the Hippodromes or Empires almost every town boasted, or at a cinema, which had probably been an Empire a few years before.

Sing As We Go, Love, Life and Laughter, Looking On The Bright Side, Look Up and Laugh, Keep Smiling - the titles were optimistic, and the films lived up to that optimism.

'Whenever there was a Gracie Fields picture showing I would be there. My word, if you were down in the dumps when you went in, you were a different person when you came out. It put new life into you', said Ethel Lord, one of her fans from those days.

Basil Dean and Maurice Elvey directed those early films, and, according to many who worked with him, Basil Dean didn't have an easy manner for comedy. Gracie said to John Loder, her co-star in *Love, Life and Laughter*, 'John, how can I be funny when Basil's watching me so seriously all the time?' John Loder suggested she meet Monty Banks, who had directed his last film. One of the results of that meeting was that Gracie's next four films (apart from *The Show Goes On*, in 1937) were directed by Monty Banks.

Meanwhile Basil Dean had shown that it wasn't only the glamorous Hollywood stars and lavish productions that made money and drew the crowds to the cinema. Gracie's fooling around and trying to put wrong things right, and her breezy cheerfulness, epitomized the way so many of her audiences would like to be. The fact that her buoyant approach was part of her offscreen personality too brought them even closer. Watching the rushes of her own pictures in the studio projection theatre during the silent close-ups of herself singing, she said, 'Eh, what a fool I do look, let's have a tune with it', and proceeded to sing with her image on the screen.

In one scene in *Looking On The Bright Side*, which called for drinks, Gracie suggested they should be the real thing to be truly authentic. 'Coloured water isn't the same', she said. They used the real thing. 'We shall probably have to change the title to "Looking On The Tight Side"', she quipped when she watched the reaction!

Looking On The Bright Side has a moving story connected with its title song. Howard Flynn wrote it after a two year stint in hospital where he had several serious operations. He was in continuous pain, and then he became deaf and a further operation was decided on to try to rectify this. From his hospital bed Howard wrote:

> I'm looking on the bright side
> Though I'm walking in the shade
> Sticking out my chest, hoping for the best,
> Looking on the bright side of life.

One of his publishing friends visited him the day before the operation and said he would show the song to Gracie. The operation was successful, and Howard slowly recovered, while the song he wrote from the depths of his pain went round the world to cheer and inspire millions of people who heard it.

Another interesting snippet is the fact that the biggest set built in English pictures up to that time (1932) was made for *Looking On The Bright Side*. It consisted of a block of tenement flats named 'Parkers Peace' (where Gracie lived in the film) and she had to throw copies of her sweetheart's new song to the people below.

Margaret Hazell, who worked at Ealing Studios in those days, said that when the crowd of extras often could not afford to eat in the canteen on the little they earned, Gracie told them to go ahead and have what they needed and she would foot the bill. They used to troop in and say, 'Gracie will pay', which she did the whole time they were there.

When *Queen of Hearts* was finished she gave everyone at the studios a present. For each of the ladies there was a leather photoframe with a still from the film inside it, and for the men an engraved fountain pen.

Gracie's films always did better in the provinces than in London, and while the critics were quick to praise her as a performer, many of the stories had a rough ride. Here is part of a review of *Sally In Our Alley* when it was showing at the Leicester Square Theatre:

Against a background most aggressively cockney, the chirpy, sentimental, jauntily capable personality of Gracie Fields contrives dominatingly to overshadow the faults of this sketchy talkie. Lancashire rises triumphant above a story that is a story in name only, and direction which is not worthy of Maurice Elvey, even though he is handicapped by the weakest of plots. Elvey, with admirable commonsense, declines to fight a losing battle with a poor narrative, and confines all his efforts to placing Gracie Fields in the limelight and keeping her there. He succeeds in this without much trouble, and

Gracie does the rest with all her usual enthusiasm. The result is a talkie which never begins to be a film but is sound entertainment of the roast-beef-and-yorkshire-pudding variety. Just to add a little diversity to the film, a newcomer, Florence Desmond, gives a fine performance as a quite moral, screenstuck waif; and thereby demands for herself the future attention of producers who want a girl with acting ability and personality. The rest of the cast is just competent... You'll like Gracie Fields and a few scenes of the picture which are really well done. There is enough entertainment here to help you to forgive the weaknesses.

The Leicester Square Theatre was at that time doing what it called a '50-50 Show': Gracie Fields in *Sally In Our Alley* on the screen, and Jack Hulbert's live 'exclusive song and dance show on the revolving stage.' The prices of admission ranged from 1/6 to 8/6, and all seats were bookable.

Gracie made her Ealing Studio films on a share of the profits basis, and as all her films did well in cinemas around the country, she made more money than by taking a salary. Basil Dean said in 1933, 'In cinemas where three day runs were the rule, *Sally In Our Alley* stayed for three weeks.'

The only British comedy star who came near Gracie in the thirties was George Formby (in the forties he surpassed her box-office drawing power), who began his film career with Basil Dean in 1934. The film magazines and comics all featured Gracie - *The Film Star* telling 'the long complete story of Gracie Fields new picture' in several issues. *Film Pictorial*, *Picturegoer* and *Film Weekly* presented her frequently, with interviews, pictures and reviews. No matter how poorly the critics rated the story of the picture, and mostly they did, they awarded it marks for 'entertainment value.'

'The public go to these films to see and hear Gracie Fields,' one critic wrote, 'the story doesn't matter to them.'

Although the stories were, for the most part, flimsy and unreal, Gracie's personality breezed through the pictures - she made people laugh and actually believe that the most lowly of a factory's employees, the poorest down-and-out, the humblest citizen of the world, could, with cheerfulness, song and a dash of down-to-earth common sense, solve not only her own problems but those of the community in which she was involved.

Most of the critics, after two or three films said, 'She is good - please let her have a better story next time.'

Gracie herself wanted to do more acting - not to give up singing, but to do a play or film without music sometimes, as she eventually did in *Holy Matrimony*.

'You had real words to say which the author enjoyed writing, and so you enjoyed them too', she said of this script.

She won an award on American television for her part in Barrie's *The Old Lady Shows Her Medals* in 1955, and high praise from the critics whenever she had the slightest chance to show her paces in the acting field.

Later she made four films in America, all in quite a different tempo from her English ones. *Holy Matrimony*, the one she did with Monty Woolley in 1943, was adapted from Arnold Bennett's *Buried Alive*, a case of mistaken identity between a famous artist and his valet, the ensuing romance and repercussions.

This film won much praise in the USA: 'The Woolley-Fields team is a potential goldmine' said the *New York Daily Mirror*, 'For much of the picture's velvet we can thank Mr Woolley and Miss Fields', stated the *New York Times*. The film reached the ten best films of the year list.

We're Going To Be Rich, in 1937 (in America it was called *He Was Her Man*) co-starred Victor McLaglen and Brian Donlevy and was a story about the South African gold rush.

Molly and Me, which she made in 1945, was again with Monty Woolley. In this she is an out-of-work actress, who becomes a housekeeper and revolutionizes the big house. There is a lovely scene in a pub with Gracie and her friends singing to a concertina accompaniment.

Madame Pimpernel, which was called *Paris Underground* in America, was not the type of film usually associated with Gracie.

It was the story of two women (Constance Bennett and Gracie Fields) who were resistance workers during the war. Gracie had a real chance to show her acting capabilities in this film, and she came through with flying colours, giving a superb and moving performance. Constance Bennett, as producer as well as co-star, actually cut some of Gracie's scenes because her acting was so good.

James Agate said in 1934 after seeing her at the Palladium, 'No other music hall artiste could invest this howling defiant drivel with such exquisite pathos and sincerity. This fine actress could play Carmen or any role. She should be given a chance to play St. Joan.'

Because of her magnificent voice Gracie suffered from typecasting. In the singing films her personality was so strong that it came through. In many of the films they never changed her name even - the character she played was simply called Grace or Gracie. If she had been able to get into a part, as she indeed did in *Holy Matrimony* and *Madame Pimpernel*, she would have submerged this forcefulness into the role. Today I believe a producer would take a chance and let her do both types of film. She did two completely different styles of singing on stage - from the sublime to the ridiculous - and although people argued over it, they flocked to see her. It is a matter for regret that the actress in Gracie wasn't given a vehicle worthy of the talent more often.

Nevertheless, her films gave great happiness to vast numbers of people. They were right for the times, helping folk to keep cheerful against the dark background of the Depression. 'Come on, luv, your chin's touching your knees', she used to say to her friend Nell Whitwell in her own poor days if Nell looked miserable. In her films Gracie said just that to everyone who ventured into the cinema.

Filming earned her a great deal of money, and it seemed that the more reluctant she was to do it, the more she was offered. She said many times that she felt imprisoned in the film studio and found all the waiting about and repeats tedious. She used to tell a story about dancing up and down a flight of stairs every morning for eight weeks. 'I never saw the finished film until a year afterwards. When it came to that scene, the sight of those stairs so exhausted me that I felt I'd done the whole thing over once more, and when I got up to leave I found my knees were so weak that I had to sit down again.' This was a slight exaggeration, but Gracie could always tell a good story. She did all her own stunts, 'Basil Dean insisted, and after all I was being well paid.'

She received £50,000 a picture for four films from 20th Century Fox, and the newspapers reported that, although Mae West was the highest paid actress in the USA, Gracie Fields was the highest paid in the world! Gracie accepted the American contract for two reasons, one highly practical. At the time she owed a lot of money in tax to the Inland Revenue, for during the preceding boom years she had spent heavily, buying property and settling money on her family. The second reason was that, having once been so poor, she 'felt it would be wicked to turn away such an offer.'

The film critic C.A. Lejeune said of her, 'She has the art, like Chaplin, of touching an accessory and bringing it to life. She can sing *Walter* like a pantomime Dame, *The Sweetest Song In The World* and make it sound like a Victorian posy, and *Music Maestro Please* and make it - almost - resemble high dramatic art.'

The same lady, writing in the *Sunday Observer* in 1939, said Gracie was:

> a star of the theatre, the radio, the films, and now television, she is as much part of English life as tea and football pools, our green hedged fields and the Nelson column. She has been mobbed by more crowds and held up more traffic than any other film star except, possibly, Robert Taylor. She has had to slip out of buildings by fire escapes and be rescued by police in a Black Maria. She has been decorated at Buckingham Palace and sung to workmen up a scaffolding. She is enormously kind and endlessly generous. Rich people send her roses and poor people knit her tea cosies. When she comes in front of

the tabs to sing her final number, the house roars like a great hungry beast and won't let her go.

Some day the best English film biography ever made will be done on the life of Gracie Fields, and I hope that Gracie herself will be the one to do it. There will be nothing sentimental about it - a sheer story of hard work done with humour and courage. In its way it will be the complete English microcosmography of the twentieth century, a story of north and south, fame and the inarticulate, of the people who work and move in the front page limelight and the others who live behind lace curtains and an aspidistra in a suburban row.

6. A Smile and a Song

The Aspidistra was, of course, one of Gracie's famous songs. It was written by Jimmy Harper, Will Haines and Tommie Connor, three names which constantly crop up in Gracie's numbers. Tommie Connor says the inspiration for it came when he was walking along a London street and saw a woman by her window with a huge green watering can.

'As I watched her watering an equally huge plant I thought, my goodness, that's the biggest aspidistra in the world. I knew at once it was the title for a song, and began working it out in my head. By the time I got to the tram the first verse was written, and I finished it as soon as I reached my office.' He contacted Jimmy Harper, who wrote the music, then Bill Haines showed it to Gracie. The rest is history.

It was a good song, and the fact that Gracie and some of her fans who weren't as keen on her comic songs grew sick to death of it in no way detracts from its merits as a comic number.

This type was more difficult to find than any other. Gracie could sing ballads already in existence, but the funny numbers were more specialised. The three names above are on many of the comic song music sheets, plus Harry Castling, Noel Forrester, J.P. Long, Leo Towers, Maurice Beresford, Robert Rutherford, Leslie Elliott, Noel Gay, Desmond Carter and Reg Low. Bill Haines owned the Cameo Music Publishing Company and was associated with many of Gracie's songs. Although others could have sung them, because she never bought them outright, they seldom did. Mostly the songs were written with Gracie in mind, and her interpretation was the one that prevailed.

Not many comedy songs look funny in print, the words need the light and shade of a human voice. Max Kester says that *Turn 'Erbert's Face To The Wall Mother* put a roof over his head.

'The money I made from that song enabled me to put down a deposit on my first house, yet at the time Gracie wasn't too keen about the number.'

'Well I'll try it,' she said, 'but I'm not sure. Not sure at all.'

Gracie gave most songs three or four airings, and if they hadn't caught on then, she threw them out. One which she used to sing in the earlier days was *'Enery, 'Erbert, 'Epplethwaite*, but she stopped doing it after a while because it was so difficult to time. 'Some folk laughed more than others,' she said, 'and we couldn't get it right. You've got to time properly on the variety stage or you overrun.'

This was the old music hall tradition - never overrun, for others have to earn their living too. Gracie was always the complete professional. She listened to advice, although she didn't always take it, often preferring to trust her instinct (which seldom let her down where it concerned audiences) but she kept the unwritten rules.

Although many of her comedy numbers were loud, not all of them involved screeching. *Walter, He's Dead But He Won't Lie Down, She Fought Like A Tiger For 'Er Honour*, they made folk laugh, and Gracie sang them with gusto, but not everything was so highpitched. In *The Co-op Shop* she raced the band with good effect, and it was very topical when she was singing it.

There was gentle comedy, satirical comedy and the simple comedy of everyday things. *Got To Keep Up With The Joneses* (whose title speaks for itself), *The Nudist* (the tale about trying to buy a birthday present for a nudist - 'A watchchain would look silly, draped across the front of Willie'), and *I Took My Harp To A Party (And Nobody Asked Me To Play)* - which has happened to so many of us at some time, maybe not with a harp but with our own particular equivalent.

When Gracie was urging us to *All Talk Posh*, there was a greater division in the way people spoke and lived than there is now. Music hall has always been a working-class entertainment, and Gracie was a wonderful music hall artiste. Her songs and sketches were about the lives of everyday folk, ordinary people who worked and married and brought up their families - about

people who 'got on', and people who had bad luck, about babies
and marriage, arguments and making up, about poor people
who wanted to be rich, town people who wanted to live in the
country, and some people whose dream was to live anywhere
as long as they had a roof over their heads. Some of the songs
were a bit saucy, some were hilariously funny, especially with
her actions, and some were tremendously moving.

The late Russell Harty remembered being at a concert with
his mother. 'The first time I saw Gracie Fields I sat in the two
shilling seats in King Georges Hall, Blackburn, with my mother
crying on one side and my Auntie Alice crying on the other.
Gracie was on the stage, in a white frock, kneeling, her hands
clasped, singing the Lord's Prayer. It sounds vulgar. It wasn't.
It was almost unbearable. I whispered to my mother to ask
why she was crying, and she whispered back, "Because she's
doing it right."'

When Madame Tetrazzini heard Gracie singing at the Lyceum
she asked her to sing the aria from La Traviata. 'I was in a
panic,' Gracie said at the time:

> I had learnt all the arias from listening to Galli-Curci's records.
> I couldn't understand any of the Italian or French, so I'd
> sung comical gibberish, intermingled with the real thing. But
> I loved Grand Opera, and I loved Tetrazzini's voice too much
> to want to ridicule great music in front of her. To me opera
> was only for singers who were properly trained. I should
> have loved to learn, but when I was young we didn't have
> the money for lessons. When I understood operatic music
> more I wouldn't attempt it unless I could do it perfectly.

Gracie sang the aria in the role of the character she was playing
in that particular sketch - a charlady, and afterwards Madame
Tetrazzini tried to persuade her towards opera, 'but I stayed
where I knew I belonged', Gracie said, 'although I always
cherished the memory.'

Dame Eva Turner said in 1982:

> In my opinion she had an exceptional voice which she used to great advantage. Her sense of timing was excellent, and she never unduly abused her voice which is evidenced by reason of the length of time it served her. Right up to the end of her career she was able to fill the bill and put it over. I recall she once asked me whether she made a mistake in not becoming a "serious singer" and at that time I told her in view of her great success in her particular field, she had certainly done the right thing by working on the lines she did. I do think, however, she could have made a career as a "serious singer" had she so wished.

An American opera singer once said to her, 'You are a wicked girl. You should have been in opera with a voice like yours.' Once, when she was very young she wanted this, but by then she was happy with her unique place in entertainment. 'Didn't have to worry if I got a bit of dust in my throat, I could laugh it off. Couldn't have done so in opera', she commented.

As 'Stana' Fields, another variation of her original name, Gracie wrote and translated songs herself, among them *Lancashire Blues*, *Song of The Mountains*, and *Cor'n'Grata*.

Gracie worked with few props, often without any. She didn't need them. All that was necessary for her was an audience, and all that was necessary for them was Gracie.

On stage she usually had a simple setting. A piano, the stage drapes, and in her hands a scarf, often matching her dress.

Gracie never wasted time on stage. The audience had come to hear her sing, and she got on with the job quickly in true music hall fashion. She used to stop the welcome applause with her famous whistle and go straight into the songs. Often she wore round her shoulders a white fur, which she threw across the piano after the opening number. 'Only wore it for swank.' 'Hope someone dusted the piano', or 'You've all seen it now so I needn't bother', she'd say. Song followed song, and if the audience clapped too loud or long, she whistled for 'hush' again or told them to 'Cease, cease.'

Steadily she worked her way through from the hilarity of *The Rochdale Hounds* to the comic pathos of *The Birthday Song* and the little boy whose day was less than perfect. Nervously twiddling her scarf, with slightly pouting lips she told of the frustrations the six year old suffered and how he reacted, 'Then I showed 'em if I could be sick or not - every room.'

From the rollicking fun of *The Spaniard That Blighted My Life* she went on to the sending up of *Oh I Never Cried So Much In All Me Life*, then a sudden switch to the drama of *The Nuns' Chorus*, or the peace of *Ave Maria*. No messing about here - Gracie always sang the sacred songs straight. Then she would be fooling about with her voice, doing 'cod opera', throwing her long rope of pearls round her neck in a mock choke, yet as she hit those high notes you knew what opera had missed. Next a romantic number, and just as you were feeling all misty-eyed, she decides to burlesque it and instead has you almost crying with laughter.

Her voice was versatile, the range and depth of her singing amazing: from comic numbers to romantic, from simple to sophisticated, from innocent to saucy. She got away with some daring lines during the twenties and thirties, possibly because no one could really take offence at them for she made them such fun.

In 1933 at the Holborn Empire she said to the vast audience (three thousand people), 'Right, we'll forget we're at the Holborn Empire. Imagine we're in our front room and we're having a bit of a "do". We've had a nice tea - some boiled ham and lettuce, and a tin of salmon, and we're all right now', and they sang and sang with her, just as though they really were at 'a bit of a do' in their front room. She could reduce the biggest theatre to everyone's front room, and turn everyone's front room into the biggest theatre.

Let's imagine for a moment that we have gone to the theatre to see Gracie. In the foyer her picture smiles at us from the posters. We go to our seats, buying a programme on the way, and settle down to read it.

The overture, then two young dancers open the show, a pianist, a comic, a magician, a tenor, and a couple of acrobats... As the theatre fills with people, you can sense the excitement in the atmosphere. Smiles are exchanged with folk we have not met before, and, as the orchestra files in, the packed theatre fairly hums with anticipation.

It is a good bill and we applaud well, but most of us are there to see Gracie, and when the safety curtain falls during the interval, we know we have not much longer to wait, for she is doing all the second half.

Everybody is back in their seat as the orchestra strikes up, 'Sally, Sally...' The curtains open, and Gracie comes on singing... 'Pride of our alley...'; the applause is thunderous, but her voice soars above it, 'You're more than the whole world to me. Thank you, thank you very much', and she launches immediately into a quickfire medley - *Sing As We Go, Walter, Walter, Lead Me To The Altar, Pedro The Fisherman, I Never Cried So Much In All Me Life, Roses Of Picardy...*

Her expressive hands tie her scarf round her head for the next number, and when she takes it off again, she runs her fingers through her hair, using them as a comb. A stillness comes over her, and the theatre is hushed and reverent as she sings *Ave Maria.*

Absolute silence while we return from that glimpse of heaven in her voice, then the solid sound of thousands of clapping hands. Gracie holds her own hand up, 'Enough', she says. 'We're now going on a trip round the world, and if you know the words you can join in', and she transforms herself quickly into an Irish colleen, a Scots lass, French, Spanish, Italian: 'It's Lancashire Italian', she says with a laugh, speaking "off" for a moment, and it isn't just her accent which is good, it's her gestures and expressions - for the duration of the song she becomes that person completely.

Sometimes she talks to us between numbers, in her surprisingly deep voice. 'A long time ago I brought a song back from New Zealand with me', and in a cracked and wheezy voice she sings the first line of *Now Is The Hour* - then, briskly, 'Well we're *not* going to sing that one.' The laughter mingles with her next words, and by the time she really *is* singing her sign-off song: 'Now is the hour for me to say goodbye...', we are still clapping and cheering.

She blows kisses, and the curtain comes down on another performance. We talk to each other as we jostle for the doors. We go out smiling, humming, revitalized for the coming days. We smile back at her picture in the foyer, and if there is time before the last bus or train, or if we have come by car, we might go round to the stage door and join the crowd waiting for her. For days afterwards we are carried along by the memory of that wonderful evening.

This is how it was so many times for so many people. This is why Gracie's concerts were always sold out. It is hard to describe to any who never saw her what a performance by Gracie was like. In more modern parlance I suppose you would say it 'turned you on, got you high'. Her voice held all the joy and sorrow in the world, the richnesses, the sadnesses - it was all there in the depths and tones of Gracie's singing.

One critic wrote, 'Her performances aren't so much a theatrical occasion as an emotionally charged reunion.'

Another (Anthea Goddard) talked about her 'ripe voice - from poignant sob to hysterical falsetto, and suddenly to a disconcerting unladylike hoot. Gracie has never lost the art of knowing exactly when and how to dissolve the tears into laughter. Just as the sentiment of *Sonny Boy*, or *White Haired Granny* is at its stickiest she saves the situation with that piercing hoot, then launches a vocal attack on the biggest aspidistra in the world.'

She was such an original - when she sang a song it was hers, whether you liked it that way or not. She sang *Waltzing Matilda* slower than most, 'It's too pretty to rush through,' she said, 'so I do it slowly.'

When she sang *Over The Rainbow*, she sounded as unlike Judy Garland as possible. In *White Christmas* she echoed the longing for an English Christmas. You may prefer one recording to another, but Gracie never tried to sing a song in the way it had been sung by someone else. It was always her version - even if somebody else was associated with the song. A critic once said, 'They go into the sieve, and come out as Gracie Fields numbers.'

She stayed true to her earlier prophecy of sometimes altering the phrasing, singing it just that little bit differently to the last time. 'Well your mood isn't always the same, and naturally your interpretation varies...'

It didn't stop the mimics, and her manager issued a statement to the effect that they would sue anyone impersonating Gracie without permission. 'We don't wish to stop the sincere artiste, only the many cruel caricatures which are being perpetuated...' There were exceptions. Florence Desmond was one person Gracie allowed to imitate her, she even helped Florence to get the right balance and phrasing.

Sometimes Gracie sent herself up, and in a way this emphasised the two personalities. GF, which she often referred to herself as, and Gracie the actress, who could mimic GF. The great difference when she did this was that she usually finished by hitting the top notes with an ease and clarity not many could achieve.

Her control of an audience was complete. I believe that, if she had told them to stand on their seats, all those physically capable of doing it would have done so, but Gracie would never have made people look silly, not to that extent. She controlled them with love, with the mutual desire to have a good evening's fun which she, and they, knew she was going to lead. She was a natural. She respected her audience, knew they wanted the fun of her comedy and the beauty of her serious voice, and knew too that she was capable of maintaining this balance.

George Black wrote in the *Sunday Chronicle* in 1935:

Seven years ago I took over the London Palladium and to have Gracie Fields on my opening bill was great good fortune, for I had always seen in her the living embodiment of all the great traditions of variety. Marie Lloyd at the top of her career was never more popular than this ex-mill girl had become. Her power over the laughter and tears of an audience was greater than that of Elsie Janis* or Florence Mills** I studied Gracie as she worked. That was something I had often done. From the day I had first seen her at Barrow-in-Furness long before, when she was quite unknown - I had tried to discover the secret of her charm and power. It eluded me then, and even today I cannot say wherein it lies. What she has is so peculiarly her own that none can copy it. It is something that cannot be learned in schools of acting. She breaks all the rules and can never do a thing wrong.

She broke a cardinal rule that night. Any manager could have told her that to turn her back on the audience and walk upstage before the applause and laughter were over was one certain way of ruining an act. She did it and it was one of the most remarkable things I have ever seen her do. With her back still to the audience she paused a moment and began to sing. The crowd, prepared to laugh again, were brought to silence by the clear, liquid notes, that third voice of hers, of a plaintive melody, *Three Green Bonnets*.

At exactly the right moment, known to her by instinct, she turned her head, and began to walk slowly down the stage singing. The house was hushed, breathless. As the last notes died away I heard a gasp. And I, who had been a hardboiled showman since boyhood, and thought I knew all the tricks of the trade, felt what the audience felt. For here was no trick. This was blazing sincerity - a heart speaking to the hearts of the world.

* American actress, singer, lyricist, producer, mimic, 1889 - 1956.
** Negro singer and dancer, 1895 - 1927.

Wally Singer, a friend and fan says he has listened very closely to Gracie's voice and tried to analyse it. The nearest he can get is that it was like a finely tuned violin.

There was the other side, the people who 'could not stand Gracie Fields screeching,' but they were few against the hundreds of thousands who loved her voice.

She has been called 'common'; if making folk laugh with no matter how loud a voice is common, then she was. But if they, the common people, understood her humour, they also understood her other side and were more reverent than a church congregation when she sang the sacred songs.

When the critics chastised her for rock-and-rolling to *Born To Be Your Baby* at a Royal Variety Show which was televised, she said, 'The public expect me to mix it up, now serious, now larking. I always have and I always will - that's me. These TV critics don't understand that I'm not singing to them, but to all the folk in their family parlours. I can't do things by tricks, I have to feel it or nowt happens.'

This was something that went very deep with her. Years before, she had sung *Little Old Lady* at a Command Performance and when a critic said it was a ridiculous song for such an occasion she 'started picking at it', and thought, yes, he's right. Next time she sang it she sent it up and the audience were furious. 'After that I never messed about. What the audience liked I sang.'

She sent up the rich and poor equally - she had personal experience of both sides of that coin, and although she was rich for the greater part of her life, she never forgot the poor days. Her voice has been variously described as 'a unique and glorious soprano' and 'the great coloratura of the century.' It was an operatic voice, yet, because of lack of funds when she was young, she never trained for the opera. By the time she had enough money, she thought it was too late, and she was established in a different field.

Some thought it almost a sin to waste that glorious voice on numbers a lesser one could do. Musical comedy would have been another possibility yet she never did it. C.B. Cochran was going to team her with Richard Tauber once in a musical at the Lyceum, but that idea fell through, mostly because it was the period when Gracie was getting to know Monty Banks and wanted to be free of further long-term commitments for a while.

There was talk of her doing *Me and My Gal*, but she shied away from possible long runs, perhaps her seven years with *Mr Tower of London* had put her off. In 1947 she was offered the part of Annie Oakley in *Annie Get Your Gun*, but turned that down because she thought the character would have to be too drastically changed to suit her age.

Eventually she was a one woman show, combining all the fields in her performance. She misused her voice to a devastating extent without any disastrous results. No matter how she croaked and wheezed in some of the comedy numbers, when she wanted a good note she achieved it. It was a powerful voice, carrying to the farthest corner of great concert halls even before the days of the constant use of the microphone.

'She made the Palladium stage her own. She explored parts of it which other singers, rooted to their microphones, never visit', said a *Daily Express* reviewer in 1948.

She moved all over it in 1929 too, when she appeared in a sketch in *The Show's The Thing*, which involved scrubbing the stage while singing. She tackled a different section each night until it was finished, then began again. 'Might as well make myself useful while I'm out there', she joked.

Her diction was good. 'I can't abide not being able to understand the words', she used to say, 'I've been to concerts when you'd have thought they were singing a lot of gibberish, or a foreign language.' She laughed at the memory of her own Lancashire Spanish and Rochdale Italian.

'OK if you do it for laughs, but not out of laziness. Folk pay their money and should be able to understand what you're on about.'

Gracie could sing in several languages. 'You can learn a song without being able to speak the lingo', she said. Nevertheless, when she went to France, to the Apollo Theatre, Paris in 1928, she sang her songs to the French waiters at the Café Royal first, to check the sound, and many of the reviews commented on 'her perfect French accent.'

On a tour of Wales she learnt Welsh from a Welshman, and she put her knowledge to good use when she was in Christchurch, New Zealand, at a civic reception, by singing *Land Of My Fathers* in Welsh when she discovered the Mayor's original hometown.

From her early days she was a good mimic, and she was always a great professional, so she worked at and polished her accent and pronunciation when singing in another language, and the unsure part of her nature encouraged her to joke with her audience about it.

'Ee, that were a difficult line to learn.'

'We'll take a deep breath and hope for best.'

'How are we doing - all reet?'

And the voice, and the accent, came across perfectly and with an ease and assurance that made light of the preparatory work she always did in pursuit of giving good value 'to the customers'.

'I wanted everyone to go out happy and feel they've had what I would call a good meal. I wouldn't like to go on and think - I'm just going to do that show, and they've got to take it or leave it. I couldn't do that ever, I have to give everything I've got then I can sleep happy.'

7. Honours and Awards

For many years in the thirties Gracie did a week's work a year in Rochdale for local charities. In 1931 she raised £1,673, in 1933 £1,117, and in 1934 £1,629. A phenomenal amount of money in those times of depression, and from an area that was amongst the hardest hit with unemployment. The money was divided among many causes ranging from young people to old. In both 1933 and 1934 the People's Service Guild received over £500. The Guild established workshops for various crafts, to help the unemployed, and each year Gracie visited the centre and talked to the men. She had been poor and out of work, and she understood and did something about it.

Her sympathy was of a practical kind, and she gave not only money raised through her concerts and appearances but also her time and interest. When one man said to her, 'We are trying to look on the bright side', she answered sadly and genuinely, 'It must be hard sometimes, lad.'

In 1933 Gracie opened an orphanage at Peacehaven in Sussex. This was because the Theatrical Ladies Guild (now the Variety Artistes Ladies Guild) needed somewhere for the children of actors and actresses who had either died or were ill and temporarily unable to provide for them. The home was to 'keep, clothe and educate needy children of professional people until they reach an age where they are capable of looking after themselves, to give them a happier, sunnier outlook on life, and to strive to maintain that outlook after they leave it to make room for other little ones.'

Gracie's mother and father, her manager Bert Aza, her two sisters, Edie and Betty, and their husbands were all present at the opening ceremony, as were many celebrities of the day - music hall artistes Charles Coburn, Robb Wilton, Norman Long and Charles Austin, and Sir Harry Preston and Dominions

Secretary Mr J.H. Thomas. Gracie made a little speech, then the guests all had tea in the large dining room before departing.

Twelve children were the nucleus of the orphanage, which was originally the first house that Gracie had bought for her parents. They had found it 'a bit far from pub and fish and chip shop, lass,' so she bought another one for them nearer to the good things of life, and, with additions, the first house became the Peacehaven Orphanage. The Guild ran it, and Gracie financed it until 1967, when it closed through lack of children needing it. The two remaining were found homes in the area, and the house was sold (it is now a rest home).

The number of children fluctuated through the years between twelve and twenty-five. Gracie went to see them frequently and kept in touch with the matron about the welfare of her charges. 'I should like to be the matron', she said once, 'I suppose that sounds funny, but it's true. I love kids and I'd see they were all one big, happy family.'

Most of her visits were private ones - when she lived in Telscombe, at The Haven, during the latter half of the thirties, it was near enough for her to pop in for a while, and she did this often. When she broadcast, all the 'repeat' fees went to the orphanage, and when she was asked to open anything, from a store to a cinema or holiday camp, she usually asked that the fee, whether it was £15 or £250, go to the orphanage fund.

During the war, mothers and children were evacuated from London to the orphanage. Later, when they and the orphanage children were evacuated to the country, the Navy took over the house.

The Haven, in Telscombe was one of Gracie's favourite homes. Her bedroom there was decorated in dark grey moire silk, and had a marble washstand. The bathroom was pale green. In the large oak-beamed sitting room was a white Bluthner grand piano, a bookcase and a well stocked bar. A comfortable sofa and armchairs stood on the wooden floor near the open brick fireplace, and the shelves held some of the fine china she loved to collect.

Outside the back of the house was designed to look like a ship, with decks and outside stairs leading to two flat roofs, and another staircase down to the lawns. It was a happy house.

Many things have been named after Gracie: a ship, bus, aeroplane, theatre, cocktail, rose, a canal boat, once even an elephant and a horse.

Gracie's ship was launched on 8th April 1936 at Southampton. *Gracie Fields* - a 393 ton paddle steamer - was built by John I. Thorneycroft. She cost £35,740, and her captain was N.R. Larkin.

As the *Gracie Fields* glided into the water her namesake led the watching crowds in *Sing As We Go*. Several thousand people watched the launch, and Gracie, from her position by the microphone, gave those at the back a running commentary on the scene from where she stood.

Two hundred guests sat down to a luncheon afterwards at the South Western Hotel, where a novel feature was the naming of the tables after principal marks in the waterway served by the ships of the Red Funnel Company. The top table was called Southampton Water, while the others became the Solent, Spithead, the Needles, Cowes Roads, Sandown Bay, St Catherine's Point and Christchurch Bay.

The Red Funnel Company, whose flag is blue, green, red and white, and whose first four ships were named *Sapphire*, *Emerald*, *Ruby* and *Pearl*, presented Gracie with a brooch in the shape of the flag and incorporating these four gems, and she treasured and wore it frequently until it was stolen when she was in America many, many years afterwards, and never recovered. Gracie also received a silver christening mug and a lifebelt inscribed with the name of her ship from Sir John Thorneycroft, and from the Portsmouth and District Lancashire Society, an ornamental clog inscribed 'To Our Gracie with best wishes', and an enormous bunch of red roses.

The *Gracie Fields* was on the Southampton to Isle of Wight service, and soon after her launching Gracie took all the children from her orphanage for a trip in her.

On July 15th 1939 the steamer was involved in an incident with a flying boat. As she was leaving Southampton for Ryde, filled with holiday-makers, at the mouth of Southampton Water, an RAF flying boat from Calshot struck her foremast and crashed into the sea alongside, with its starboard wing shattered. No one was hurt, although several passengers suffered shock. Jagged pieces of metal from the ripped wing were showered onto the ship, which had her foremast snapped off and her port bow damaged.

The *Gracie Fields* was called up for war service on 22nd September 1939. Putting on her warpaint at Dover she was used, as many paddle steamers were, as a minesweeper, serving with the 10th Minesweeping Flotilla.

At 2100 hours on 27th May 1940 she left Dover for Dunkirk, arriving at 0300 hours on the following day. She proceeded to transfer troops from the shore to the waiting HMS *Calcutta*. After a few trips between the shore and HMS *Calcutta*, she sailed home to Margate with 281 troops on board.

The following day she returned to Dunkirk and took about 750 troops off La Panne Beach. She was starting back across the Channel when she was attacked by dive-bombers off Middle Kerke buoy. Hit amidships by a bomb, she was unable to stop her engines and was continuing underway at six knots when her helm jammed. A small craft, the *Twentie*, secured alongside, transferring as many wounded and others as she could carry. Another craft, the *Jutland*, then steamed alongside, secured and took off more troops. After the *Jutland* had pulled away, low in the water beneath her human cargo, HMS *Pangbourne*, already damaged by near misses, and with twenty-four casualties aboard, went alongside, took off eighty troops, and, after a difficult manoeuvre, took the crippled paddler in tow.

At 0130 hours on Thursday 30th May 1940, the *Gracie Fields* reported that she was sinking. *Pangbourne* took off the stricken ship's crew, slipped the tow and abandoned her. The last call from the paddle steamer *Gracie Fields* came from 51° 20'N, 02° 05'E.

Gracie said when her ship sank, 'It makes me feel sad, but as J.B. Priestley wrote, "she went down doing her duty."'

The hybrid tea-rose named for her was deep buttercup yellow and won a gold medal for its breeder, Mr George Frederick Letts of Hadleigh, Suffolk, in 1938 when it was introduced. It had fine glossy leaves which were mildew proof, produced vigorous growth and was free flowering and an ideal bedding variety. It had a rich, fruity, sweet-briar scent, and sold, in 1938, for 2/6 a bush, 24 shillings a dozen. At 2/6 a bush it was among the more expensive roses in the catalogue, but it proved very popular.

It takes up to ten years to breed a new rose, and 'Gracie Fields' was raised from original stock of 'The Evening News,' and 'Daily Mail.' George Letts sent Gracie a bouquet of 'her roses', and she sent him back a photograph of her with them. Although he saw and heard Gracie many times, George Letts never met her. 'She was always my favourite,' he said, 'I admired her tremendously.'

In January 1938 the *Rochdale Observer* launched a Portrait Fund. They asked people to send a shilling, or as many shillings as they could, towards a portrait of 'Our Greatest Townswoman'. In a little over a month more than thirty thousand readers had contributed 15,046 shillings, making a total of £752, and forty-five year old James Gunn, later knighted as one of Britain's most eminent artists, was asked to paint the portrait which now, when it is not on loan to art galleries in different parts of the country, hangs in Rochdale Art Gallery.

Typically, when it was unveiled and presented to her, Gracie said, 'I feel that this is the most magnificent tribute that has ever been paid to any artiste. I am very, very happy and thrilled. You have proved now that you do think something about me, and I think something about you too.' Laughing, she added, 'I took three weeks off specially to pose for this picture, otherwise it would never have got done and Rochdalians would have said, "Hey! You've got our shillings - stop mucking about".' Gracie gave the painting to the art gallery right away. 'He's made me quite nice looking,' she quipped.

1938 was quite a year for public recognition. She was awarded the CBE, the first woman variety artiste to receive it.

Waiting with the other people in the ballroom at Buckingham Palace, Gracie said afterwards, was 'like something you read about, a wonderful fairy story. I watched a man being knighted, and believe me I felt a long, long way from ordinary life at that moment.'

The crowd waiting outside the palace cheered her as she came out with her medal. Shortly afterwards she was given the Order of St John of Jerusalem for her work for hospitals, and the Red Cross, the first actress to receive this award, which is never given lightly. The Priory in Clerkenwell is the headquarters of the Order of St John in England, and it was there that Gracie was invested as an Officer Sister of the Order; she left with the eight-pointed cross pinned to her dress, driving through the beautiful historic Gatehouse whose pavements were lined with her fans. A typical 'Gracie incident' happened then. She saw a little old lady peering round the corner of the arch where no one was supposed to be, and she asked for her car to be stopped, alighted and showed her the cross, which she wore frequently and treasured for the rest of her life. Many years later, on hearing of a friend's recognition also, she commented, 'Sisters in the service of mankind.'

In May the town of her birth gave her the highest honour it could bestow on a citizen. The day Gracie received the freedom of her hometown lived forever in her heart. She loved Rochdale, the Rochdale of her childhood and youth especially, because a lot of her memories were there.

Many moving and inspiring words were spoken that day, great crowds cheered her, and the nation 'listened in' to a lively interview conducted by Richard North, who was described as 'the travelling radio reporter' of the North Region staff. The broadcast also went out on Empire Transmitters to her admirers in Australia, New Zealand, Canada and South Africa.

When the ceremony was over, Gracie went onto the town hall balcony to receive the cheers and good wishes of the thousands of people who were packing the streets below. From the many lovely moments of that day (when she admitted softly, 'I'm all nerves'), three items above all else show us Gracie. The last part of her reply to the Mayor, 'Wherever I go in this big world of ours, this casket is going to go with me. I shan't need it to remind me of Rochdale, because I couldn't forget it if I tried.'

The other two were not words but deeds. Gracie had a rug made by the Disabled Men's Handicrafts Ltd and presented it to the Mayor before she left the town hall. The wool rug bore the Rochdale coat of arms. Also she suggested, and gave, three performances for local charities after the official presentation, before leaving for London around midnight on that historic day.

After the solemnity of the citation, Gracie had lunch with the Mayor and city dignitaries. Then she lightened the proceedings by riding round the town on a fire engine, in full fireman's gear, before going to the theatre for the first of her charity shows.

Eighteen years later, in 1956, when Rochdale celebrated its centenary as a borough, the magazine *Lancashire Life* asked her what Rochdale meant to her, and she wrote:

You ask what Rochdale means to me, perhaps you will think my answer strange, but to me Rochdale means first. In Rochdale I first opened my eyes. In Rochdale I first cried, first laughed, heard the birds sing for the first time. I sang too for the first time in my life. I was even spanked for the first time in Rochdale. And in Rochdale I wore my first pair of clogs.

My first, and almost my only schooling took place in Rochdale at the Parish Church School. My first tram ride around the town, my first swimming lessons in her baths, and when very young, slipping into the Ship Canal along with the other children for an extra swim during the hot summer days.

My first job was as an errand girl for a confectioner's shop, for this I got a shilling a week and my mother complained that it cost her two shillings a week to have my shoes repaired after all the walking I did on the job. My first song on a stage was sung at the Old Circus in Rochdale where now stands the Hippodrome.

My first job as a winder was in Pouches old cotton mill way down off Oldham Road. My work since then has meant travelling the world over, to great places and small, but 'Home' to me always means Rochdale and its gradely folk. My memories are ever sweet and homely. I see all Rochdale's lovely parks and gardens, the beautiful walks all so near - Healey Dell, Hollingworth Lake, and all the rest.

On my travels too I am reminded so often all over the world of home, whenever I see the machinery and products of Rochdale proudly stamped with names of her great manufacturers. Once in Naples, one of the Cirio people - they make jams and sauces - told me that the machinery in their factories came from Rochdale. You can just imagine how proud that made me.

She took great pride in the town of her birth and early years, and, although she left it when she was sixteen and never returned there to live - 'I probably would have done if it had been by the sea', she often said jokingly - in the years before the war she went back frequently, usually staying with friends.

She returned after the war too, but less often, although she always was, as Rochdale's former Member of Parliament Cyril Smith once said, 'Rochdale's greatest ambassadress.'

She mentioned the town in concerts, broadcasts and other countries, from east to west, north to south, and anyone who had ever heard of Gracie Fields always knew she originally came from Rochdale. 'Where do you live?'- 'Rochdale.' - 'Ah, Gracie Fields' town', is a common occurrence for the natives of the town in conversations with other folk all over the world.

8. Illness and Divorce

In 1935 Gracie toured South Africa. There had been a delay on the film *Queen of Hearts* when one of the actors was ill, and the film was only finished and 'in the can' at three o'clock on the morning she sailed.

For a few days she rested, then began rehearsing for the South African concerts. Gracie, superstitious over some things, wasn't over colours, and she wore a dark green dress on her arrival in South Africa. 'Friends told me it was an unlucky colour', she said later, 'but it wasn't so for me.'

Her brother Tommy went to South Africa with her. 'Her reception was phenomenal,' he said, 'I'd never seen anything like it. Every usherette from every theatre and cinema, all lined up with bouquets of flowers, bands playing... We drove from the docks in open cars, right through the whole of Cape Town, and there was the ticker tape flowing down, and thousands of people who had taken the day off work to welcome Gracie. It really was an incredible experience.'

That tour of South Africa was a surprise to Gracie too. She thought she would have to win them over but found that many people were already committed fans. 'I was totally unprepared for my reception in South Africa,' she said later, 'and their welcome unnerved me.'

They had heard her records and seen her films, and when she did a thirty-minute act for her first show in that country, the critics complained that it wasn't nearly long enough. Gracie said, 'All the criticism, instead of being directed at me, was somehow thrust onto the orchestra. It just shows you the advantage of having a reputation. If the show was a flop it couldn't be Gracie Fields - it must be the miserable, anonymous orchestra.'

She did a typical 'Gracie' thing then, invited the critics to come back at her expense and she would put on a 'better show.' She told them she had been nervous after such a welcome, and hadn't realised that they expected a longer performance, but that it had nothing to do with the orchestra and was entirely her fault. When she left Cape Town, that orchestra gave her a silver plaque which said, 'To Our Gracie from the orchestra' and there wasn't one of them who would not have followed her anywhere to play for her.

Twenty-one year old Harry Parr-Davies was with them on that tour. Gracie said, 'Four years previously a long, lanky lad walked into my dressing room at the theatre. He'd got past the stage door keeper because he looked so young, like a messenger boy. He mumbled something about a song he'd written. He seemed so nervous I let him play him his song and it was very good. The number went into my next film and Harry composed many others for me after that, as well as becoming my accompanist.'

Harry, born in Neath in 1914, had learnt to play the piano when he was six. He played for Gracie for nine years. He was grumpy and temperamental but extraordinarily talented, both as a composer and a pianist.

While they were in South Africa, Gracie saw as much of the country as she could, visiting gold and diamond mines and talking to as many people as possible.

'I'll always remember going to the diamond sorting department and holding piles of the stones, just letting them trickle through our hands,' Tommy Fields said, 'and Gracie laughing and saying how rich she felt.'

They toured from Cape Town to Johannesburg, and at each station crowds were waiting to catch a glimpse of Gracie, and so she sang from the observation platform at each stop along the line. She was in South Africa for Christmas 1935, and the BBC arranged for her to broadcast a message to people in Britain, but they could not get through, and as it was to be 'live', and not a recorded message, there was nothing to be done. The tour was so successful that it was extended by six weeks. On the day she returned she went into Broadcasting House for a short interview. The announcer simply said, 'Here she is, just back from South Africa', no names or long elaborate lead-in, and Gracie's voice went into thousands of rooms with her usual greeting, 'Hullo everybody...'

In 1930 she toured America. 'I was a flop for the first three days,' she said, 'and most unhappy. I didn't feel right.' Many British artistes have not done well in the USA, and vice versa. Humour especially does not always travel, but she was a singer as well as a comedienne.

Always nervous before she went on, and with some critics saying that the Americans would never understand her accent, she had many qualms, but Gracie enjoyed a challenge too, and by the end of the first week she really did have a success on her hands. 'The first three days were a flop,' she insisted, 'but I worked on it.'

'She has a voice packed tight with soul appeal, a gorgeous sense of comedy values and a versatility in delineation that is rarely combined in one individual. She had the Palace mob at her feet and trailed off in a dizzy array of encores. These United States will hear plenty more of the Lancashire Lassie', the American newspaper *The Billboard* enthused wordily.

This kind of thing always frightened Gracie. 'In America they billed me as Gracie Fields - The Funniest Woman In The World - that petrified me for a start', she said. She always had a wonderful reception in the USA after that.

Her brother Tommy was in New York several years after the war when Gracie was working at the Plaza Hotel, doing five shows a day. 'I'd never seen her work in America,' he said, 'so I went along. When she came onto the floor I was absolutely amazed because everybody stood up and applauded. She had a terrific reception even before she opened her mouth.'

She sometimes chided her audiences for doing this. 'You shouldn't clap too soon, you'll put me off. Wait and see if I'm worth it.'

When she made her first appearance at the Waldorf-Astoria, the audience were all talking so she said to them, 'Ready when you are.' They stopped and listened. Jack Benny, who was top of the bill, said they had never been quiet before. Gracie said, 'It was sheer cheekiness that made me do it.'

Everywhere it was the same story. Streets lined with her fans, Gracie standing up in an open car so as many as possible could see her. Whenever she went on tour, in England or abroad, it was like a royal procession. She felt a duty to the people to let them see her when they obviously wanted this so much, but she was frightened when they mobbed her.

Once, outside a theatre in Britain when this happened, she opened the car window when she had reached safety, and really went for the crowd. 'You know I usually stop, but it's a special family party tonight, and now you've torn my dress and made me late...' She didn't often fall out with her admirers. 'Some of 'em overdo it a bit', she declared, but mostly she accepted it as part of her work. 'I'm grateful they want to see me,' she said more than once, 'but there are times...'

Another occasion was when she went dashing in at the stage door and could not get through because of a small crowd waiting there. She knew most of their faces, they were regular followers. Fighting her way through she grew very cross, 'You're mad,' she said, 'hanging about here this cold weather...' It was December. She apologised when she came out and saw them there again. 'I was late and a bit edgy', then in a different tone, 'I still think you're all crazy.'

Yet they came, and Gracie saw and spoke to as many of them as she could. Her warmth and personality drew people to her, and they adored her as much as a woman as they did as a singer. 'I'm ordinary,' she said to them, 'don't raise me too high...'

Gracie and Monty Banks first met at The Haven, her home in Peacehaven. He came to see her about directing her next proposed film, *Queen of Hearts*. Monty's name was really Mario Bianchi, and he was born in Cesena, northern Italy. His first wife was Gladys Frazin, an actress with a history of mental illness. Monty had been a stunt man and an actor before his directing days. As well as being an exceedingly good director he was full of fun. He had gone to America when he was nineteen, taken part in silent films, he was one of the original Keystone Cops, and had been in England for several years directing.

Gracie was thirty-eight when she met Monty. 'It's funny, when you look back,' she says in *Sing As We Go*, 'how little you realise what a casual meeting can do to change the whole course of your life.'

For the first time Gracie came close to enjoying making a film. Monty was a natural clown, but like Gracie herself, he was a true professional and beneath the fooling he worked to achieve the results he wanted.

Queen Of Hearts, the film Gracie finished in 1936 before she went to South Africa, was a great success. She did another film with Basil Dean, *The Show Goes On*, a story superficially like her own, and then in 1937 Monty Banks directed her in *We're Going To Be Rich* (in the USA this was titled *He Was Her Man*). This was Gracie's second film with Monty directing. She still did not care for film-making, the stage was her real forte, but she was committed to the films for a while. It seems generally agreed among the critics that Monty Banks captured Gracie on film as well as anyone ever did.

She and Monty had a lot in common. Both had been poor and with talent and hard work had reached the top. He took Gracie to Hollywood to meet Daryl F. Zanuck, head of Twentieth Century Fox, who was paying her £200,000 to make four films. 'Now I know everyone's gone daft', she said to Monty and her agent Bert Aza.

It was Monty who persuaded her to buy some property in America, because she didn't like staying in hotels. La Escondita (The Hidden House) was in Santa Monica, California. It was hidden behind a tall wall, half way up the canyon side. There was a garden with lawns, flowers, trees, an aviary, swimming pool, tennis court and garden bungalow. At the side of the house was a walled courtyard with an outside staircase and three rooms above. 'Will be nice for the family for holidays too', Gracie said. Then she returned to England and more work.

Gracie was doing a film a year, tours, concerts, records, appearances at charity functions where she always 'gave 'em three penn'orth not two', to use an expression of hers. Wherever she went in a private capacity, crowds gathered and persuaded her to 'give us a song, Gracie, just one.' She nearly always did. She said more than once about her fans, 'I don't know what they'll ask me to do next, but whatever it is I'll do it.'

In 1938 she made *Keep Smiling*, with Roger Livesey as her co-star, and in 1939 the film that completed the four that she was paid £50,000 each for, *Shipyard Sally*, which also had Sydney Howard in the cast. These were made in England at her request. For months she had not been feeling well and when that last film was in the can, she went to the doctor. He sent her to hospital where they did an exploratory operation. Afterwards they told her she had cancer and they needed to operate again. It wasn't until much later she knew that if she hadn't had the operation she would have been dead within the year.

Gracie, now aged forty-one, had always wanted children. As the eldest she had mothered her two sisters and her brother, possibly more than most elder sisters because, being on the stage and away from home, she really had looked after them when Jenny sent them out to join the company on tour. When the doctor told her gently, 'I'm afraid it means a hysterectomy', her dreams in that direction were swept swiftly away.

'The hours in which I had to tell myself, "well you can't have everything" weren't all that easy,' she said later, 'but maybe I was getting a bit long in the tooth for kids anyway, yet somehow, until then I had still hoped.'

After the operation in June 1939 she was unconscious for three days, and almost without exception the nation prayed for her. In churches of all denominations prayers were offered, asking, begging, for her recovery. Half a million letters, hundreds of bunches of flowers and gifts were sent to her at the Chelsea Hospital for Women. It was an incredible demonstration of affection for this woman who had sung and clowned, but especially sung, her way into the hearts of so many people.

'Gracie gravely ill,' read the headlines, 'Miss Gracie Fields underwent an internal operation last night. Her condition is serious. As I write the nation is hanging on the news from the Chelsea Hospital for Women. It is Our Gracie who is fighting. Readers will not desire that I should say more.'

The pavements outside the hospital were covered with straw to deaden the sounds. Bulletins were issued twice daily to cope with the overwhelming flood of enquiries, and the *Daily Express* cartoonist Strube showed his famous 'Little Man', Mr Average, with bowler hat and umbrella standing outside the hospital with a bunch of flowers in his hand and looking upwards towards a partially opened window.

Slowly, very slowly, Gracie recovered. 'Whenever the pain was bad,' she said in her book, *Sing As We Go*, 'whenever I drifted away and came back again, I always saw Mary by my bedside. I think she could never have gone home. One of the most wonderful things I remember about that long illness was the sight of Mary there whenever I opened my eyes.'

Mary Barratt (later Davey) had come to work for Gracie in the middle thirties and remained one of her closest friends. Monty Banks, as well as Mary Barratt, was her constant companion while she was so ill, along with her mother and father and favourite cousin Margaret.

As soon as she could walk, she visited the other wards, sharing her flowers with all the patients, until the hospital resembled a magnificent nursery. She left hospital in July 1939 after six weeks there, to find a huge crowd waiting outside to greet her. She was pale and unsteady, and the sight of the people brought the tears to her eyes. For a moment it seemed they were about to cheer. Ballet dancer Anton Dolin was there. 'She saw this,' he said, 'or sensed it, and raised her hand to stop them. There was not a sound, and then all the men in that great crowd took their hats off. It was an incredible moment, as though she were a queen and they were paying homage.'

At that time the public were not told that Gracie had been operated on for cancer of the cervix. In 1939 the word cancer was avoided if possible, but Gracie was a wonderful example of recovery from this disease, for she lived and worked at a pretty full pace for another forty years. She went for annual checkups until 1954, when she was finally cleared.

On July 22nd 1939 her divorce petition came up. One newspaper reported the following day:

The marriage was in 1923 at The Register Office, Wandsworth, and there are no children. Petitioner's case was that because of unhappiness she was compelled to leave her husband in 1932, and since then had had no communication from him. It was alleged that respondent committed adultery with Miss Annie Lipman, his secretary, at a Hastings hotel, and they had lived together at Hampstead.

Petitioner, who gave evidence from a seat in the witness box, asked for the discretion of the court in her favour, and put in a statement which the judge read. The judge said he was satisfied it was a proper case for a decree, and he exercised discretion in the petitioner's favour. The proceedings lasted half an hour. Mr Norman Birkett KC and Mr Aitken Watson were her counsel, and Mr Pitt was represented by Mrs P.M. Cloutman.

Miss Fields arrived at the law courts in a private car, accompanied by a relative [her sister, Edith] and a nurse. It was raining heavily and few people had assembled. When the case was over her two companions, holding an arm each, assisted her from the court to the adjoining lift. They went to the ground floor and out through the judge's exit to the quadrangle, where her car was waiting. The small crowd which by this time had assembled raised a cheer and Gracie waved her hand in response. She was looking pale and rather drawn. Immediately she and her companions were seated the car drove away on the return journey to Peacehaven.

From there, a few days later, Gracie left for Capri for two years rest, as the doctors prescribed. Before she left, she broadcast to the nation, and that broadcast made history, for in the House of Commons that evening Sir Samuel Hoare said, 'Gracie Fields is on the air tonight. It is obvious that the debate must end at an early hour.'

Gracie thanked all the people who had helped her over what she described as 'the most dreadful ordeal of my forty-one years.' She thanked her surgeon, New Zealand-born Mr Searle, the doctors and nurses at the hospital, and the Bishop of Blackburn who said prayers with her. Her voice almost broke as she thanked people from all over the world for their love and gifts. Then she sang *I Love The Moon*, a song written by Paul Rubens during the First World War.

Gracie told her listeners when she sang it in 1939, 'The words express all I'm trying to say to you now', and in homes throughout the country people wept to hear that golden voice again.

I love the moon, I love the sun,
I love the forests, the flowers, the fun,
I love the wild birds - the dawn and the dew,
But best of all I love you - I love you...

9. Gracie and Monty

Six weeks later war broke out. Gracie was in love with Monty Banks, and they planned to be married once she was well again. Now Gracie's one thought was to get back from Capri to Britain and do her bit for the war effort.

They left the following day, and when Monty and Mary (Mary Barratt) remonstrated with her that she was not yet fit to work, she said, 'I must. Work will be the best tonic I could have. In some small way it will be a thank you to all the folk who've helped me through this illness.'

Basil Dean was organising ENSA (Entertainments National Service Association, which comedian Tommy Trinder laughingly changed to Every Night Something Awful) and he said later that the most requested stars for ENSA concerts were Will Fyffe, Gracie Fields and George Formby.

Gracie said she would entertain troops anywhere, and in November she was on her way to France. Mary Barratt and Monty Banks were with her. The first two concerts were planned for Douai and Arras, but before they reached their destination the car broke down and Mary and Monty had to get out and push it from the mud. They made Gracie sit still, in any case she would not have had the strength then to do anything else.

The vehicle broke down repeatedly, and on one of these occasions, near Metz, an army convoy caught them up. They recognised Gracie, who was standing by the car while the others wrestled with it, and with help from the British Army they got it going again, and Gracie gave her first concert there and then. 'How those lads sang and shouted for more', she said later, 'I was still weak, but on that road in France, leaning against the car door for some support, and surrounded by the paraphernalia of war, I knew I was back in the fray.'

The boys in that convoy also remembered, as John Graven Hughes recalls in *The Greasepaint War*. When the leading three ton truck pulled up he says a corporal shouted, 'It's Our Gracie.'

> And it was Gracie Fields with her gaiety and humour in the broad, down-to-earth idiom of Rochdale, that voice of startling clarity and irresistible quality. They crowded round to give her a welcome, and a soldier said, as they always did, 'Give us a song, Gracie.' She threw her hat to Monty Banks, stood on the running board and sang *Sally*, unaccompanied, to soldiers perched on top of tanks and on the sides of Bren gun carriers.

Gracie recalls, 'Most of the boys were like old friends. They'd seen me on the halls or heard me on the radio, and I suppose I was part of the life they left behind. The songs I sang, *When I Grow Too Old To Dream*, *The Isle of Capri* and *Little Old Lady*, were the ones they'd whistled on the way to work, and when they heard them again in France they were back home for a little while.'

They went on to their planned venues, Arras and Douai, and Gracie admitted long afterwards that she was shaking with nerves, she felt so weak. Yet in front of the footlights she came back to life.

The little party went on through France, and Gracie spent Christmas singing to the troops at Rheims. The weather was atrocious. Mary Hemingway, who was there as a reporter for a Fleet Street newspaper, wrote later in McCalls:

> Some units were tented down in the empty harvested beet fields, and although with hearty cockney humour they had named the rows between tent rows after Piccadilly and The Strand, their tents were pitched open to the prevailing west wind. Their kitchen and mess area were set up in a mud-provoking hollow. When I wondered aloud to an officer about the setup he answered jovially, 'No matter, they're not getting killed.'

Nobody was looking forward to the Christmas holidays until word got around that Gracie Fields was coming to Rheims to give a concert. Officers not invited. Only petty officers, tommies, and aircraft maintenance crews could come. Spirits ballooned. Rheims was in the centre of the champagne country and the most uncomfortable British encampments.

The Christmas Day weather wasn't too bad, and the army cooks managed to roast sides of beef for dinner. But a murderous storm whirled up that night, coating roads with ice, and camouflaging ditches with snowbanks.

'She'll never make it,' people muttered. But she did, and so did the others of her cast and the small orchestra that accompanied her. (Her chauffeur told me the drive from Paris was 'a horror', but Gracie said, 'It was nothing, ducks.')

The Rheims Opera House, its cup running over with tommies, must have quaked the town with the racket of the audience's welcome when Gracie hurried on stage. After the nasty drive she looked fresh as a fresh peach, cheerful as Father Christmas, bright as a tulip, with her blonde hair shining, and loving, loving. She was the happy essence of Home.

When the uproar subsided she sang her signature tune, *Sally*, and at its end the old roof lifted an inch or two off its pinnings. She sang all their favourites, and for the finale Gracie and her troupe on stage joined hands, advanced to the proscenium, and clasped hands with the soldiers from the front row seats, leaning out over the orchestra pit, and the whole house sang, 'Should auld acquaintance be forgot..'

Outside in the freezing air soldiers climbed into the open backs of lorries, squeezing themselves together for a twenty or thirty mile ride, like upended planks. One after another of the lorryfuls of young men picked up the tune and sang 'Roll out the barrel, we'll have a barrel of fun...' and some lorries changed it to 'we've *had* a barrel of fun', their voices echoing diminuendo in the frosty night. Gracie Fields that Christmas was one to whom I am ever grateful.

Listeners to the BBC after the nine o'clock news heard a NAAFI Variety Concert organised by ENSA, 'Gracie with Jack Payne and his band from "Somewhere in France..."'

On a couple of occasions Jack Payne and his band had transport difficulties and were delayed en route, so Gracie and Monty turned out an old sketch from her theatrical basket. They rehearsed and all went well, but when they came to the performance, which included Harry Parr-Davies (composer and Gracie's accompanist) and Mary Barratt, Basil Dean says that, Monty's startling improvisations, verbal and gymnastic, delighted the troops but reduced Gracie to such helpless laughter that she forgot to 'feed' him with the correct lines, and the so-called dramatic sketch ended in Marx Brothers confusion.

Gracie sang her way through France, then went back to Capri for a couple of weeks to recover a little. Everyone I spoke to who worked with or saw Gracie Fields during the war gave me the same picture. She went wherever was suggested as long as there were troops who needed entertainment.

Richard Murdoch and Arthur Askey worked with her in Lille and Amiens and said, 'She was a tonic, did a marvellous show, and the receptions those soldiers gave her were absolutely fantastic.'

Arthur Askey said, 'My God, she worked. Often when I'd had enough and they said, "There's a bit of an isolated camp down the road", she'd go. Twenty, thirty miles, she could be tired out, but she'd climb into the lorry, or jeep or whatever transport was taking her, and when she got on the stage, no matter how rough and improvised it might be, she seemed to shed that tiredness and become a different person.'

Gracie and Monty acquired a mobile tea-van, and at the next stop she had great fun when the boys crowded round to find it was 'Our Gracie' dishing out the tea.

In January 1940 they returned to Britain, and Gracie went to Greenock, singing to the Navy. She toured camps all over the British Isles, then went back to Capri to collect some clothes and generally put things in order.

Her parents were in America with her sister Edie and some of the grandchildren, in the property she had bought when she was over there in 1936, and although she wanted to be married in Britain, her mother's general health wasn't good, and she was going blind, so Gracie and Monty decided to marry in California where her family could be present.

They wed on March 19th 1940. Gracie wore a blue costume, white blouse, white shoes, and a smart pillbox hat for the ceremony, which was conducted by Judge Joseph Marchetti. Gracie clung to the hope that they could have a further ceremony in the church at Telscombe in Sussex where they had lived and where her orphanage was. This needed permission from the Bishop of Chichester because Monty was a Roman Catholic, and both parties had been through a divorce.

It never happened, largely because events of the outside world caught them rapidly. They both knew it might be difficult if Italy went in with Germany because Monty was still Italian. Years before, he had taken out naturalization papers to become an American citizen but had never filled them in. He had land in Italy, several farms which his sister managed, but he had spent most of his adult life in the USA.

Two days after their wedding, Gracie did a show with Maurice Chevalier at Drury Lane in London, and another in the Opera House, Paris, 'to promote goodwill between France and England.'

She and Monty both entertained the troops in France until nearly the end of May 1940, when most of the ENSA people were brought home before the German occupation. She sang a wartime version of her famous comic song, *Biggest Aspidistra*:

Then Goering saw him from afar and said to his old Frau,
Young Joe has got his blood up so the war's all over now,
'Cos they're going to string old Hitler from the very highest bough,
Of the biggest aspidistra in the world.

She was put on a blacklist and a German editor wrote, 'Gracie Fields has earned for England the equivalent of 100 new Spitfires. She is adjudged a war industry and should be treated accordingly.'

Gracie and others were recalled. She left Arras under cover of darkness and without any luggage. Two days later the hotel where they stayed was bombed by the Germans, her bedroom reduced to rubble, and seven people killed.

Back in Britain they toured the military camps and the factories. They returned to London, and Gracie was alone in their hotel when the legendary *Sunday Express* columnist Lord Castlerosse telephoned to urge Monty to go to America or Eire.

'It's most important,' he said, 'to do with his folks at home, you understand.'

When Monty returned, Gracie took a deep breath and told him, and together they faced the knowledge that, because he had never finished and filed those papers to make him a United States citizen, he would be an enemy, in technical terms, if not in thought and desire, of his wife's country.

Gracie said later, 'I loved my country and I loved my husband, and in the end I reached what seemed to me to be a fair compromise.'

On 11th June 1940 Italy entered the war on the German side, and Monty Banks immediately became 'an enemy alien'.

Gracie had managed to get a meeting with Winston Churchill and two or three other ministers, and Churchill told her the best thing she could do was to earn some dollars for Britain. 'We need all the American dollars we can get,' he said, 'You, as an Englishwoman, can travel almost anywhere, but if you want to work for Britain it's no good earning English pounds, Gracie, but if you can earn American dollars for Britain you will be doing her the greatest service you can.'

If Monty had stayed in Britain, he would have been interned because he was Italian. No wife worth her salt was going to see that happen if she could prevent it. Therefore on Thursday

30th May, wearing a red, white and blue rosette on her coat, Gracie and Monty sailed for the USA and Canada. In Canada they met more trouble. Monty, said the officials, would have to be interned. 'What about me?' Gracie asked. 'I'm his wife.'

She was there to give concerts for the Navy League, and Monty's plans were to go on to America and become a US citizen. Arguments ensued, but eventually they allowed him to travel on, and Gracie stayed in Canada with her pianist, Harry Parr-Davies, and did thirty-two concerts across the land.

That tour resulted in £170,000 for the Navy League. Gracie took no fee during the war. The only money that actually passed through her hands was a cheque for $1,000 given to her by a Frenchman after she had sung *There'll Always Be An England* at a private party. Gracie sent the cheque to Rochdale's MP, Dr H.B.W. Morgan, 'for the most needy causes of our hometown.'

Her accommodation, meals and transport were provided, but that was all. When the concerts were finished, she went to California for a week to see her husband and family. She wasn't a fit woman, and anyone who has ever undertaken journeyings of far less than the thousands of miles she did then will realise some of the strain she was experiencing. After that strenuous Canadian tour she desperately needed a rest. That was when the hounding gathered momentum.

Headlines screamed from some of the newspapers that Gracie Fields had deserted her country, had taken all her money and jewellery abroad. Traitor and cheat are strong words - both were used against her, and the wounds went deep.

Monty wanted her to give up everything and live in America, but Gracie knew she could never do that. 'My conscience is clear,' she said when she returned to Canada for her second Navy League tour the following week, and the reporters rattled their questions at her. 'If I have done anything I shouldn't have done, I will go and put it right. I'm going back to England when I've finished this tour anyway, but what have I done wrong?'

In her heart she knew it was because she was married to an Italian. 'Monty was practically the cause of the war according to the papers', she said bitterly afterwards.

Mr J.J. Davidson, the MP for Maryhill, Glasgow, tabled a question in the House of Commons asking why Miss Gracie Fields was allowed to take £8,000 out of the country in October 1939, and Monty Banks, her husband, to take £20,000. The reply was that permission to take out the money had been applied for the previous October.

> The application was supported by a strong medical recommendation. It was decided that the sum asked for was excessive, but permission was given for the sum of £8,000. This was a large amount, but the circumstances were unusual and it was expected that Miss Fields, after her recovery, would earn dollars in America which would be surrendered to the state. Miss Fields was also granted a sum for the support of her parents in the United States, and a further sum to meet life insurance premiums payable under prewar contracts. These allocations were in accordance with normal practice.

Gracie had to take out a huge medical insurance to work overseas because she was working against medical advice. The answer continued, 'The restriction on taking out jewellery imposed on July 1st 1940, did not exist when Miss Fields left the country.'

Monty Banks, angry at what he saw as grossly unfair, and anxious about Gracie's poor health, said in an interview with Associated Press:

> I am not a British citizen and it is my own money. Anyway we followed the usual procedure, making regular application for permission to take our money with us. It is just because I am Italian that they are trying to make things disagreeable for Miss Fields. I wish they would cease. She has been giving very generously of her time and her talents. If they bother us

any more I am going to telephone to her to come home and live like a normal person.

That statement didn't endear him to the British press nor the British people, and Gracie, hurt and bewildered, said in a telephone interview with a Canadian newspaper:

All my assets are in England. I don't see why I should be persecuted like this. Let the government look up their files, they will soon find out I haven't taken everything out of the country. I have been working harder in the past few months than I have ever done before, and it has not been for myself. I am getting sick and tired of it, it's all so unpleasant. My home is in England and I intend going back. I can't understand it, everything I have, and the same applies to my husband, is the government's whenever they want it. My husband didn't do anything wrong and neither did I. I haven't earned a penny for myself since the war started. I'm disgusted with the whole thing.

Then she got on with the business of entertaining and raising money for the war effort, while at home the arguments continued. Her accountants in London issued a statement saying, 'It is within our knowledge that she has left substantial assets here.'

Dr Morgan, Rochdale's MP, asked for the question to be withdrawn, suggesting that the information required could have been obtained 'with less publicity and without a parliamentary reference to a great native.'

It wasn't withdrawn, and part of Dr Morgan's reply was, 'Her patriotism and loyalty are unchallengeable, an unfair reflection on a very good and fine lady beloved by numerous democrats in Great Britain.'

From America, where she had moved on to raise money for British War Relief, Gracie answered the Scottish MP:

At this grave hour of crisis which our country is going through, when all our thoughts and efforts are united in the common cause, I feel that your investigations of financial matters are most praiseworthy. But I am sure that in my case you have been misinformed. Can easily comprehend that, as since Italy declared war we have suffered numerous other embarrassments. Appreciate if you ask manager Clydesdale Bank Lombard Street, London for copy of my husband's letter to him dated May 22nd. Also statement from Bank of England showing amounts allowed me by them since war started. I hope this information will clear the position. Before Monty Banks left England he paid his income tax in full.

Mr Davidson said, 'I see no reason to follow Miss Field's suggestion that I should consult her banker. The Home Secretary's reply will be sufficient. There is plenty of work for all stage artistes who want to do their bit in this country.'

Gracie also wrote to Dr Morgan, thanking him for championing her.

Dear Dr Morgan, I do thank you for your very great kindness in standing by me during the Glasgow MP's nasty business. I guess there's always somebody trying to make trouble, as if there isn't enough in the world already. If some folks would work as hard as other folks maybe we'd be getting this awful war over much quicker.

There has been nothing taken out of England without permission of the banks, and what I was allowed is being spent in expenses doing my job. I have used my own money for all expenses since the war began, and I haven't received one penny from anyone.

I'm very happy to tell you that my Canadian tour up to now is a great success, and it looks like we shall attain our desire of making over £50,000 - a quarter of a million dollars, for our Navy League and Red Cross etc. Anything that I can attend that will help our country I have done, and I might add that I've never worked overtime so much in all my life. I only hope I can keep well and fit to continue my job. My very kindest regards to you, and again I thank you.

In February 1941 Gracie acknowledged the Mayor and Mayoress of Rochdale's Christmas and New Year greetings with a letter which included the following passage:

> I had hoped to return to England at the conclusion of my Canadian tour, but I was advised by the British officials here that I should continue to do the same charitable concert tour through America, because as well as raising a large amount of money for our needy ones at home, it would also help tremendously in creating international goodwill between ourselves and the Americans. I am very happy to say that both these endeavours have exceeded my expectations, and I am enclosing a few clippings which I thought might be of interest to you. It means a great deal to me personally to feel that I am doing my little bit to help my country, and no matter how strenuous my job may be I shall continue until the time comes when peace and sanity are again restored.

In a letter to a friend, May Snowden, in March 1941, she says:

> I've been going steadily for a couple of months doing the whole show myself, one hour and three-quarters singing. My sisters and their children are in Hollywood, and Mother and Dad... Please God this dreadful war will soon be over, so we can all go back to our normal way of living. Forgive the scribble and pencil, pens go funny on planes and that's what I'm writing to you on now, keep safe and well...

The cuttings she enclosed are worth reprinting here in part. The *Portland Oregonian* said:

> Gracie Fields of the honey-colored voice virtually paralysed a capacity audience in the public auditorium at her benefit performance for British Civilian Relief. The pert English comedienne, whose performance here netted approximately

5,000 dollars for her countrymen, alternately stilled the jammed house with a voice whose quality was the texture of living satin, or brought gales of laughter that swept from the gallery to the main floor with ballads delivered in the several English dialects. Her ability to turn from sublime singing to the raucous rendering of a cockney ballad in the tenor of a fishwife was little short of amazing to an audience that arrived totally unprepared for the chameleon-like repertoire of the talented singer.

Virginia Boren in the *Seattle Times* wrote:

I've never been a hero worshipper. But I'm a fanatical, fervent, feverish one right now. I'm crazy about Gracie. The program said, 'Gracie Fields, the toast of the army and navy, the idol of the RAF, and Commander of the Order of the British Empire.' And that's not half enough! Call it brotherly love. Call it the love of one democratic nation for another democratic nation. Call it international goodwill. Call it 'Hands across the sea'. But whatever it was it swept up with Homeric grandeur across the footlights to Gracie Fields, the lass of Lancashire who knows how to make broad humor buy food for bombed children... It made England and America one. It made the sponsors give Gracie 1,000 dollars *extra* for the fund she's raising for the children in Britain's bombed areas.

On their first wedding anniversary Monty met her in Salt Lake City, where she was giving a concert for British War Relief. They had a precious night together, then she moved onto her next venue and he returned to the film he was making in Hollywood, *Blood and Sand*.

'Monty courted me for four years,' Gracie joked to her audience, 'but we never saw much of each other, we were both so busy. We thought after we were married things would be different, but...' she pulled a face and blew him a kiss.

Gracie travelled across America under the banner of The British War Relief Society - through Canada under the auspices of the Navy League of Canada War Fund, everywhere singing and talking to thousands upon thousands of people, many of whom had heard her on records only until that time.

These concert tours made one and a half million dollars (almost £500,000) for Britain. That wasn't widely reported in the British press, yet it earned Gracie the Navy League's highest decoration, the Award of Service Medal.

Writing in 1952, the late Godfrey Winn said about that time:

Now in the calm and comparative peace of the aftermath let us be fair. The blitz had not yet commenced when Gracie put her duty as a wife first and went with her husband to America. A year later when the bombing was still at its height she returned to Europe and spent three months touring the camps and factories of England.

That return is now conveniently forgotten by her critics with such long memories, but it should not be so. Nor the certainty too that whatever money she was allowed to take out of the country she paid back a thousand times over by the performances she gave throughout America and Canada to raise money for British Relief Funds.

How the men in the fighting zone welcomed her. There was no criticism in their hearts as they listened to the old familiar songs reminding them of home. And what must have been in her own heart as she heard their applause coming back in great waves towards her, isolated under a spotlight on the stage?

'They want to crucify me', she said to Anton Dolin. 'Oh God, they don't know what they've done, they've given me hell. I'll get over it and I shall come back. Back to my dear London, my beloved England some day. I'm working every minute I can, as you are, yet still it's not enough - they don't know what they've done.'

She wrote to Monty, her beloved Mario, who from November 1940, was officially a USA citizen, sending him the following song she had composed and written on the back of one of her photographs one night when she couldn't sleep.

> You'll have me, I'll always cling to you,
> You'll have me, I'll always sing to you,
> Life gave us our awful blow,
> But my dear, we'll live to show
> The world what love can do,
> You'll have me forever by your side
> We will never, ever lose our pride,
> So darling, only realise I'm forever by your side,
> You'll have me forever - I love you.

10. Wartime

We need Our Gracie more than ever in these troubled days,
The Nightingale of Rochdale with her bright and cheery ways,
For when that golden voice comes trilling out upon the air,
We smile awhile and quite forget our worries and our care.

Comedienne, philanthropist, great lady all in one,
Adored, and yet unspoiled by fame and riches, she has won,
A lasting place deep in the heart of all true English folk,
The Lancashire Lassie who conquered the world,
With a song and a smile and a joke.

Patience Strong

In 1941 Gracie came home to tour the camps and factories in
Britain. Basil Dean, who organised the tour, received
anonymous letters about what would happen should she set
foot in this country again.

To show the other side, I quote here from a private letter
sent to May Snowden on 19th May 1941, from Mr W.H. (Bill)
Mooring of Odhams Press.

Take it from me Gracie did nothing wrong, unless it could
be called 'wrong' on her part to have stuck by her husband
in spite of the fact that he happened to be born an Italian.

Personally I admire that, and having known Monty and
Gracie very well long before they knew each other I was
infuriated by unfair, and often untruthful stories printed in
the British press about them. One point has never been made
clear in the British press, and Gracie herself is not in a position
to stress it. London newspaper editors however, could, if they
chose, secure confirmation from the Ministry of Information
concerning the national value of the work Gracie has been
doing, and still is doing, on this side (the USA).

Those of us who have experienced the gradual change in American public sentiment since the beginning of the war, realise fully how strong was the feeling in USA against granting Britain any kind of aid. This attitude was quite understandable because many millions of Americans desired above all other things that their country should not become involved in, what at the time seemed to be, a foreign political squabble.

It is my belief, based on my observations over a long period, that no one individual has done as much as Gracie to help cultivate amongst Americans interest in the British character and sympathy for the British cause. That is something quite apart from the enormous amount of work she has done on concert tours across Canada and USA, which still continue. Last Sunday she flew in from nine concerts, the audiences of which varied from American university students to 7,000 munition workers now building planes for us.

She had hoped, during May and June, to make a flying goodwill tour back home, and she tried to secure the necessary preferential travelling permit, so that she would not be held up in Lisbon. In fact she asked me to accompany her to manage the tour. Official information this week indicates a long delay in Lisbon to be unavoidable, and this would mean Gracie would have to let down the organisers of another giant tour of Canada which she is due to start soon, and which is to be followed immediately by another cross country tour of USA, all of course for war charities.

I explain this in case you should see reports to the contrary in the British press. These are facts beyond dispute, and if you should see printed anything to the contrary, you might perhaps like to write the editors correcting them, also get as many of your friends to do likewise. Unless the loyal Fields public rallies to her defence I am afraid it would be sometime before the British press shows her genuine fair play.

Gracie arrived in England on 8th July, after difficulties with her air passage and a long wait in Lisbon, where her money ran out. Lisbon was in a neutral country, and during the war many people passed through. Anna Neagle and Herbert Wilcox were also at the airport waiting and were able to lend Gracie some money.

She landed at Bristol airport during the afternoon, where a bevy of airmen, waafs, and mechanics raced across to her plane and cheered. Later at a press conference she said, 'I know what they've said, and I know that they are wrong. My conscience is completely clear, otherwise I should not be here.'

Because she was married to an Italian who had become a naturalized American there was speculation as to whether she was still British. 'I came here on a British passport. I'm British and always shall be', she said, her blue eyes bright in anger.

Journalist Beverley Nichols was present afterwards when she lay on the sofa to rest before her trip north. 'Basil Dean said to her, "Gracie, would you like a sip of brandy?" In faint, but fervant tones she replied, "For heaven's sake, luv, don't put such ideas into my head. Next thing they'll say is, she's taken t'bottle!"'

The tour was to begin in Rochdale, which was a wise decision in view of the happenings of the previous year. They drove up and were met at the boundary by the Chief Constable and the Town Clerk, then continued their journey to the town hall. Basil Dean said that people stood at the gates of their houses to see her go by, this time because she had been at the centre of such a controversy.

They reached the town hall, the square was packed, and, as Gracie came out onto the balcony, not yet knowing what sort of reception she would have, a roar of welcome went up and the factory whistles sounded a salute.

The tour, which took in the north of England, Greenock, Rosyth, Orkney, Inverness, Ipswich, Harwich, Chatham, Folkestone and London, lasted thirty-nine days, and she gave concerts on thirty-four of them, sometimes twice and three times a day. Eighty-six full concerts were given, and the audience figures were in excess of 410,000.

Monty hadn't been allowed into Britain, and this caused a fair amount of trouble and embarrassment. He insisted that Gracie must have two days rest out of the seven because he was very concerned for her health. She said herself some time later that it was a full three years before she began to feel right again. She refused to rest, however, wanting to do as much as she could, so they compromised and she had one day off a week, which was usually spent travelling.

The last stop on the tour was a big concert in aid of Red Cross and St John's War Organisation at the Albert Hall, London, on 17th August. The *Manchester Guardian* critic wrote afterwards:

> There has probably been nothing quite like the peculiar enthusiasm she evokes since the days of Charles Dickens' public readings. And indeed this artiste in her own line has many of Dickens' personal characteristics - the immense vitality, the rich theatrical exuberance, the sheer fun, and a popular sentiment which we are about to call unabashed, when she suddenly abashes it by turning round and mocking her own seriousness. That is a peculiar art of which even Dickens had not the trick.

Her manager, Bert Aza, and theatre historian W. Macqueen Pope helped to arrange the tour, working closely with Basil Dean so she could cover as much ground as possible all over the country. The BBC tried, unsuccessfully, to get her for a broadcast, but she only did the ENSA shows, then back to the USA because she was committed to an American radio show in aid of British air-raid victims. This was called Carnival For Britain. It was organised by the British War Relief Society and the American Theatre and featured Gracie, Gertrude Lawrence, George Burns and Gracie Allen in New York; Noel Coward, Sir Cedric Hardwicke and Robert Montgomery in Hollywood; Vivien Leigh, Laurence Olivier, Beatrice Lillie and Leslie Howard in London.

After that it was another War Relief tour which took her in September 1941 to the Masonic Auditorium, Detroit, where she sang Noel Coward's latest song, *London Pride*, to a packed house.

The bombing of Pearl Harbor in 1941 brought America into the war, and Gracie said she would now divide her earnings between the two countries.

In July 1942 she accepted an engagement in an all-star show in New York to be called *Top Notchers*, for one month. She 'needed some cash', she explained to reporters who questioned her, as she had 'a lot of commitments, and I haven't earned anything for myself since the war began.' After the furore of her financial arrangements in 1940, she was careful to give her reasons to the papers. It was the line of least resistance, and it was the truth.

However, she became ill and had to give up her part and go to her Santa Monica home for a rest. The doctors advised several months, but Gracie said she would 'see how it went' and was in fact back on her war relief work within two months.

In 1943 she returned to Britain to do another factory and camp tour. Her husband, Monty Banks, had appeared in a couple of films and was now running a restaurant in New York 'because we have to earn a living.'

The 1943 tour also began in Rochdale, where she had a rapturous welcome. 'Well,' she told her closest friends, 'I belong there, it would be terrible if they weren't pleased to see me.' But she was welcomed elsewhere too - by the soldiers, sailors and airmen in the camps she visited, and by the factory workers all around the British Isles.

'Good old Gracie, we're winning, you know', they shouted. In spite of all the troubles, she still identified with the people.

At one factory during the tour the manager was very nervous, saying it was a dodgy audience - the previous week Noel Coward had sung *I'll See You Again*, and they had answered, 'You bloody well won't...' When she came off, amid cheers and shouts for more, he said, 'I'll never believe what I read in the papers again.'

She brought with her a new song called *The Wings Of England*:

The Wings of England are spreading across the sky,
The hopes of England are still flying high,
The Wings of England are like the lion's roar,
That sings of England for ever more.

She did broadcast during the 1943 tour, and the Central Overseas Audience Research Department reported the following:

There is no doubt at all about the popularity of Gracie Fields at home, with both civilian and forces listeners. Her recent live programme attained a peak audience, and whenever her records are included in a programme the figures show a leap up.

The BBC played her records to counter the Nazi propaganda of Lord Haw-Haw (William Joyce). No matter what they read about her, when they saw and heard her again, vast numbers of people knew beyond any doubt that she was still 'their Gracie', the woman who could reach their hearts and emotions.

Inevitably of course some of the mud that was thrown stuck, and years afterwards there were people who said, 'I liked her until she married Monty Banks during the war.'

Those who championed her said, 'What about the others, the ones who have left and are sitting out the war in a safe place? She's not doing that.'

She returned to the USA between her wartime tours, but she was working for Britain almost exclusively. The only money she earned for herself was on two of the three films she made then. *Holy Matrimony* in 1943, and *Molly and Me* in 1945, both of which were already contracted. For the rest the dollars came back to Britain. The money from her brief appearance in *Stage Door Canteen* (1943) went to the Ladies Guild and Orphanage.

In *Stage Door Canteen* she sang *The Machine Gun Song* and *The Lord's Prayer*. In Britain *The Lord's Prayer* was removed from the film, as unsuitable.

On July 10th 1943 the Eighth Army, under General Montgomery, and the Seventh Army under General Patton, landed in Sicily. The battle for Sicily went on for five weeks, and in mid August the island was ours, and the troops went on into southern Italy. On September 3rd, Allied forces crossed the Straits of Messina and landed at Reggio di Calabria.

Gracie reached Sicily two months later and made a surprise appearance at a hospital show with Waldini's band. According to Richard Fawkes in *Fighting For A Laugh*:

> 800 people filled the hall. In the centre with their nurses were the seriously wounded and the stretcher cases. A breathless pause when Waldini announced Gracie, they did not know if it was true or not. Then she walked on. She made them roar with laughter for half an hour, then she sang *Ave Maria* and had us all in tears. Then a laugh to finish.

Ex-signalman Cecil Gilmore saw her in Sicily:

> My Div, the 50th (N) Division, were waiting for a ship to take us home to prepare for the invasion of France. We'd had a pretty hectic time, but then we were stationed in a luxury hotel in what is now a well known holiday resort. Every day we used to go down and swim in the bay. There was an old ship there, and most of us used to climb up onto the rigging, swing out and drop into the sea. We never wore any clothes.
> One day a group of us were swimming around when a broad Lancashire voice called out, 'Hi lads, enjoying yourselves?' Yes, it was Our Gracie, and that evening she gave us a wonderful show. I'll never forget it.

Harry Parr-Davies, now in the army, had been posted as her official pianist, but was suffering from exhaustion and Ivor Newton was her pianist on that tour. Ivor said:

> I wouldn't have missed it for the world. It was exciting to accompany her and impossible to be indifferent to the genuine love and affection she commanded. Her energy was incredible,

and unlike singers I normally worked with, the idea of saving or nursing her voice never occurred to her. ENSA had so many requests for Gracie, and her only regret was that it was physically impossible to do more than she already was.

In *The Greasepaint War*, J. Graven Hughes tells the story of an impromptu show put together when Georgie Wood met Gracie in Tunis. He suggested they get together with Al Jolson and Jack Benny and put on a show at an airbase in Algiers. Although ENSA didn't allow artistes to appear in USO shows, the ADC in Algiers explained matters to General Eisenhower and it was authorised. 'It really was a terrific show', he said.

In Rangoon Gracie gave two concerts one day, and the next she kicked off at a football match and also sang from the football stand. Just after the Battle of Tunis she was there. In Singapore she visited the hospital, and in Athens she appeared twice on the day she arrived (she reached there at 2pm), twice on the Sunday, and twice on the Monday before moving on to Salonica, Patras and Araxes (in the Peloponnese).

Wherever she went, she simply wanted to get on with the job. There were many stars and many not so well known actors, actresses and entertainers who also did a grand job during the war, but, as this is part of Gracie's story it must concentrate on her efforts.

Illusionist Will Ayling was Major W. Ayling, Officer Commanding ENSA Services and Entertainments, in 1945 when Gracie arrived at Dum Dum Airport.

It was the first time I had met her. She stepped from the plane clad in bush jacket and drill trousers, her hair tussled and packed beneath a wide brimmed service hat, the band surrounding the crown stitched with the badges of the units and divs she had visited en route. She was to be in Calcutta for a few days, and the only place large enough for her concerts was the race-course. A floodlit, wooden, portable structure, built as a small theatre stage, stood isolated before a packed stand, the illumination spilling onto the olive-green uniformed troops. I sat beside her on the improvised steps at the rear of the staging, whilst her husband, Monty Banks, did his stuff as a compere before introducing her.

'Listen to my old man,' she whispered, grinning at me, 'gets more like a ruddy ham each day.' It was affectionately said, and during the next three days I witnessed their happy relationship, although I did see him sulk in a corner for a short time after a mild disagreement. It didn't last long, she soon won him over.

For that concert she wore a long black dress, over which was a beautiful ivory crochet cotton overgarment. Really two items, the top being in the form of a short coatee, the other a reversed skirt, open at the front. It was ingeniously designed in fairly large circular patterns which, although of considerable open work, served to camouflage the dress proper. Gracie confided that it was easily carried in a holdall bag and could, on removal, be shaken out and worn over a normal dress which might have been badly creased. 'A bit of instant glamour', she said, laughing.

She gladly toured hospital wards, stopped at each bed greeting the occupant either boisterously, with a joke or two, or quietly, as the circumstance required. Before leaving she would sing, often in answer to a request, without accompaniment, just so naturally. It was a great experience.

She sang on the football field in Singapore too, as Donald Sinden recalls.

I had to fight to get in, and I was sitting high up in one of the stands. All the stands were packed, and the pitch was covered with the wounded and the POWs. It was only four days after Singapore was ours again. Down in the middle, on a tiny stage like a boxing ring, Gracie sang her heart out. I reckon it was one of the best performances of her life. She gave us everything, and when she started the first few notes of *Sally* I looked at all the faces around me. Tough men who had seen a lot of war were crying...

As Gracie said, 'I represented home...' Before that, though, there had been more carping. *The Crusader*, one of the Eighth Army newspapers, carried an article slating Gracie for not staying longer in North Africa and Sicily.

Naomi Jacob, who was with ENSA on the organising side, also wrote a piece for the *Union Jack*. She called it 'Mind Your Own Business'. 'We had a storm stirred up', she wrote. 'I use that word stirred advisedly, concerning Gracie Fields. Gracie crammed every hour of the day with work. No place, no audience was too small, no gathering of men in some vast amphitheatre too large...'

On November 10th 1943, Prime Minister Winston Churchill intervened and ordered that 'in future all articles appearing in the Eighth Army News be submitted for censorship.' Mr Churchill felt it unfair that Gracie should be singled out in this manner for an attack in a newspaper published for the troops.

Georgie Wood says in his autobiography, *I Had To Be Wee*:

> We arrived at Maison Blanche Airport outside Algiers. We were all hungry, dusk was falling rapidly, and there was no transport. We wandered off to the Toc H canteen and they implored us to give a show. Now here is one of the many occasions when Gracie showed not only her real wish to work, but her willingness to work under any conditions. Two tables were pushed together, and between us we did a show of over two hours.

The next day they played to over six thousand servicemen at the Base Open Theatre at Maison Blanche, and the following one gave four more shows before moving on.

11. Letters from the Far East

When the war in Europe was over in May 1945, Gracie went to sing for SEAC (South East Asia Command). Monty Banks went too, and during this tour she wrote long letters home to her family. Before that much of her correspondence had been postcards, and spasmodic. These are extracts from some of the letters from that time. They were away for just over four months.

May 22nd 1945

We leave here next Tuesday morning and go right through, and are supposed to arrive in Australia Friday. I'm supposed to start my first concert within two days, but there's the nuisance of having to find a new accompanist immediately on arrival, as my accompanist doesn't want 'war work'. He didn't mind going just to Australia, but for this he wanted a nice renumeration in American dollars, which of course we couldn't afford so we'll just pick a new Australian lad. I'm so sorry they didn't let me have that Australian boy who played for me in England - Hal Stead. He's really very upset that ENSA hasn't helped him to join me because he would have done the whole tour with me afterwards.

I think I told you in my previous letter they are trying to switch the tour around starting off from England, but I haven't heard a line since I told them to go ahead, whatever they did would suit me. But to get our priorities on the airplane we had to promise ten weeks in the Pacific under USO. It doesn't make any difference anyway to me so long as I keep moving around and my work is pleasing to whoever sees and hears me. Seeing as it's over in Europe, we should really entertain the kids who are in the thick of it in the Pacific.

I'm dictating this letter on my way to Los Angeles, going down to the clinic to get a shot for yellow fever. I have to have thirteen shots of different things. I have had four up to now, typhoid, cholera, and I don't know what the devil the others were for, and the vaccination. We won't be able to get all the shots in before leaving but I am told that we get them at all the stops. In any case we have the whole lot before entering any of the areas where certain things may be picked up.

August 16th 1945 Piva, Bougainville

Here we are on the day of celebration. This morning I sang The Lord's Prayer at thanksgiving service, and it was very impressive.

I've given five small concerts in five different hospital wards, and tonight we give a big show to about 15,000 - about 1,000 American boys will also be there. My pianist's [Eric Fox] young lady is a Gilbert and Sullivan opera singer and she does her bit, also a squeeze-box hurdy-gurdy boy to play a few tunes, and a man singer, and we do the old servant sketch when and where it's possible.

It's dreadfully sticky hot, it's all jungle and so different to all the other theatres of war I've sung in. You can just imagine what the poor lads have gone through and it's usually raining, something awful sometimes, easily 6 inches of rain. We are lucky, it's fine for us today, they say it rains every afternoon.

Of course there's plenty of different kinds of crawlers, and three times the size of our ants and spiders, etc. But Monty and I are very lucky here, we have been given the hut that was specially built for the Duke of Gloucester, and it's beautifully netted, roof thatched by the natives, so it's fairly cool. Also we have an ice box and it's full of beer and coca-cola, and today the Americans brought me a huge can of milk they had flown from the mainland. We also had a shower and hot water specially fixed for us.

Well, we just hope we keep well and free from fevers, etc. Now I'm going to have a wee rest before the big show starts.

The American Colonel Fox has just told Monty he's leaving with all his lads to go right on to Tokyo tomorrow, every American leaving the island, and what a thrill for them to be moving and getting near to returning home.

Saturday August 19th 1945

Here's our next stop at Jacquinot Bay on the island of New Britain, and Pa and I had to sleep in different sheds, the lav a half mile away, and so many bugs and mosquitoes! It poured with heavy rain all day yesterday, and all last night, and thank heaven it's fine this morning so we were able to leave. We thought we were going to be stuck here awhile, we had a dreadful flight yesterday morning, the Pilot unable to see more than 50 yards and by a miracle he landed us safely on this island. Today we go to Lae, Madang. It's quite interesting but will Mamma Fields-Banks and Papa be glad to get back to our lovely home.

There were quite a number of natives on our last stop and they make the billets and do lots of odd jobs. They say when they were first requisitioned they were delighted - they thought an order had come to do their head-hunting which had been stopped for some time. They say they put on a good show fighting the Japs. The Japs don't yet know it's over - they're saying a Japanese prince has to come and tell them. So far as the army is concerned they still have to be on the alert.

PS. If you saw Monty in his uniform you'd scream - and his big hat which now he's made look like Napoleon's or Nelson's.

Sunday August 20th 1945

Here I am again - we are on New Guinea, this is Lae, and thank heaven, our quarters are lovely. Another hut that was especially built for the Duke of Gloucester. Thank goodness I'm GF! Our last stop was absolutely awful but I hear this is the last place built for the nobs. We'll just have to keep our fingers crossed and hope for the best. The bugs and mosquitoes, of course, get in through the nets. I nearly suffocate myself sleeping with me head under the sheets. It's so sticky hot. My hair is dreadful, feels like it has been combed with syrup or glue.

I got a shock last night, one of my many mosquito bites was all open and a strange little white crabby-looking animal was eating away at the sore. Monty went immediately to see the Doctor who gave him some Metholated Spirit, and said it would be OK. Well, loves, I do hope so, there's so many different diseases about these islands. Peggy Shea, the little girl who is on tour with me - she sings - has a rash on her ankle. We're both going to sing at the hospital this afternoon and have our sores attended to after the concert.

Our three big concerts have been a grand success. I did about five 15 minute shows the first day in Bougainville - The Lord's Prayer at the Peace Service and a big show 35 minutes at night, all in the open air. The next day about three 15 minute shows in the hospital wards and a big show again in the evening. Yesterday we had only one big show in the evening for which I was glad, as I still am struggling with a cold since the big open air matinee in Sydney, where a tremendous wind blew down my throat.

It's a pleasure to be here in this lovely hut. We are both together here. A soldier guards us all night in case of any nonsense, though they don't expect any trouble around here. There are 70,000 Japs on the island but last night the General had word from the General in Bougainville that the Jap General had been there to surrender. Still there are a number of Japs in the bushes who are sent out for a month or two months to make nuisance fights, so it may be a couple of weeks before these know it's over, although they've dropped leaflets all over the place declaring the Peace, so as far as the Army is concerned, they still have to be on the alert.

Today was to be a day's complete rest but we're going just the same to sing at the hospital at 2.30. So to bed early tonight to be ready for our next stop. God bless you and all our friends - hope you're all well. We are both OK, my cold has nearly left me, every day it's betterer and I'm so glad I managed to get on all right with my earlier shows, telling lots of stories and singing in a low key. Last night's show from me was much more like a good GF show and I don't feel any effects from me bites, so maybe the meths spirits killed my trouble, I hope so anyway. Today I feel fine.

I'm glad I came here, it's really so fully rewarding to hear the poor lads enjoy everything. Some of my good stories are old, but Tripe, Irishman, Jock, a Scotchman and Maternity are OK. Also the 3 soldiers and 2 girls gag gets a big yell from the lads. Monty and the pianist Eric Fox do the handshaking routine the lads did at my radio shows and the boys love it.

Oh, I had a sweet shell necklace and bangle given to me last night after the show from one of the lads. They get them alive from the shore and bury them in the sand, then next day gather them and polish them and they are very pretty. Then they wire 'em together and make these pretty trinkets. I'm enclosing his lovely letter he gave me with the present inside so you can keep it for me.

On plane to Wewak from Madang, New Guinea, August 21st 1945
We have just left Madang and we had the best time of our trip through there - mostly Air Force. We gave two hospital concerts, 15 minute shows and a 45 minute show from GF at the big evening show, about 4,000 boys, and we had lunch with all the boys lined up along side of them all. Our bunks were on the water's edge so we got

a swim. One of the nurses lent me a swimsuit. It was grand, so lovely and warm the sea. Also a sea captain took us a short sea trip after our afternoon concerts.

It's been the most lovely spot we've struck - a moon shining through the tall coconut trees. There's a very big plantation of coconut trees and lots of them have been destroyed through the fighting. A native went up a tree and threw down the coconuts and we took snaps of him.

The boys made a lovely heartshaped cake with "Thanks, Gracie, for coming to sing for us" written round the edge of the cake. We didn't get any bites from bugs either and a fairly nice cool breeze at night. They say it's hotter at Wewak and farther up north where we're going. I hope there's not too many mosquitoes - my legs and arms are bitten to pieces.

Wewak, August 21st 1945

Well, we were surprised with nice quarters at Wewak. They'd built a special place for the Duke of Gloucester, not as good as the last ones, but at least Mario and I were together though we had separate bedrooms. At least I was able to unpack a few things and hang them out to get a bit of fresh air. Everything gets dreadfully damp and mildewed if you don't watch out, it's so hot and sticky, so as there was a slight breeze from the ocean I grabbed the opportunity to hang up my fur coat which I have to travel with as I'm sure to need it when I get to Italy.

By the way, I shipped a whole lot of stuff to Mary's headquarters and I hope she gets it safely. Three cases, one rather large, a tin one and two smaller ones. Anyway three in all, and there's most of our things in them, also lots of new woollen underwear for the poor people in Italy.*

Well, the others took a wee trip on a launch, I stayed in camp and made myself a bathing suit out of a yard of material I'd got for a turban headdress and I hope to wear it at our next stop, Aitape.

* Gracie quietly looked after the poor all her life.

Aitape, August 22nd 1945.

Here we are in Aitape and I was given a very nice blue bathing suit. We've a concert after lunch for the hospital patients and one big one tonight (we'd only one big concert in Wewak - 15,000 troops attended, the biggest yet). I'm going out in a launch after the concert to a small island and having a swim from there.

LATER. Had a wonderful day in Aitape. The island was lovely, all nice white sand, we all swam about for an hour, beautiful Capri clear water, but there's some kind of sea bug which you can't see but it gives a little sting. Monty got it first and shouted, 'Oh, I've been bitten.' I got scared and swam out to him, I thought it was a shark, as there's lots around these islands and one has to swim where the bottom of the ocean can be seen. Well, we all got these small stings though they're not harmful, just a kind of a quick pin prick.

We were on our way back when we passed a native boat, so Monty and I got aboard and it was most interesting. Made out of a tree trunk all hollowed out, and cane across. A fire burning on some sand and wet sacks, cooking sweet potatoes and some other stuff all in rags being smoked. Four men Fuzzie-Wuzzies and a Mare, they call the women. Fairly old people, the Mare's bosoms small and all dropped flabby. We had a couple of snaps taken, hope they turn out good as I don't suppose we'll ever get another like that in our lives.

We've had another big concert - the poor lads, some of them had sat there all night so as to get a good seat and brought along lots of grub. We leave tomorrow for Morotai.

On plane to Morotai, August 23rd 1945

We get the snaps of the 'Lacatoy', that's the name of the native boat. I'll bet the name came from the missionaries' 'like a toy'. I forgot to tell you the old man with the oar spoke quite a bit of English. He said

missionaries teach him and he now teaches little children
ABCs, but he got a bit mixed up after that.

We're not performing today as the journey is quite a
long one, between 7 and 8 hours, and tomorrow we go
to Tarakan. We just stop and sleep in Morotai and get
our plane attended to, returning to Morotai later.

We've just landed on our way to Morotai at an
enormous American Airfield to refuel, and a chap took
us around for a jeep ride. We've never seen so many types
of planes, it was one of the big starting places for all the
big air raids on Japan. It was called Burack. An Australian
boy took us around, and Monty was trying to locate a
mess to get some American cigarettes and coffee, but we
couldn't find one so here we are, all aboard our plane
and drinking the mucky Australian coffee we brought
from Aitape. Still it tastes good, also the canned meats
and bread and butter - we're all starving!

August 26th 1945

We have just left Morotai and it's been marvellous.
General Blamey was there, and his wife, Lady Blamey
also. She's working for the Red Cross and we were their
guests, so we've had a very grand time. We were supposed
to rest there and return for two days and work then.
Well, of course, Lady Fields said, 'let's do a hospital at
least so we'll feel we've done our good deed for the day',
so we did and the poor lads did enjoy it. They had a stage
set up and brought all the lads on stretchers. These poor
lads had been right through the war, and had lost legs
and arms. It does make me feel sick when the poor kids
ask me to autograph their plaster of Paris around their
arms and legs, but they always ask for Monty and I to do
it and you couldn't refuse, but as I said, it does make you
feel awful inside.

Well, after our concert we went for a cruise with the
General and his high ranking officers, and Lady Blamey,
her friend, a Matron of one of the hospitals and the

Matron-in-Chief of the whole of Australia and battlefronts. We went to a small island, and a boat being pulled on the end of ours with half a dozen big strong black men. These fellows went off to fish and we all swam in the beautiful clear water for about an hour, then a small motor boat which had accompanied us to the island took us out to where these black men were fishing.

They throw out a stick of dynamite in the sea, then all dive under and bring oh, so many fish that have been killed and stunned, and such beautiful coloured fishes, some they called Parrot fish, every wonderful colour you could wish for, hence the name. I haven't even seen a Parrot fish in an aquarium.

Well, they caught plenty and we had a very grand dinner last night with the General and everyone, and the Army Band played about 100 yards away all through dinner. We had all the songs from Oklahoma, which he's crazy over. Monty did the Mexican General, wearing the General's hat, and the General and his wife and friends just yelled - he did so many funny things! We went to bed about 11 o'clock, and yesterday Peggy, who's billeted at the hospital, told us the General went round there and was just having lots of fun with all the nurses and was there till 3am. He's certainly a card, the officers say they can't keep up with him.

Our last night's dinner finished up with a toast to His Majesty, the band playing The King, then the General sent for the Band Master who conducted the band, to come and sit between the General and myself and have a glass of port. After, we all went out and joined the band boys in a few songs, then Monty took the baton and did an imitation of Toscanini and had everyone in stitches, even me who has seen him do it before. We finally went to bed about 12 midnight, completely wacked, but it had been a grand day.

August 27th 1945

We're just leaving Tarakan Island. We had over 10,000 lads to the concert and it was a great night for all of us. The boys had built a lovely stage and dressing room and dolled it up with flowers. One boy came to where Peggy and I were and presented me with a lovely corsage of orchids which he'd been out in the bush to gather.

After the show finished a boy came on the stage and presented me with a lovely heart-shaped brooch with To Gracie From The Boys Of Tarakan scratched in silver over plastic. We had, I should think, our very best reception here and goodness knows, all the others have been wonderful. Monty and Eric had bunks near the Brigadier-General and we stayed with the nurses.

August 27th 1945

We've just left Balikpapan and what a mess the place is! All the oil tanks blown to bits and all the tiny villages - you can hardly tell where they were. In fact, there's absolutely nothing for miles, only burned out and shattered shacks.

The Australian lads had a very hard time to land as first the Dutch people had mined all around the sea, then the Japs mined it again, and the Aussies had to drop mines so the Japs couldn't get away but the Air Force and the ships gave the place a good pasting. It was our worst place for food. I had the Matron of the Hospital's tent to sleep in and Peggy shared a tent with the Matron.

We had a couple of shows on top of a truck to the patients in Hospital and last night was our biggest crowd ever... nearly 25,000. You could see cigarettes being lighted for miles it seemed, and what a grand audience they were. We had the usual troop concert party 'drawn from their own lads', then we did the last half. [It was here that Gracie asked them all to strike a match and for those in front to look back and see the wonderful picture she could see.]

They gave me a pretty serviette ring with 'To Gracie from Balikpapan'. We got some laundry done, but the damp heat just makes everything soggy in no time. Tarakan and Balikpapan have been the poorest places for food with the exception of breakfast, and I felt awful as at each place they gave me two eggs, and I feel I'm taking it away from the poor lads, so I left one untouched.

Peggy and I had a room together at Tarakan, it was nice and clean. I've got prickly heat spots all over my body and it itches like the devil. They gave me some stuff to dab on, hope I get rid of it soon. Otherwise we're all O.K. in spite of our strenuous programme. We're now on our way to Brunei, expect to land there in half an hour.

August 28th 1945

Just left Brunei, Labuan Island, Borneo. Had dreadful food, these last places. Tarakan, Balikpapan and Labuan have been the last places taken and haven't been able to get fresh food yet, and oh boy, the bully-beef cooked in seventeen different positions! Well, it got us down a bit after the other places, and of course, Monty and I had to be split up. Neither he nor I like that, still the nurses did their best to make us comfortable. They are a grand lot of nurses everywhere, and believe me, it must have been pretty rough, and tough for them starting and building up these hospitals, but they never grouse - bless 'em all.

Peggy and I had the Matron's tent between us at Labuan Island and I've been awake all night chasing a B***** Big Mosquito with my nearly blind eyes. Unfortunately I couldn't find him so one of my knees has the map of Ireland on, and oh, don't it itch! Just hope it doesn't turn into any funny business. They say the malaria mosquito doesn't make a noise, and this one did - he was dive-bombing trying to get my nose all night, so at 4am I got up and took the blasted net off, it had got inside and couldn't get out. So I suffocated myself under the sheet just leaving enough room for my nostrils to breath and did I sweat. But he didn't get me nose! Or my face, thank goodness.

We're on our way back to Morotai, we're supposed to rest tonight as it's a six or seven hour plane journey. I hope that General Blamey isn't there, he's a marvellous chap, but I was nearly unconscious when we left there last time. We do three nights there. Our concert last night was the first time we had rain. You could hardly hear yourself shouting and that's what I had to do to overcome the storm. Nobody moved or left their seats and everyone was completely drenched, but it just shows you what these concerts mean to them.

Monty and I are together in a nice hut on Morotai and it's pretty free from bugs, although I did get a small bite. But at least we have our own lavatory and shower. It's awful to go to the lavs at the last places - I was afraid to sit down.

September 6th 1945

Here we are on our way from Leyte, we did five shows, and a hospital matinee. There we had dinner with General Miller of the Wild Cat Division, and played to his troops that first evening. The Wild Cat troops carry a real wild cat in a cage always with them into battle. I saw it and it was wild indeed, never got friendly even with his keeper who feeds him every day. He was in his cage with native matting to protect him from the sun and bags of ice put on top to help keep him cool.

We had a chap for MC and he was on stage for hours it seemed, saying nothing; A young girl contortionist - she was 24 but looked 14, fresh and extraordinarily clever. She didn't make you feel squirmy like some of these contortionist make one feel. Also a young fellow tap dancer who was especially good but who just stayed on and worked too hard, poor devil.

Age 12 - touring.

A singer's long, slender throat.

1940. Hon Captain. Women's Volunteer Reserve Corps.
Photograph courtesy of Central Press Photos.

1941. With Scottish shipbuilders.
Photograph courtesy of the Daily Record.

Entertaining the troops.

The Gracie Fields - launched April 1936.

Gracie and Monty - so in love.

A Smile and a Song.

I'll Always Sing To You - the photograph Gracie sent to Monty with her song on the back.

On the terrace of Canzone del Mare, Capri.

1950s. With niece Grace - going on tour.
Photograph courtesy of The Press Association Ltd.

With Boris at their home - Canzone del Mare, Capri.

Pleased to see you (in background: Dannie La Rue and Frankie Howard).
Photograph courtesy of Doug McKenzie Photographic Services Ltd.

1978. Rochdale Concert (including Ben Warris, Larry Grayson and Sandy Powell).

There Is Nothing Like A Dame.
Photograph courtesy of Central Press Photos Ltd.

Our shows on Leyte went well. The next concert was given on a nearby island for the sailors, and this was nearly the end. The MC pleaded for the sailors to be quiet, then got sarcastic, pleaded again, but they just shouted all the time he was trying to talk. Then to crown all, several radio calls to tell the lads to get back to their ships, and also someone shouted the beer's on (it had been off especially for our concert) so up jumped bunches of them and ran for the beer, bringing it back to their places.

Well, I had to go on just as they were in a devil of a drunken shouting state. I gave them about twenty minutes of popular songs which they seemed to enjoy and the whole show wasn't longer than three quarters of an hour, and the lads didn't mind, and we were all happy to get back to the motor boat that took us there. The lads waiting on the jetty to get boats to take them to their ships all had at least half a dozen cans of beer they were carrying back, and they began to throw them onto our boat for us to drink.

At Leyte I was staying with the Major Nurse and her friend. They were very nice and hospitable. Our food was taken at the Officer's Mess and it was a messy mess. They had a nice dance floor adjoining it and had dances every Saturday. I didn't go to it but Pop went. The food was not good there.

There was an enormous lizard outside our bungalow, three feet long, in fact it looked like a young crocodile. There was a river at the side of the bungalow.

Batangas, September 7th 1945

Well, I'm again staying with the head Captain of Nurses. Papa shares a tent with the Captain of U.S.O. who will accompany us through our tour. He's very sweet, Captain Bradshaw, and he's married to an English girl who, he says, tries to sell him London. But he says he's winning - she's in New York which he says is the best place. The pianist also shares their tent. He's Mr Private Buckowsky, a tall Polish chap, not too hot on the piano accompaniments but the old girl will sing whatever she starts and the pianists can all play what they like!

We all meet at the mess for meals and our shows. Monty did his jokes and did very well although he's not used to doing this kind of work, the lads liked him.

Batangas seems to be quite cultivated, there's a real feeling of civilized people here. The natives are energetic and get things done, and there was quite a nice little town and square that has been badly bombed. But it's rained cats and dogs, so we're up to our necks in mud. Your feet disappear into it getting into the jeep that takes us to our shows, and the poor jeep swings and skids all over the place, which I suppose will be good for the liver. Good job I'm not in the family way - I'd sure lose it in these jeeps.

Leyte was dry so we had more dust than we've ever seen - it was thick. I'd prefer mud any time to this awful dust you get on all the islands when they've had a dry spell.

We hope to get through our tour about the 20th September and get to India and Italy before it gets too far into the winter over there. I'm not taking any rest days they had set for me so I won't leave out any of the shows the U.S.O has set for us. This will cut about nine to ten days, all being well.

Batangas was quite interesting. They had a market, the natives selling fruits, poultry, etc, and lots of souvenir shops, but they're going daft everywhere with their big prices for everything. The lads pay for anything that they want even to a coca-cola which costs $1.25, and 10/- if they get it at their own canteens. I got some wooden slippers - they cost $5.00, worth about $2 at most. The cloth bust as soon as I wore them and I nearly broke me neck. We went to see a Filipino VJ dance in the big square and it was a lovely sight. The girls wore glorious dresses, all hand embroidered. I'd love to get one. A Red Cross girl had bought one, giving $105 for it, but the work is perfect - hope I can get one.

We have a small band drawn from the troops doing a half hour show, and two girls, and an Italian girl plays a squeeze-box very well, and accompanies the other girl in modern songs. It's just rained cats and dogs during our shows here but the lads and nurses and Red Cross girls, they don't bother about it, and sit just as if the sun was shining, yet they're absolutely sopping wet. They are marvellous, anyway they must be enjoying it when they sit in storms like we had during the show. It was very tricky and hard to sing and talk over the noise the storm was making, but they laughed in the right places so I knew it was going over OK.

September 10th 1945

We arrived in Manila and had lunch with General Marshall. He invited us to dine at what looks like the only place left standing in Manila. This city has taken a bashing - it's definately the worst place I've seen, even worse than places in Sicily. It evidently was a very rich city, beautiful buildings and lovely houses all along the seafront, great wide roads and streets, and it's now all rubble. Never have I seen such a mess.

We had a lovely lunch - General Marshall was very nice, and I thought it strange he has an English girl as secretary. Her husband is a P.O.W. in Japan. They, she and her husband, were caught I think she said in Singapore, and had to split and hope for the best for one of them at least to get away, and he was caught. She's very sweet but waits patiently for every batch of P.O.W.s hoping he'll get here soon, as she heard he was alive.

We left after lunch to catch our plane to Lingayen, and after travelling about one and a half hours, had to go back to Manila. We were just a half hour away but the storm was too thick, the pilot couldn't see twenty yards in front of him, and was afraid, as it was getting worse every minute, that he wouldn't be able to see to land. So we spent the night at the Rosario apartments, where we had lunch, and I was glad of the rest for my voice. The cold I got from the Sydney outdoor concerts seems to be around me all the time but, touch wood, my voice has been, and is, OK. The bedroom was a large one and quite bare of any furniture, just the bed. Monty had a room adjoining with a shower and water closet which was a treat.

Lingayen, September 11th 1945

We left and had a nice journey this time, and did two hospital shows in the afternoon and a big show outside at night. I stayed with a couple of nurses, they had quite a nice place but a couple of lizards were in my bedroom during the rest I had between shows, so the nurse informed me they were OK and eat the mosquitoes. One they called Oscar. During the middle of the night, Oscar or his pal walked across my feet outside my net. I shook all the bedclothes, feeling dopey and sleepy, I was sure he was inside my net. We go to Baigui, fifty miles up into the hills, it's about 7,000 feet up, tomorrow.

Baigui, September 12th 1945

A very interesting motor journey, and cooler all the way. We passed a lot of mountain natives, queer Chinese-Japanese-Filipino people. We saw a couple with a half a dozen smooth haired dogs on leashes, only the leashes were bamboo sticks, and we were informed that they were selling them. The mountain folk eat them - awful?

I have a little New York Italian-French girl, she's a soprano with a small hospital unit, about four fellows who do comedy, play instruments and comedy songs. She's a very sweet kid, she told us our fortunes, read our hands - good too!

We stayed in General Lyman's house. He had a sitting room, three bedrooms and a bath. We dined with him that evening. They say he's a full-blooded Hawaiian, very Chinese-looking and so nice and kind. We did two indoor shows. It's mainly hospital lads there convalescing in the cool of Baigui. It made our shows nice and easy, not having to make too much noise like you have to outside, especially in the rain.

The town of Baigui has been wrecked just as badly as Manila. This was a rich little town, homes of rich Filipinos and lovely schools, and churches. I went to a Catholic broken-down school run by Belgian nuns, they had been educating the mountain folks since the last war, and said the kids were all so keen to learn everything, and one hour each day was given for beautiful silver filigree lacy jewellery (like the Mexicans do but much finer). I put in an order for a couple of bangles, ring and brooch but they can't be ready before next April as they have so many orders. The money from this work goes toward helping keep the school going.

There was one nun, an English woman, and I had to go upstairs to talk to her, she came from around Manchester and was so shy. She said she didn't like to come downstairs as there were so many soldiers and she got nervous. I'm still doing my best to get a Filipino dress - no luck in Baigui!

We left Baigui at 5am this morning to catch the plane at the Lingayen Airport at 8am, but we didn't see a plane. Stuck around until 11am, and a Colonel from Virginia invited us to his tent to have a beer whilst waiting and trying to find out what's wrong. We had lunch at the mess hall with the Colonel, and he asked me if I'd sing a couple of songs for the few lads dining there, so Monty did his routine and I sang half a dozen songs, and at 1pm Captain Bradshaw and Monty decided we should all motor to Manila as it was impossible to get any information in Lingayen - and what a long drive, 280 miles! Was me poor back stiff, and were we hungry!? We got there nearly ll o'clock that night and slept at the Rosario Apartments in our same rooms.(The Rosario Apartments are kept for P.O.W. Officers arriving.) We were lucky to stay there again. Monty brought me a coffee and a boiled egg - a rarity around these parts, eggs are, and some toast.

September 14th 1945

Left Manila in a C16 plane for Okinawa. We were hours on the airstrip whilst the lads were packing everything they could get onto the plane. We had a nice jeep inside with us. Our pilot had his pet dog, always travels with him. A wire haired terrier, an independent little tyke, suppose it's swollen headed having done over 600 hours air travel. They provided me with a canvas stretcher to lie on so I took a nice nap, and we arrived in Okinawa about 6 o clock that evening. Were too late to do a show, for which I wasn't sorry.

We expected to have our worst quarters to live in, and to our surprise we found the best. It's a four bedroom and sitting room hotel they call it. Our shower and La-La outside, and the mess hall were pleasant. First time I've seen tablecloths since I came to the Phillipines. The American isn't near as fussy as the British except when we dined with General Marshall.

Did four big shows in two days, and was to do two the next day, BUT we had a hurricane. The wind and rain blew for four hours at more than 100 miles an hour. Very exciting and scaring, expecting to be blown, the hotel as well, right down the hillside (where the hotel was pitched) and had to get up at least five times in the night to move the bed away from the rain that was coming in everywhere.

Our floors were young lakes, sitting room too. We were the only occupants of the place and slept in the two bedrooms on the left. The two on the right were quite dry, so next night we moved into the right side, and lo and behold, the wind and rain decided to change and we were just as bad as the previous night. It wouldn't have been possible to do any more shows, as all the stages had been blown away, and everywhere knee deep in mud, and so we left for Manila.

Manila, September 19th 1945

We're staying this time at the once very elegant Manila Hotel, three floors being usable, and they've certainly been good to us. We have a nice double bedroom and sitting room. We did several shows at the different camps and hospitals and met quite a number of P.O.Ws, British and American, and even Rochdalians. Poor devils, they looked dreadful, so bony you just wonder how they could have survived at all, the state they're in. The lousy Japs gave them rice and grass to eat, and even cut down that ration three months ago. The Red Cross and Hospitals were certainly taking good care of them, giving them the best fresh food, chicken broth, etc.

Well, I managed to get me a Filipino dress, two in fact were presented to me by the Y.W.C.A. The lady I shared a bedroom with on Leyte being one of the head workers for it, had me meet some of the richer Filipino ladies, and they performed their dances for me - very interesting, and gave me a basket of fruit, so Pop and I gave them a cheque for the Y.W.C.A. of $100. We left Manila after I'd been for a ride around seeing the markets. Lanny Ross who works for the U.S.O took me.

We left for Morotai at 8.30am, but landed in Leyte and had to stay the night there with the Major Nurse again and left for Morotai on the 23rd at 6am, arrived Morotai 12 o'clock, had lunch and shower and left at 1.30pm for Darwin, where we spent the night at General Murray's house.

We're travelling in a small private Boford plane. It was dreadfully cold in the air as we were up very high over the sea, so we unpacked our warm coats, me fur one. Today we are on our way again to Sydney, where I hope to post this nice long letter. Touch wood, we are very well, and just waiting patiently to get to Capri and take a wee rest there. Colonel Fairfax is waiting in Sydney for us, and we're supposed to leave for Singapore tomorrow, the 24th September. Hope you're all well - I'm longing to see you again.

PS. Just arrived in Sydney, had two stops, bad weather so got here this morning. Had our first hot bath for over five weeks, felt good too! I'm now going to get my hair fixed, I hope, a good colour - it's like Joseph's coat now.

*

In November 1945, on Armistice Day, Gracie was back in Capri and was asked to go over to Naples to do two concerts, one at the San Carlo Opera House and one at the Bellini Theatre. For three days the sea between Capri and Naples had been too rough for the boats to run, and it didn't seem as if she would be able to get over. She was also still recovering from flu, but when the Royal Navy came to the rescue with a motor launch at twenty past six that evening, she wrapped herself in the oilskins they provided and made the crossing in one of the worst seas in the area for many years.

Isadore Green wrote in the Tunis edition of the *Union Jack*, 'I watched her dragging herself up the stairs. She looked ill, white, haggard, in a state of utter exhaustion.'

'I'm not a good sailor', Gracie said. Monty Banks had made the journey too, and he helped her to the dressing room. Ten minutes later she went out onto the stage and sang *Land of Hope and Glory* to a packed Opera House. The audience clapped and cheered, then she sang again before departing for the Bellini. Isadore Green said, 'The drive took a minute and a half. Gracie was in a state of collapse. She could speak only in gasps, she was blowing like a boxer who has gone through fifteen rounds of tough fighting...'

At the Bellini she walked on, whistled to the audience and cried, 'Hullo, lads, I've made it.' Then she gave a full show, cracking jokes and ending with *Sally*.

Gracie herself always said that when she walked onto a stage, something happened to her. She became a different person. It is not unknown - Marie Lloyd and George Robey are two more who, when their music played, seemed reborn and able to rise above their sickness and soar to the heights, no matter how ill or tired they seemed offstage.

After the war, with the traumas of nationality and loyalties behind them, Monty went with Gracie to the White House, at the invitation of the President, happy to see this acknowledgement of the way she had worked. The President thanked her for what she had done for the morale of all the forces she had visited, 'your own and ours. My boys have come back from the Pacific Islands and said how wonderful you've been. They love you as much as their own, in fact they only wish you were their own. Now,' he went on, 'I, being an American, you realise I can't create a title for you or anything like that, we just don't have those over here; but I'm going to present you with twenty-five gold pieces. Each piece is worth twenty-five dollars. These are now extinct. There are possibly about 150 of these only in the world, and so you see they are rare. I shall be pleased and happy to give you these in recognition of what you have done for our boys.'

During the war many of the American boys had been among the twenty thousand odd troops in Gracie's audience in Algiers when a wind storm blew up.

'The piano only had about half a dozen playable notes', Gracie recalled later. 'Tonight you'll just have to sing popular songs, comedy ones and those that have a story line - you can't possibly sing any of the good ballads or religious songs,' her pianist said, 'the notes simply aren't there.'

Gracie had been on stage only a few minutes when the storm blew up.

The few copies of music we had on the piano were blown all through the audience, so I began a community singsong to try and drown out the noise of the windstorm, which was really frightful while it lasted. Those lads joined in with enthusiasm, but 20,000 voices singing as loudly as they could with me only just beat the noise of the wind. It lasted about twenty minutes, then stopped as suddenly as it had started.

We finished singing, and for a moment or two there was an almost unearthly silence. Suddenly a voice called out, 'Gounod's Ave Maria.' My poor pianist was beside himself worrying about the music, the noteless piano, and the sand in his eyes, so I sang Ave Maria without musical accompaniment, alone, in the utter stillness that came over everything. Never, I think, has a prayer been so sincerely and thankfully felt as by all those twenty thousand boys. It was one of the most thrilling moments I have known.

12. Working Party

After the war Gracie talked about retiring. She had these plans to retire all her life but often admitted, at that time anyway, 'After a few months I might find myself itching to go again, I'm still full of vitality.'

In 1947 she did a tour of New Zealand and brought home with her a Maori farewell song, *Haere Ras* (Now Is The Hour), which she introduced to us in July in the first concert of her new radio series. She was forty-nine years old when she toured Britain with this series, titled 'Gracie's Working Party'. The BBC were extremely enthusiastic about it. They had done their research well and said in a letter to her manager, 'From all the indications, her reputation stands very high in this country.'

There were, however, problems to overcome, not least being Gracie's reluctance to lay herself open to criticism again. Another letter suggested, 'She would probably respond to an appeal made on grounds of national emergency in a way no other artiste would.' And again, 'In view of her unique position she is the only artiste suitable for this series of programmes.'

Although the war had been over for two years, many conditions were still warlike. Food rationing, for instance, went on (although it eased) until 1954, and men and women who worked in the factories had to stay until they were given their 'release.' 1947 produced one of the coldest winters and hottest summers for several decades. Austerity was still rife, there was an acute coal shortage, and the initial euphoria of victory was two years in the past.

Gracie was paid £2,000 for the twelve programmes into which the idea of the Working Party eventually developed. Originally six were designed, and the payment to her was to be £1,000. She gave all her fees, including reproduction ones, to the Variety Artistes Federation Benevolent Fund.

The tour began in Rochdale in July 1947, and went on to Liverpool, Middlesborough, Newcastle, Huddersfield, Sheffield, Glasgow, Belfast, Coventry, the Potteries, South Wales and London. It started with a lot of unwelcome publicity from her point of view, because the Variety Artistes' Federation argued with the BBC about whether to charge an entrance fee to the concerts, and naturally enough the newspapers used Gracie as the headline.

Theatre managers sent a deputation to the then Postmaster General (Mr W.T. Paling) protesting against free admission. 'It is one thing for the BBC to admit the public free to its own studios, but quite another for it to take a cinema or hall and set up in direct competition with us', they said. The BBC answered, 'It is our normal practice to admit audiences to variety shows. Their numbers are negligible compared with the millions who listen to the broadcasts.'

Reporters asked Gracie to comment. 'I should have stuck to my instinct', she said. 'I don't want to be involved in another scrap.'

'It's not you personally the protests are over', said the BBC. In any case there wasn't much she could do about it at that stage because the contracts were signed. 'Except to go to it with my chin out and my thumbs up,' she said to her friends, 'but I wish there didn't have to be such a *fuss.*'

The dispute was settled, and J.B. Priestley wrote 'A Pen Portrait' in the 18 July *Radio Times*, which was much more than a publicity feature to herald the start of the series, rather an in-depth look from a craftsman as supreme in his field as she was in hers.

> Her colossal reputation, unique in its period, puzzles many persons who do not understand popular entertainment. There are, broadly, two reasons for it, and one is technical and the other psychological. The technical explanation is that while she fused two different kinds of appeal, one sentimental and the other comic, into one unique style of performance, she was also compelled to dominate her audience more thoroughly than any other variety artiste.

It is easy to see why she had to do this. To combine sentiment and broad comedy, to alternate them as she does, so that at one minute the monster audience wants to cry and the next minute finds itself laughing uproariously, demands complete domination or it will be a ghastly failure.

Notice how Gracie can slide from an almost naive but powerful sincerity, which turns some Tin Pan Alley ballad into something like a folk song, into burlesque that, before you know where you are, is gloriously funny. And to do this a performer must have the audience completely subjugated, eager to obey the slightest gesture of command. And an audience so dominated has its response raised to a higher level. It enjoys an *experience*. And for such an experience it is instantly and profoundly grateful.

Again the Gracie Fields who thus became a great variety star also became a symbolic figure. She expressed far more than herself. Just as Marie Lloyd had been the symbolic figure of the London of the nineties and the Edwardian era, so now Gracie became symbolic of the industrial North. She was the Lancashire or Yorkshire mill girl immensely enlarged and intensified by talent and art. She sang her head off, as they do or would like to do. She was independent, saucy, sharply humorous, bossy, maternal, blunt in manner but deeply feminine in her rapid alternations of sentiment and derisive laughter.

She was the people in all the little back streets, now with a full orchestra and the lid off. And in the years just before the war, when she was often ailing and desperately tired, she was compelled to maintain this character, off as well as on the stage, to be both candid and high spirited, generous with her time and attention, often at a very severe cost to herself. It is no joke to be an uncrowned and unguarded queen...

'Gracie's Working Party' was produced by Mr Bowker Andrews. It involved a lot of organisation, travelling and working together. It sparked off criticism among those who harboured resentment against Gracie for the war years, and it gave the BBC 'the only series which is earning anything like a peak listening figure', according to one BBC memo which described her as 'this truly astonishing woman.'

It featured local amateur artistes in the towns they played, and boosted the morale of Britain's workers, even if it almost ran the whole Working Party team, from star to office boy, into the ground.

When she was asked to do another series in 1948, Gracie cabled succinctly from her home in Capri, 'Thanks very much. Impossible to do another Working Party. Imperative take rest.' She was at that time suffering from severe sinus trouble and exhaustion.

Reginald Jordan, BBC man and old friend, said after a concert where the crowds almost mobbed her, 'Surely she is the only woman in the world who can start her own riot, and with one piercing whistle, stop it!'

In 1948 she came to the Palladium for a fortnight. She was nervous and asked Monty, Lillian, Bert, Mary - all those closest to her - not to go to the rehearsals because she didn't want conflicting suggestions. She said she would work out her own programme.

'Gracie had an instinct for choosing the right song for the right occasion', Lillian said. 'She did it in 1939 with *I Love The Moon*, and she did it again in 1948 when she came out to face four thousand people.'

It was nearly ten years since she had appeared on that stage and heard the 'Palladium roar'. Some of them were dramatic, heartbreaking years for her. She sang *Take Me To Your Heart Again*, simply, honestly - not throbbing sobstuff but with a moving sincerity.

She and her audience, for they were *her* audience especially on that night, were one. As she came to the end of the song, tears were running down the faces of most of them, and Gracie was crying too. Recovering quickly, without further ado she went into the next song, and the next, and the next. Hers was always a truly music hall approach, no wasted time, no messing about, but a quickfire attack.

She turned cartwheels across the Palladium stage that night and ended the evening singing with the great crowd - or were they singing with her?

> I'll always love you,
> Promise that you'll love me.
> I'll always love you,
> Thro' all eternity,
> So long as the world goes on,
> Whatever the future be,
> I'll always love you,
> Knowing that you love me.

It was an emotional first night - almost like a reunion between lovers, the one in the glaring spotlight and the multitude in the softness of the shadows.

After that she appeared again every year, topping the bill for two weeks at one of the meccas of variety, the London Palladium.

In 1949, under the management of Claude Langdon, she gave eight concerts at the Empress Hall, then toured Britain and Canada, meeting with success after success and knowing, after her years in the wilderness, that she was still loved where it mattered most to her.

Her nephew, Tony Parry, remembers being taken to the Palladium when he was a child and living with his grandparents in Peacehaven.

Aunt Gracie's dressing room was the brightest place on earth. It smelled of sweet perfume, greasepaint, cold cream, flowers and tobacco. Cups of tea were continually being poured, and plates of thin sliced sandwiches with the crusts removed were always there, as were fancy pastries and cream chocolates. All I ever saw Aunt Gracie eat and drink was half a sandwich and a cup of tea. The rest was there for visitors.

13. Widowhood

After the war Monty Banks played the Mayor in *A Bell For Adano*. He had good notices. He also began work on the swimming pool and restaurant they planned below the villa.

The building of the pool caused a lot of bad feeling in Capri. People protested when the blasting of the cliffs and terraces surrounding the villa went on. 'It turned the sea into a filthy yellow mess for a time,' Gracie said, 'but everything settled down again when it was finished.'

Although Monty did not intend to be the chef for the Capri restaurant he was an excellent cook and loved spending time in the kitchen. One year he prepared and cooked a traditional English Christmas meal for fifteen people, most of them his relatives through marriage.

When the time came for serving they all sat round the large table, noses twitching with anticipation as the succulent aroma preceded Monty, who was proudly carrying the turkey.

Jenny looked: 'What, no gravy?' she said, 'Eeh, Monty,' and one of the family was despatched to see to the gravy. Roy Parry (Betty's husband) later captured that scene in two beautiful sketches which the family treasure.

Now though, Monty was looking forward to having the restaurant and swimming pool operational and he and Gracie being together in their own home at last.

They were very much in love. He flirted and he gambled, but 'that was Monty, that was his nature,' Gracie said. 'The flirting was harmless most of the time. He was a natural charmer with the women, but that was as far as it went. It was good for his ego, and I always knew it was me he loved. We made a great team. The gambling was difficult and did worry me. It was like an addiction, he'd put a bet on almost anything, and like most gamblers, lost more than he won.'

Life became fun again with Monty. Brash, noisy, warmhearted and lovable, he and Gracie, although from different countries, had come from the same hardworking backgrounds and they understood each others fears and joys.

They spent the Christmas of 1949 in Britain with Jenny and Fred. (The Stansfields had moved back after the war and settled in Sussex.) Christmas was always a crowded, happy time. Gracie loved to have her family around her, and she blossomed in the atmosphere. Monty loved this too and was on very good terms with them all. There was a mass of talent among them and they enjoyed charades and singsongs round the piano, all joining in, the older and younger generation too.

Gracie and Monty left Britain in January 1950 to go to Monty's family in Cesena for Gracie's birthday celebrations on the 9th. They were to spend a few days with Monty's sister (Maria) and her husband before returning to Capri. They travelled on the overnight Simplon-Orient Express, and on the Saturday afternoon, soon after the train had gone through the Simplon tunnel, Monty Banks collapsed with a heart attack.

Gracie had the train stopped at Arona, and an ambulance waiting, but nothing could be done. Monty died in her arms. Heartbroken, Gracie accompanied his body to his birthplace, Cesena, for the funeral, the day after her birthday.

There was a two mile procession. Monty, although he had been away so long, was popular. Gracie had some black blouses, but no proper black outfit, 'Mario hated me wearing black, he liked bright colours. This skirt was scarlet. Mario liked me to wear it all the time in Capri. It was the first thing I put my hand on. I had it dyed', she said, still in shock.

Monty, whom she usually called by his Italian name of Mario when they were together (and often they were 'mama' and 'papa' to each other), was only fifty. They had been married for ten drama-packed years. Now, at fifty-two, Gracie had to face life as a widow.

She returned to Capri with Mary Davey, her secretary and companion, who had flown out to be with her. Her fans wrote, many of the letters suggested work to help her over the loneliness, and she knew they were right. She could not have stayed at home doing nothing, especially after all their planning.

It isn't easy to be married to a big star, but Monty coped with that. There was no professional jealousy, he was very proud of her. They had a great companionship, as well as great love in their marriage. There were quarrels, sometimes explosive ones, for Monty had an excitable nature, but there was such a lot of love and warmth and laughter.

After Monty's death she fulfilled her existing contracts, and accepted touring engagements in Canada, America and Great Britain. Whenever she returned from touring, some of her family or friends went to stay.

'I was never alone, and I was terribly lonely', she said of that time. 'I knew I'd have to get used to it, plenty of others did, and so should I. It doesn't do to start feeling sorry for yourself', she told her friends. 'Of course I miss Mario. It was so sudden, it's hard to believe, but we had ten years. I knew him for twelve, and that's longer than a lot of people had during the war. I *have* to remember that and try to get used to being alone again.'

One of the things she dreaded was being alone. 'Maybe some of us are meant to be loners', she said. 'Perhaps the good Lord planned it so, but I don't like it.'

She knew that those closest to her tried to make sure there was someone there after the tours. She felt guilty about this, and didn't want the pity of them saying, 'Must make sure Grace isn't on her own.'

Two months after Monty's death, Gracie came to Britain to record some programmes for radio impresario Harry Alan Towers. He urged her to change any of the songs which she had already chosen (it had been planned when she and Monty were over for Christmas), but she didn't. She said she would have to change them all because of the words, or because they were the special ones he liked her to sing.

Godfrey Winn went along to interview her afterwards. He sat quietly through the recordings, as he tells here.

All set to go, Gracie? She went. First into one of those Lancashire stories that don't sound funny when anyone else tells them. Then into a number entitled, *I'm One Of The Little Orphans Of The Storm*. It was the old familiar line, and she was codding with her voice in the old cartwheeling style. Then suddenly the surprise came.

'Now I will sing for you *Oh My Beloved Father*, by Puccini.' The impact was startling. I told myself it was because I hadn't heard this lovely thing in English before. But it wasn't that. She sang the final words, 'Father, I pray... Father, I pray...', in a way that you don't expect, even from a great artiste, in a broadcasting studio.

Later, when I congratulated her, Gracie smiled her old, wide, brimming smile. 'I'll tell you the secret, luv. I've had the Puccini put down a tone. Gives me more of a chance. Don't have to do any screeching. My, but I want a cup of tea. Coming?'

She didn't want any fuss, there had been enough of that when she and Monty were married. She told Godfrey Winn, 'After my operation they told me not to work for two years but I started after two months. They told me I'd be sorry, but I never have been. So don't feel sorry for me because I've started work again after two months.'

She said that when she was touring and Monty was home or in Hollywood working on a film the telephone rang whenever she returned from somewhere, and it was Monty. It was uncanny, she said, how he timed her arrival, and it was wonderful to hear his voice and she missed this so much.

I didn't mind the tours any more. The phone would ring, I'd lift the receiver and he was there in the room. Now when the telephone rings I don't want to answer it.

One of my happiest memories is the last year of the war when we were working together. We just went where they sent us, it was tough going, but we felt like kids on a 2/9

tour. I sang and he cracked jokes. I told him he was an awful
ham comedian, but how we laughed. It was so good to be
working together. But once the war was over I began to think
of retiring. It was Mario who wouldn't let me. He persuaded
me to sign, at Christmas, for this big coast to coast Canadian
tour I'm doing after the broadcasts. He was always saying to
me, 'Gracie, if you don't work, you'll die.' Now I'm a very
lonely woman. I have lost my anchorage.

Everything Monty did was larger than life. Gracie said when
he was there the villa was full of life. He was such a happy
spirit and she felt his spirit around her when he died. For him,
the tiniest thing, making a cup of tea, boiling an egg, was carried
out as though he were staging a big production. He threw
himself into everything heart and soul.

She went to supervise the selling of Monty's five farms just
outside Cesena. His sister and her husband lived in the tall
farmhouse, and they moved into Cesena. Gracie sold the
property to an orphanage. Then she came home to try to pick
up the threads of her life again. She knew she had to work. 'I
missed him so much. It was all I had now, life had married me
to my work.'

In the September, Edie's seventeen year old daughter, Grace,
went to Capri for a month. In the family they were known as
Big Grace and Little Grace. They even had two bicycles marked
on the handlebars, Big Grace and Little Grace.

In the autumn of that year, 1950, Gracie returned to the
Palladium, her first appearance there since her husband's death.
The theatre had had a succession of American acts, and the
critics awaited eagerly the return of a star who almost always
stole the notices whether it was a simple concert or a Command
Performance.

'Palladium audiences, however enthusiastically they may
cheer, scream, or sigh for the Kayes and the Sinatras, always
hold in reserve a special kind of reception for Gracie Fields',
wrote critic Elizabeth Frank.

Last night, on the occasion of her first return after the death of her husband, it was possible to feel the waves of warmth and affection sweeping from the auditorium to the stage, where a Gracie who seemed just the same as ever, held them all in the palm of her hand. But there was something different. The closely cropped curly hair was grey, the approach to the audience quieter and more intimate, and there was a new dignity and graciousness about her whole demeanour.

She has, of course, still that bland audacity which is all her own, of sandwiching a prayer, sung with nunlike demureness, between the sad story of *Our Nellie*, and that everlasting giant aspidistra; of being yearningly sentimental at one moment and completely outrageous the next...

'Gracie Fields was in tears at the end of her act,' reviewer John Barber wrote, "You've made me cry," she sobbed into heart-moving applause. "Stop it, stop it." It is her first appearance here since her husband, Monty Banks died in January this year. Gracie is a bit sadder, her tight curls are a bit greyer. But at 52 she is triumphantly handsome. She wears a white tulle dress, girlish as her high, clear voice. Some of her serious songs are new, but they drench the house in the old emotion...'

Gracie's white tulle dress had a leaf design of green sequins across the bodice. 'I paid £40 for it in Capri,' she said, 'cheapest stage dress I ever bought, but it made me feel like the girl on top of the birthday cake.'

At the end of that first night, when the audience were still crying, applauding and shouting for *Sally*, while the stage was rapidly filling up round her with bouquets of flowers, Gracie brushed the tears from her own eyes to sing it for them. 'Come on, everybody', she called, the power once more returning, and nearly three thousand people stood and sang *Sally* with her.

The heart she always put into her singing, and the audience's reaction on this occasion, drained her, but their love also renewed her courage.

In November she was again chosen for the Royal Variety Show, her fifth, and that year, 1950, she was voted one of the people of the year in a *Daily Express* ballot. Readers were asked to name one person only, under various headings.

'Man of 1950 - Britain' was Winston Churchill. 'Woman of 1950 - Britain' was Princess Elizabeth (our present Queen). 'Man of 1950 - World' was General MacArthur. 'Man of 1950 - Leisure' was Ted Ray. 'Woman of 1950 - Leisure' was Gracie Fields. There were thousands of entries, and the *Express* commented when announcing the results, 'It was never a question of twenty, ten, or even five people in any group competing closely for the winning vote. Every one of the five names shown here had a runaway win, the voting was overwhelmingly for them.'

Christmas was spent in Capri with some of her family, among them Little Grace and Monty's sister, Maria, and her husband.

In January 1951 Kenneth Adams, then Controller of the Light Programme of the BBC, wrote to Gracie to invite her to 'take part, and in fact to occupy your proper place at the top of the bill for the Festival of Variety. May I press you to make yourself available to us for this programme which could not be truly representative without you', the letter continued.

Gracie accepted and wound up the Festival of Variety which the BBC organised to celebrate the Festival of Britain. The concert took place on 6 May 1951, and she was introduced by Wilfred Pickles, who said, 'I'm going to say very little indeed about the next artiste. I welcome, on your behalf, and with all my heart, the greatest lady of the variety stage. I need only say two words more, "Our Gracie".'

She came on to the kind of ovation which had caused her to say in the past, 'They clap too long and too soon...'

Nevertheless, this was one of her favourite broadcasts. She included *Sing As We Go, Mocking Bird Hill, I Never Cried So Much In All My Life, So In Love, The Biggest Aspidistra* and *At The End Of the Day* (the first performance of this). She sang them all in quick succession, finishing with *Land of Hope and Glory*, 'Come on, everybody', she said half way through, and the voices of that huge audience joined hers to a glorious and stirring finish.

The rehearsal in the afternoon was another example of the great contrast between the inner and outer woman. She walked in, wearing a smart but ordinary coat, a scarf over her grey curls, and her glasses on. When a BBC official questioned what she was doing there, she answered quietly, 'Well, I was asked to come, luv, my name's Gracie Fields.'

Mr Alfred Richman, who was at the rehearsal, said in his report, 'Gracie bobbed and weaved and clowned on the stage, she said, "By Goom", lost her music, kicked the microphone, and sang *Land of Hope and Glory* so beautifully that hardbitten professionals applauded, and Wilfred Pickles blew his nose.'

Kenneth Adams wrote to thank her on 7 May, and in his letter he said:

> Ever since, as a Manchester Guardian reporter, I stood by your side on the balcony of the Town Hall at Rochdale for your "homecoming" in 1931, I have dreamed dreams of your some time or other appearing for me on my show. Well, last night it happened, and the Festival of Variety came to its only fitting climax with you. Thank you for being the same as ever, and so unique. I don't know what your plans are, and I don't want to bother you. But please remember that, if you do feel you would like to broadcast, the Light Programme is at your disposal, any time, any place. Its audience is the people, the great mass of the people, and it is in their hearts you are enthroned.

The Festival of Britain in 1951 had something of the grandeur of the old Empire building days about it. Gracie toured the exhibition while it was on, and went down the river to Battersea and sang with the band which played for the dancers at the great funfair at Battersea Park.

She was booked for a concert tour of the USA and Canada immediately afterwards, and took her niece Grace with her. 'I had very few duties', Grace said, 'mostly I was in the wings

making lists of songs. She always thought she could find the
perfect rotation, but as she was such a master of atmosphere
and audience mood the songs came out in a different order
every night. I pitied the poor pianist.'

They met J.B. Priestley on board ship. Gracie knew him from
before the war when he had written the script for two of her
films. (*Sing As We Go* and *Look Up and Laugh*.) When he had
talked to her about the script he'd said rather grandly, 'Well, I
think it'll be a success.'

'That's a bit of a negative attitude,' she said

'Well, we authors don't like to assume it will sell well.'

Gracie laughed, 'What the heck are you writing it for then?'

She was often frank to the point of rudeness if she thought
someone was saying something for effect, or being particularly
pompous.

Now he was on a lecture tour and asked if he could stay at
her Santa Monica home while there.

'Well you'll have to muck in because I've no help in the house
and I shall be busy selling up and sending my furniture back to
Capri', she told him.

Three days after they arrived at La Escondita, Priestley turned
up. Each morning he came down to breakfast wearing pyjamas
and dressing gown and waited for Gracie to cook his bacon
and eggs. He stayed nearly three weeks and Gracie recalled her
grandmother Chip Sarah's lodgers. 'Must run in the family,
we make them too comfortable!'

In November she appeared in *The Cavalcade of Variety* at the
Palladium. The show, sponsored by the *News of the World*, was
put on by the Grand Order of Water Rats and Lady Ratlings,
an organisation which raises thousands of pounds every year
for charity. The occasion was graced by a galaxy of glittering
stars. Comedian Ted Ray, who was King Rat (Chairman) that
year, sat on the stage wearing his chain of office and surrounded
by fellow artistes and representatives of the variety world. Bud
Flanagan, Leonard Jones, Sir Noel Curtis-Bennett, Georgie
Wood, Albert Whelan, G.H. Elliott, Tom Moss, Nat Mills,
Bunny Doyle, Alf Pearson, Barry Lupino, Fred Russell (at

eighty-eight he was the eldest among them), Sir Louis Sterling, Talbot O'Farrell, Cyril Smith, Dave Carter, Lupino Lane, Ben Warriss, Serge Canjou, Jimmy Jewel, Vera Lynn, Max Miller, Arthur English, Jimmy Bailey...

Gracie seemed completely back in favour with the press and public, but she always had at the back of her mind the thought that she was getting older and would not be able to go on singing forever. Not on the concert platform anyway.

'I have to be sure I can give the same slap bang-up performance', she said more than once; yet there was a part of her that could not say no. Her voice was still good and she could get people to 'raise the roof' in a manner few others achieved.

14. Gracie and Boris

Gracie had built small bungalows in the grounds and on the terraces of the Canzone del Mare (Song of the Sea), her Capri villa, and after Monty died they were filled with friends and relatives. She had lived on Capri intermittently since 1936, and Boris Alperovici had lived there almost permanently (apart from the war years) since 1927. It seems incredible on an island as small as Capri, but, although they had seen each other, they had never met.

'In fact Boris was among those who wrote to the authorities complaining about the mess Monty and I were making of the Mediterranean Sea when we built the pool', Gracie recalled later.

Boris, originally from Bessarabia, a country which no longer exists separately but is part of Russia, went to Capri as Gracie once had, to see an island he had read about. He was on holiday at the time and went over from Naples for the day.

Boris was brought up by his two sisters, his mother having died when he was three years old, and his father when he was seven. He was a student of architecture in Rome when he first visited Capri, but became more interested in what was then a new invention - wireless. He became expert at building sets and experimenting with many branches of communication through the medium of electricity, and through his work in this area he met Prince Colonna, who introduced him to Dr George Cerio and his brother Edwin Cerio.

The Cerio brothers lived on Capri and had a marvellously equipped workroom and laboratory where they experimented with sounds and pictures. Boris left university without finishing the course and went to work in Capri with them. He became like one of their own family and immersed himself in the work he loved, inventing and experimenting. He and Edwin Cerio built a television set as early as the beginning of the thirties, and in 1934, when Gracie Fields appeared on those first wavery pictures from Crystal Palace, Boris and Edwin Cerio saw her on their screen in Capri and wrote to tell the BBC.

During the war Boris had to leave Capri, which became a military zone. Like Monty, who had to leave Britain, he had nationality trouble. He held a Romanian passport, for although he had lived in Italy for so long, he had not then become an Italian citizen. He moved to a small village near Naples but could not continue with his radio work because 'It would have caused suspicion that I was spying', he said.

In 1943 Boris became attached to the Eighth Army through both his linguistic and engineering abilities. They needed an interpreter who also knew the technical terms involved, and he fitted the bill perfectly. He spent the rest of the war as a sergeant in the Royal Engineers. In 1945 he was one of the troops packed into the Opera House in Naples when Gracie gave her concert there.

'*Land of Hope and Glory* was magnificent,' he said, 'then she sang two comic songs which I didn't like.'

In the summer of 1951 Gracie's nephew Tony Parry (Betty's son), his wife Peggy, and children were living with Gracie and managing the restaurant when her record player broke. Tony suggested asking 'Mr Boris' to have a look at it. 'He's a wizard with electrical things', he said.

Boris did come and mend the record player, which is probably where the story started that he was a radio repairer. He never was. Boris was an engineer and inventor, as Tony Parry said on that first occasion, 'a wizard with electrical things.'

Because she thought he didn't speak English, Gracie simply smiled at him while he was working on her machine and left it at that. She immersed herself in work after Monty's death, and it was after another tour of Canada that she returned to find that the children had been playing with her tape-recorder and it wasn't working properly. This time when 'Mr Boris', Boris Abraham Alperovici to give him his full name, came to look at it, Gracie discovered that he did speak English, and several other languages too. In the ensuing weeks they came to know each other better, and they fell in love.

Gracie was fifty-four and Boris forty-eight. She had behind her two marriages, one disastrous and one happy, and he was a bachelor. They kept their romance as secret as possible to begin with for Gracie knew only too well the traumas and dangers of publicity.

She was due to come back to Britain in the autumn of 1951 to appear at the Palladium for a month, and she said in her book, *Sing As We Go*, 'I've had many crazy weeks in my life, but none quite as crazy as those. Everything seemed absurdly wonderful. The London buses, the faces of people in the street, the thought of the journey back to Capri, the songs I sang. And all the time I kept thinking of Boris.'

The Palladium season was another great success. Then she returned to Capri. They thought well about the difficulties which could ensue. 'I was very severe with myself,' Gracie said. 'I realised my loneliness could lead me to read more into my feelings than I should.'

She admitted she had never liked living alone, and, although she liked being alone sometimes, she enjoyed having someone 'belonging' about.

Their lifestyles were very different, as were their backgrounds and quite often their tastes. Gracie's were particularly catholic. She found beauty in many areas. Boris had led a quiet life, while she, in comparison, a very noisy one, but they were in love and ready to take a chance.

Boris had his first taste of what it could be like when they announced their engagement on Christmas Eve 1951. Reporters converged on the island during the next few weeks, and Gracie and Boris eventually went to Rome for a few days to get some peace and do some shopping. What the papers didn't know they guessed, and Gracie's previous marriages were looked up and discussed, even her religion. Articles headed "Will Gracie Fields become a Catholic?" "Gracie will take Boris's religion when she marries." In fact none of this happened. Gracie did not embrace the Catholic religion.

She was booked for a tour of Germany, parts of which were to be recorded for commercial radio. In Hamburg and Berlin troops protested at being charged admission to hear these commercial broadcasts recorded. Gracie herself was not paid for the shows she did in Germany but was to receive a fee for the radio broadcasts of them.

Before going on stage at a Berlin cinema, she said, 'I think the lads should get in free', and after the recording she went to Wavell Barracks and sang to the troops there for another hour - free.

That wasn't the end of the storms, for when Mr Gordon Crier, Gracie's producer, left Berlin, with Radio Luxembourg man Peter Wilson and a British Army driver, for Minden, they took a wrong turning, ending up in the Russian zone where they were detained because they had no permits.

Gracie, who had flown from Berlin to Minden for her next concert, said angrily, 'It's ridiculous, Mr Crier is working for commercial radio, not the BBC. It's a political issue', adding for good measure, 'I'm mad at everybody, I wish I could get hold of the chap that did it and bang him round the ear. Why don't we grab any of their people?' Then she went on to give her concert.

Meanwhile Lillian Aza flew out to Germany to ask her not to rush into marriage with Boris, who, while he might be a very nice man, was the unknown quantity as far as everyone in Britain was concerned. 'Wait twelve months to make sure you're doing the right thing,' she suggested.

But Gracie was in no mood to listen. She was in love again and wanted more than anything else at that time to be married quietly in church, in a ceremony that would be, to use her own words, 'quiet enough for me to really listen to the words of the service.'

On 6th February King George died, and Princess Elizabeth and her husband, the Duke of Edinburgh, returned from Kenya, where they were on tour, to a country in mourning, immensely saddened by the loss of a good and well-loved monarch.

Gracie and Boris, beseiged by newspaper men in Capri, escaped to Rome again. Reporters followed them, and Gracie turned on them angrily, 'Let's get it straight,' she said after reports in the papers that they had parted, 'Boris and I haven't quarrelled, we shall get married quietly and without fuss.'

'They're turning our wedding into a peepshow,' she said tearfully a little later. To dodge reporters they got married two days later than originally planned, and some of their family and friends missed the service, which was upsetting for them all.

The ceremony took place in the church of San Stefano in Capri on 18th February 1952. Gracie made her responses in a low voice, almost a whisper, but Boris spoke out loudly.

After the service they came from the church to the cheers and good wishes of several hundred people who were waiting outside. This was too much for Gracie and she burst into tears. She recovered quickly, her public self coming to the fore again when someone gave her a bunch of red carnations. Turning to her new husband she said, 'Red for passion, that's us, eh?'

They had a simple reception at her home afterwards and gave the money a huge 'do' would have cost to the poorer people on the island. As an extra wedding present Boris fixed the underwater lighting in the swimming pool on the first morning of his honeymoon. This was something that had been planned before Monty died, and afterwards not completed.

They didn't 'live happily ever after' straight away, although they did eventually. There was a great deal of adjusting to do on both sides.

'The first two or three years were often stormy,' Gracie said later, 'Boris wanted to keep me all to himself, and I sometimes was very restless for the theatre.'

Archie and Monty had both been actively involved in the theatre and in Gracie's career, which was established and pretty much unalterable by the time she met Boris.

Because his knowledge of electrical equipment and its effects was so good, Boris often interfered during recording sessions, and this caused ructions all round. Gracie had a reputation for being an easy person to work with professionally. She was a perfectionist, but not a finicky one. She wanted everyone to do their best, and she would go to infinite trouble to get it right, but, 'I'm not a fusser, luv. If it doesn't work we'll do a different song that does.'

Boris and Gracie made each other happy too. Their 'romance' caught the public's imagination and they clamoured for Boris at concerts. She seemed to encourage this attitude, bringing him on and beaming at him as he acknowledged *his* applause. In her public life she had always found it easy to take the lead, but in private less so. His own round of applause may have made up a little for some times being addressed as Mr Fields.

Boris wasn't keen on comedy and wished she would concentrate on the serious numbers. 'He would have preferred me to be an opera singer,' Gracie often said, 'he reveres them.' Their humour was quite different. Gracie found a chuckle in many things. She looked for the lighter side and sought the sunshine in life because she knew only too well that the tears came anyway.

'I want my private life, Boris too wants this,' she said, 'but I try to explain to him that I also belong, and always will, to my dying day, to the people who have given me everything I possess.'

Gracie was a deeply religious woman. She didn't go to church regularly, but she said her prayers. They were the first ones she learnt as a child in Rochdale, and were followed by others she gathered as she grew older. She had to remember them all before she could rest. 'If I happen to fall asleep and then wake up I know it's because I haven't finished my prayers.'

'I believe in religion', she said, 'I believe in it terribly strongly.' She talked about God as a friend. 'The Good Lord always seems to be there , watching over me,' she would say, or, 'The Good Lord put all the notes there.'

During the war I usually had to end up with *The Holy City*, *The Lord's Prayer* or *Ave Maria*. No matter what I had sung before, the boys would start calling for one of those three. By that time I'd be exhausted and thinking I couldn't even speak a word, let alone sing it. Then I'd ask God to give me a bit of added strength, something so I could give them the song they wanted. That strength always came. Suddenly my voice would come back and I'd sing better than I had before. Where that strength or voice came from I don't know, but I asked for it and it came.

During the war, suffering from exhaustion, she became really ill but no one outside those travelling with her knew. Troops were moved on unexpectedly and this gave her five days rest. 'The Good Lord always helped so I never made any excuses. I stayed in bed and relaxed, then I was fine to carry on again.'

She always said a prayer before going on stage, and Neva Hecker, her American secretary, said that, no matter how late it was or how tired she felt, Gracie said her prayers before going to sleep.

Sometimes she went to church with Boris, 'but I find I get nothing out of it, but in the prayers I say every night of my life I find comfort, a wonderful comfort.'

In an interview for the BBC she talked about a scripture lesson she remembered from her schooldays. 'It was about Jesus dying, and by the tomb his clothes were left in a tidy heap.' After that she used to pick up her own clothes, and her two sisters', even if it made them late for school.

'I wanted to please,' she said, 'I tried to please.' And although during her long career Gracie often made fun of and sent up all kinds of songs, she always sang the sacred ones straight. 'Her religion was inside her,' one of her friends said, 'and it was always there.'

She gave her time for churches of all denominations. If there was a job she could do, she did it, from opening a garden party to helping raise funds for the roof of a Roman Catholic, Anglican, Jewish or any other faith's church. 'Live and let live' was one of her beliefs. Another which she occasionally quoted was 'Do unto others as you would be done by.'

In 1960, when Father Borelli from Naples asked her to sing to the homeless children of the area, the 'scugnizzi', she went. The concert took place in an old, crumbling church in Naples which Father Borelli had turned into a home. It was known as 'The House of the Urchins.'

'What could I sing to a bunch of boys and youths hardened to a ruthless fight for existence before they were ten?' she said. 'Not love songs; not sad songs; gay ones then.' And she did, beginning with a bright Neapolitan song which she sang in Italian. She sang loudly, as she had in her own childhood, when Jenny was urging her on. 'Come on,' she shouted to them, 'Canta.' And they did sing. She stopped them in her own style with her errand-boy whistle, and although she did not change their way of life, she undoubtedly brightened it for some of them.

In November 1970 Gracie appeared on her first *Stars on Sunday* programme. Jess Yates, whose idea the programme was, and who was its first presenter and producer, went over to Capri specially to ask her because there had been so many requests from viewers. At first she would not agree.

'My voice isn't what it once was, I'm not sure I could *give* as I should. I haven't got the breath control I used to have.' Eventually she agreed to do it, and it was the first of many appearances Gracie would make; singing her 'Sunday Songs' was how she phrased it.

Of course she was right: by 1970 her voice wasn't what it once had been, but it was still a remarkable voice, and, if it was lower and gentler than before, the people she was singing to were also older and mellower. During rehearsals she mentioned the costumes she would need to sort out, 'Lord I wish I was like Piaf and became famous in one dress', she said. 'Sometimes it would be nice not to have to get dressed up.'

When she came over to record the programme, tying it in with the Christmas Day one she was doing, she also sang other songs for inclusion in future *Stars on Sunday* programmes. It happened to be Boris's sixty-seventh birthday, and Yorkshire

Television canteen staff made a special birthday cake for him. When it was brought in during a break in recording, he and Gracie were sitting together talking. Jess Yates played Happy Birthday, everyone present sang, then Boris blew out the candles on his birthday cake and shared it round.

By then, Boris had seen Gracie work many times and had toured with her ('he's better at washing the smalls than I am', Gracie often joked), but the first time he came to London with her was in 1952, the year they were married, when she was one of the artistes in a Midnight Matinee at the Coliseum for the Lynmouth Flood Disaster Fund. He sat in a box with Bert and Lillian Aza and slipped down to the dressing room in time to greet her as she came off. 'Gracie, you are a very great artiste', he said. That was probably the first time Boris saw and felt her magic working on the stage. That concert raised nearly £10,000 for the fund for the relatives of the victims of the floods, and to help people salvage what was left of their homes. The cast included many famous names - Vera Lynn, Mary Martin, Billie Worth, Kay Hammond, John Clements, Jimmy Jewel and Ben Warriss, and the Sadler's Wells Ballet Company.

Gracie was always one of the first artistes to offer her services in cases like this. She was at the King's Theatre in Southsea in 1951 in a concert raising money for relatives of the crew of HMS *Affray* which sank in the Channel south of the Isle of Wight. During that evening she was given various articles to auction, and, when she ran out someone called to her, 'Your stole, Gracie - auction your stole.' Without hesitation she whipped it from her shoulders - it was palest pink, very delicate, with hand-painted butterflies all over it, and, amid laughter at her 'auctioneering manner', she sold it for £15.

She often sold her hats. In South Africa she appeared as a guest at a charity show in a packed hall. 'Whew, it's hot', she said to the audience, taking off her hat and ruffling her hair. Then, 'Here you are, anyone can have it if they pay for it', and a few more pounds went to the St Dunstan's Aftercare Fund. The following day Gracie bought another hat for 4s 11d.

Gracie could not bear to see suffering she could do nothing about. If she could help in any way, she was the first one there, but if she couldn't she got out of the way as quickly as possible. Her compassion took a practical form, her sympathy for anyone in pain or trouble was so tremendous it sapped her. If she did a show for very sick or unfortunate people, she always told the management she had another engagement immediately afterwards, even when she hadn't, because, unless she could do something to ease their pain or make their lives a little brighter, she wouldn't stay and watch. Gracie was never an accident gloater, she helped if she could, cheered where she could, then quietly went on to the next thing.

She found it hard to do shows which put such a strain on her, but she never demurred. She went on and gave everything she had to give. Her concerts often left her very emotional. 'You have to control it,' she said, 'otherwise you can't do your work properly.' She put herself so completely into the role of the song that when it was finished the tears often came. Mrs Wood of Blackpool was one of the waitresses for a reception in 1957 at Rochdale. 'Gracie sang *Three Green Bonnets* from the Town Hall balcony,' she said, 'and when she turned to come in, tears were running down her cheeks, and the crowd in the square below were still cheering and clapping.'

Mr Bowker Andrews, who was with Gracie on her 1947 Working Party broadcasts, said that in the twelve weeks she covered over 2,000 miles and did six direct broadcasts and six recorded shows. He said the tour was 'a period packed with unforgettable memories' and that wherever they went they had receptions filled with so much affection for her that over and over again she remarked to him that the responsibility of repaying so much was quite beyond her, but that she was determined to do her best.

The first Royal Command Performance, the only true Royal Command (they are now called Royal Variety Shows), was held on 1 July 1912, at the Palace Theatre, Shaftesbury Avenue. King George V and Queen Mary attended. Queen Mary was dressed in lavender silk, and King George wore a flower in the buttonhole of his dress suit. The theatre was filled with roses; from the stage to the royal box, over the proscenium arch, there were pink, red and golden roses. In the foyer were more flowers, banks of lilies and pink hydrangeas forming an avenue of beauty to welcome the royal guests. One hundred and forty-two artistes took part, many only walking on for the finale which was called 'Varieties Garden Party' and then to sing the National Anthem.

Gracie was fourteen then, an unknown, with most of the triumphs and tragedies still before her. A tall young girl, one of 'Charburn's Young Stars', full of bounce and energy and that enormous talent which was eventually to take her to the top of variety's highest tree of stars.

Gracie appeared in ten Royal Variety Shows (she was invited to eleven but the 1956 one was cancelled because of the Suez crisis). The first was in 1928 and the last in 1978, when she closed the show at the Palladium as the surprise of the evening. Royal Variety Shows are usually nerve-racking experiences, as the late Clarkson Rose remembered. He was in the 1928 one, his first as well as Gracie's.

'Eeh, Clarkie luv, how do you feel?' she asked him at the final rehearsal. He told her he was nervous; 'How about you?' he said.

'I feel as if I know nowt about owt,' was the reply.

That show was also before King George V and Queen Mary, and afterwards, when she was presented to Their Majesties, Queen Mary told Gracie she preferred the serious songs to the comedy ones.

Anton Dolin was also in that 1928 show. 'It was the first time I had met Gracie,' he said, 'and it was a first Royal Variety Show for us both. We had adjoining dressing rooms at the Coliseum. We both arrived about six o'clock, terribly nervous, and tried to console each other. We peeped through the curtains together to watch the King and Queen arrive, which was rather naughty and gave us a thrill, but made us even more nervous!'

Most of the reviews for Command Performances she was in mentioned her in glowing terms: 'Biggest cheers were for Gracie', 'A Stardust night of triumph for Our Gracie', 'Hits of the Royal show were Gracie Fields and the Crazy Gang'. In 1957 though, John Lambert interviewed Gracie the morning after the performance in which she flopped. 'Frankly,' she told him, 'I wonder if I'm finished. I wonder if anybody does want me any more.'

She had sung modern songs, presented an altogether more up-to-date image, and in a show where people have paid tremendously high prices for their seats, where they are acknowledged to be among the hardest audiences to win...

'I know,' she said, 'I made a mistake. But it is making that sort of mistake that makes me wonder if I'm finished. If I'm out of touch with what the public wants now.' Later in the interview she said, 'I know I'm an old woman now,' [she was two months away from her sixtieth birthday] 'old in years anyway, if not in the way I feel. And perhaps my voice may be going a bit.' She grumbled about the short time, nine minutes, which she had. 'All the while I was worrying about whether I was going on too long. Nine minutes and that's your lot. No time to build with your audience. Another thing, I've been singing songs like *Walter* and *The Biggest Aspidistra* for years, do people really want to hear the same old things all the time?' This was an aspect she often could not fathom. 'Over five hundred songs in my repertoire and they always want those few.'

'I still think it's the greatest honour an artiste can have', she told John Lambert quietly, 'to be chosen for the Royal Variety Show, so I just do as the producer tells me.'

He asked her if she was serious about giving up. 'I have three television appearances lined up for December', she said. 'The way I feel at the moment I wish I could get out of them, I don't want to go on just as a bit of nostalgia.'

Seven years later Gracie did another Royal Show, and critic James Green wrote, 'It was a confrontation of Queens. One Queen had been driven from Buckingham Palace and was in the Royal Box. The other Queen was on stage, showing why she has won the honorary title Queen of the Music Hall. Be as cynical as you like about Gracie Fields. What is beyond dispute is that all her life she has been a marvel, and now, almost 67, she is a ruddy marvel...'

This time she took no chances. She sang *Sally* as she came on, *Getting To Know You*, *Glocca Morra*, *Scarlet Ribbons*, *September Song*, and *The Ugly Duckling*, and went off to *Wish Me Luck As You Wave Me Goodbye*. Afterwards, at the presentations, the Queen said to Gracie, 'It is so nice to see you back once again', Gracie replied, 'It's nice to be back, ma'am - it's like the horse that's been let out of the stable once more.'

One Royal Show, in which 'Cheeky Chappie' Max Miller was told to do eight minutes and overran to the extent of doing eighteen, caused consternation for everyone connected with it. Max felt that the American acts were getting a better deal than the British ones, and he did a different, and much longer turn than the one he had rehearsed that morning. As something timed to the second as the Royal Variety Show is, it was embarrassing and upsetting for management, artistes and backstage staff. American singer Dinah Shore, already worked up to tension pitch and waiting in the wings, began to cry. It was Gracie who walked over, cuddled her and told her to dry her tears for it would all work out. Which it did, and Dinah was a big hit when she eventually appeared.

Liberace was another who cried on Gracie's shoulder when the 1956 Variety Performance was cancelled just after the dress rehearsal, due to the Suez crisis. It was his first trip to Britain and would have been his first Royal Show.

In 1952 after Gracie and Gigli had done their single acts, they sang together, in Italian, *Come Back To Sorrento*. When he flirted with her during the love song, she joked, 'I'll make you prove it afterwards' - and, without pausing, carried on singing. After the duet Gigli presented her with a giant basket of roses.

'Theatre history was made last night when Our Gracie and Beniamino Gigli sang together for the Queen,' wrote the reviewers.

Gracie's stage dresses were elegant . Sometimes rich-looking, sometimes simple, but always right for the occasion. One Royal Variety Show frock was covered with several thousand sequins which she and her secretary, Mary Davey, helped to sew on. 'Every spare minute we had we were stitching like mad', she said when complimented on the dress after the show. Over the years she wore black velvet, pink tulle, gold lame, white satin and in 1978 a blue and gold kaftan.

The 1978 show was Lord Delfont's last one as organiser and, with an all British cast, was a special tribute to Queen Elizabeth the Queen Mother. Gracie was thrilled and nervous. She practised and exercised her voice thoroughly, working on it every day from the time she knew she had been chosen again.

As the show drew near to the finish, compere David Jacobs introduced her as the surprise of the evening. The orchestra went into her signature tune and she stepped forward.

That final 'Sally', when her voice seemed to have gathered in all the richness of her eighty years experience - when, half way through, she broke off to say to us, 'I've been singing a man's song all me life', and Danny La Rue rocked with laughter as his deep, throaty chuckle came clearly through the mike to mingle with our own laughter and tears as everyone joined in - in that one chorus it was as though Gracie was giving the people a glimpse of all her voice had achieved in days gone by. The essence of her personality was there in all its richness in that last Command Performance.

She had a standing ovation, and as the applause echoed through the theatre, she gave her errand-boy whistle to stop. 'Cease, cease', she said, then, turning towards the Royal Box, Our Gracie led everyone in singing *God Save Our Queen*.

15. Two Gracies or One?

We all have more than one character, although often one aspect is dominant, and people sometimes wrongly assume that this is all there is.

To succeed as she did, Gracie had to be a powerful person on several levels. She was. As she said more than once, 'I'm a strong, hardy daughter of the north, and folk expect certain qualities.' She also had a tender side. So much so that she turned it into her 'don't let us be sloppy' side, when she would suddenly switch from the romantic to the ridiculous, the sad to the silly, the grand to the gauche. It was a way of getting over the emotional part of her nature in public.

In the world of theatre there is sometimes much falseness, often beneath the gloss is a different person. Gracie was two people. Gracie Fields the superstar, and Grace Stansfield the woman. Both were genuine; only she could adequately separate them, and over the years the two merged closer together, held strongly by that golden cord of sincerity and genuineness that was the heart of both Gracies.

Myths grew around her. Often she wanted people to know what she was like, yet she could not show them 'the ordinary person I am outside of my voice.' She was naturally forthright and intelligent, and the two forces - the honest-to-goodness Gracie who *wanted* to believe in fairy tales, and the blunt and sharp one who realised she was often being used - clashed and made her a very lonely person. Because she understood this and disliked being alone for too long, she tried to come to terms with it, but her innate honesty with herself prevented her from accepting less than she gave.

In her audiences she found the devotion she sought. It is one thing to love an audience while you are in the theatre and together, quite another to do so when they have scattered and gone their separate ways. Gracie needed individual love as well, at times desperately.

She had attention, this was always present, even as a small child when her mother was working on getting her on the stage. This attention was a form of love, it was Jenny's dream and therefore the best way she could prove her love for her family. Grace was the first and she could sing, that was all Jenny needed to propel her toward the top.

Her sister, Betty, said, 'Grace was never a child.' She was away from home a lot from an early age and learned to be tough. Life was a struggle and she had to stay on top of it.

The outgoing, exuberant personality the public knew was also the shy, retiring lady who wanted peace and quiet and above all, loving companionship.

She would often not ask for a cup of tea, her favourite beverage, in case it put someone out, and when she visited her agent, she seldom let her know - just turned up, having already eaten either a sandwich or a pork pie in a cafe along the road. Then she could truthfully say 'I've already eaten.' Sometimes it was simply 'doing her own thing', and not having to be at a certain place at a certain time.

Quite often she forgot appointments, being utterly engrossed in something else. At a prearranged dinner party once, everyone was assembled except Gracie. All these people hoping to meet her, and she had gone out to dinner with Norman Wisdom! She had attended the Ice Show at the Empress Hall, and in the finale, when the cast lined up to acknowledge the applause, Norman was lost behind most of them.

Henry Hall came onto the stage to give a speech of thanks and said, 'May I give a special welcome to our guest of honour, Miss Gracie Fields.' People waved and called to her, 'Sing us a song, Gracie', and she rose and carefully made her way across the ice to the stage.

Henry thought she might sing and handed her the microphone. Instead she cleared a path through the cast until she reached Norman, hidden away at the back, 'She took me by the hand,' he said, 'led me to the front, kissed me on the cheek and said into the mike, "In a couple of years this lad is going to be the biggest comedian in Britain."

'She started to make her way back and Henry Hall jerked a thumb. I scurried down and walked that lovely lady back across the ice to her seat. "That was really kind of you", I said. "Don't worry, I'm an old professional," she said, "I saw what was going on..."'

When he asked her to go out to dinner with him, she said everything else went from her mind. The following day she telephoned to apologise about the dinner party, and, being Gracie, she not only did so to her manager who had tried to organise it but also rang each guest individually.

In her professional life she was always punctual and reliable, but she loved to do things on the spur of the moment at other times. 'It was always difficult to arrange any kind of a "do" for her,' Lillian Aza said, 'because on her way to it she was likely to notice a film she hadn't seen and slip into the cinema instead.'

Exasperating as this was, part of the reason could have been that she knew there were going to be other people there, and she thought one less would not make much difference. She never didn't turn up anywhere deliberately, because she could not bear to let people down. She was often afraid they would find her less exciting than they expected. 'I'm very ordinary', she said, while admitting that on stage she was a different person. She knew she changed, vibrated a power over the audience which she suspected came from outside herself, and it often worried her.

In 1971, when she had been very under the weather for several weeks, she wrote to her family: 'I've spoken to Lillian today on the phone, asking her to cancel the "Stars on Sunday" job I made a verbal promise I'd do, so I hope she can talk 'em out of it nicely (it's the first time I've ever done this, not live up to my promise). The contract isn't signed, so when I hear how they've taken the disappointing news - if it is disappointing?????'

She was one of the most approachable of stars, and never thought the formality of a special evening was necessary for people to meet her. She gave most people who wanted to talk to her a quarter of an hour so that as many as possible could do so, and maybe also because she was unsure of herself. 'They might rumble me, I'm nothing like the paragon they think I am.'

In Capri, though, when a fresh coachload of visitors arrived to see her, she used to go down to the pool (there were nearly one hundred steps from Gracie's villa to her swimming pool) and sometimes she did this three or four times a day during the summer.

'It must be a thrill for your fans,' someone said to her once, 'but it's a long way down, don't you get tired of it?'

Gracie smiled. 'They come all this way and look up at my terrace hoping to catch a glimpse. If they still think that much of me, why shouldn't I go down to see them? I wouldn't go looking for them, I'm too shy to do that, but if they've asked for me, well that's different.'

She was on home ground here and probably felt more secure. She knew from the letters she received that many came hoping she would be there, and she understood their sentiments so well. Basically hers had been a Cinderella story, poverty to riches, mill to Mediterranean island. She knew that many of them ignored or were oblivious of the bits in between, but she was happy to share with them that glimpse of what it was possible to achieve.

When a holidaymaker asked if he could dip his feet in the swimming pool, 'because I've come two thousand miles to do just that', she knew what he meant. 'Go on lad, have a bash', she told him. Nevertheless she was embarrassed when crowds having tea shouted 'Hullo, Gracie', as she came into sight. She never knew what to do then. On stage there was no problem - she commanded and they obeyed. The shy side of her was uppermost when faced with outside situations. At a loss she usually joked and became the loud, noisy woman who was only a tiny part of the real Gracie.

During one interview she was asked if she sang at the tables in her restaurant. She said, 'No, luv. I sang for the bricks, now the bricks can sing for me.' Noticing Boris watching her she said, 'You don't like me saying that, do you? Well, it's true.'

When she had anyone to tea in the villa, she walked to the gate with them. 'I'll come and see you off. Must let you see I've been brought up proper', and she would laugh and maybe even pull a face at them, but she would be there with a smile and a wave when you turned round.

In 1973-4, when Sir Anton Dolin was living in Capri for six months, he gave a party and invited Gracie. She wasn't a great party goer, but she attended a few. The party was spread out over two rooms, and Gracie sat in a huge armchair while people milled around her talking, and eventually someone said, 'Will you sing for us, Gracie?'

She looked across to her host, who added his voice to the others.

'Got a piano?'

'No.'

'A guitar?'

'No.'

'Never mind.'

She smiled and started to sing unaccompanied, very quietly at first, and people were silent, listening. Those from the other room heard the pure notes gather volume and expression, and crept along the hallway to crowd into that room and hear her. She sang for twenty minutes, all new songs, and they gave her a wonderful ovation, which of course she loved.

Afterwards Anton said to her, 'Gracie, come over and do a concert. You could fill the Palladium for two weeks.'

'I'd love to,' she said, 'if I can do new songs. I'm not going to sing those old ones any more. If they'll let me do new ones... but they won't. And there's the microphone, that's another thing. They'll think they can't hear if I don't use it, and I don't like the b***** thing. It's fine for a small voice, but I can send mine all over the theatre, we always had to. No, luv, if I came, I'd have to use the mike and sing only oldies. I'm happy enough here, but I *would* love to do a programme of modern songs...'

Gracie always thanked people. She had natural good manners without any of the affected words or gestures that seem so false. 'Thank you for asking me', she said to Michael Parkinson when she was a guest on his show with Sir John Betjeman in 1977.

She never presumed folk would be glad to see her. She thought they would, hoped they would, yet never took them for granted. If they took her for granted, or took what she considered liberties, she showed her disapproval.

Once, when some fans were helping her to stow china into a new cabinet which had arrived, and she climbed onto a chair to fix something at the top, one of them playfully smacked her bottom. She was furious and well and truly ticked her off.

She loved bright colours and often wore them all together. Perhaps it was bravado to wear such brilliant colours for she was always nervous meeting new people. On stage she was completely at home and could put them at ease, but offstage her personality was such that she often hid the shyness beneath the loudness.

She loved pastel shades too. Again there was the contrast, the loud and the soft, the harsh and the delicate. Gracie loved pretty things, exquisite china, lovely pictures, fine glass and porcelain. She adored pink, liked pretty underwear, and never lost her love for tartan.

Although she developed a sound dress sense in her later years, when she was young this was lacking. George Black, manager of the Palladium from 1928 until his death in 1945, said about this in 1935, 'Either she has no sense of dress or she is not interested in it... the latter I think, for she has a natural love of beauty in pictures and music. But she goes about in any sort of clothes without the slightest regard for her appearance.'

Monty Banks' influence showed in her clothes for they were far more sophisticated and right for her during the period of their marriage (1940 - 1950) than they had been when she was with Archie Pitt. But her own natural instinct was good when she chose to exercise it.

'Gracie was never vain,' Hazel Provost, another friend said, 'but she knew when she looked all right, and she could, when she desired, look the picture of elegance.'

Of course, in the early days she could not afford very much, and she was working flat out for the show, not having the time or the energy to spend on her own wardrobe.

In 1928 she made her Command Performance dress, and when the Cotton Textile Exhibition was on in London, she attended in a dress made from Lancashire cotton which had been a gift to her from the mill girls.

Often she referred to herself in letters and talk as GF. As Gracie Fields, people expected her to be funny, to break into song and entertain them; it was natural to her and she had done it all her life, but it wasn't everything. There were all the other parts which went to make the whole person. GF had to be the most dominant. She had a strong personality, and it took over whether her audience was one person or a thousand.

Another aspect was her quiet moods, when it was necessary for her to be alone for a while. She gave out so much that she needed to catch up from time to time, to recharge her batteries. She didn't want long, but simply wanted to stride out (and she did stride, even in her seventies), usually a couple of dogs with her, to 'be quiet and peaceful', she used to say. She could cope with the crowds and the noise for part of her was noisy and she revelled in it, but the quiet bits needed expression too.

Her dogs were an important part of her life, and sometimes she acquired them through impulse. In the summer of 1973 she opened an English fete for the officers' wives and children in Naples. One officer had a puppy in his arms and was trying to find a home for it. In a letter home she said, 'Daft me said, "he's for me". He's the cutest little chap, but a so and so, tearing up the garden. Everything he can chew is chewed and he's only two and a half months old. He's a mongrel, half Alsation, and the other half is devil!'

Shopping was a bit of a hazard because Gracie was usually recognised. She seldom actively disguised herself, dark glasses sometimes, but that was all. She liked to wander round the shops if she felt in the mood to. In Brighton one day, when she went in to buy a leather jacket, the assistant said, 'Has anyone ever told you how much like Gracie Fields you are?'

'I am Gracie Fields.'

He glanced towards her uncertainly, then grinned. 'You're not.'

'I am', Gracie said, enjoying the encounter now.

He nudged her, 'Go on with you, you're not, but you do look like her.'

Gracie began to sing *Sally*, and the man nearly dropped the tape measure he was about to put round her. 'You are,' he whispered, 'Oh my goodness, you really are.'

She had spells of 'having it in' for different people, according to those who lived closest to her. She would sit at her dressing table with her hand on her cheek and keep moving her tongue round her jaw. When she was like this with someone, they could not do anything right for her. She went all round, her manager, the conductor, her friends.

'I usually kept out of her way when I noticed her doing it while I was there,' Lillian said, 'and sometimes, after a while, when I looked in, she'd say, "Where have you been - haven't seen you for days?"'

Like her grandmother, Chip Sarah, who she said referred to her customers in the chip shop as 'Sloppy Clogs', 'Ma Big Ears' or 'Cold Again Joe', Gracie had nicknames for many people, some of them to do with their job, which made it easier for her to remember them amongst all the folk she met, some to do with their physical appearance, and some to do with their speech. Not all of these were complimentary!

She didn't often talk about her inner feelings. 'I don't like a fuss', she said all through her life, but her personality and standing were such that it was impossible to avoid it. When she sang to prisoners in Pentonville in the thirties, the street was packed solid with her fans when she came out, and extra police had to be drafted into the area. If she went shopping or for a walk and was recognised, not simply a few dozen folk gathered round her but hundreds.

When she visited a youth centre run by the Reverend Jimmy Butterworth, a few hours before her last night at the Palladium in May 1953, to unveil a plate named after her in honour of Variety, a crowd of over two thousand jammed the pavements as she emerged, and when they called for a song, she said, 'It's such a long time since I was down here, I did not think you would know me with my white hair.' She sang *Sally*, unaccompanied except for the huge throng who joined in, bringing traffic to a standstill as hundreds more rushed across the road to see her when they heard that voice that, as one man said, 'could only be our darling Gracie's.'

She had a tremendous rapport with the ordinary people, if there is such a person as an 'ordinary' one. She was interested in them, in their lives and circumstances. 'Everyone's so different, yet most of us have similar sorts of dreams for ourselves and our families', she said.

16. Beyond the Mask

The woman was often hidden beneath the artiste. The performer was so dominant that the woman sometimes became swamped, but she was there, and many found her. She was in the letters Gracie wrote, in the hugs and handclasps, and in the thoughts and prayers she generated.

When she allowed a boys' club to camp in the grounds of Canzone del Mare in 1954, one of the lads fell ill. Gracie nursed him for ten days, until he could rejoin the others on the outings.

It was the same at the orphanage Gracie founded and supported in Peacehaven. She loved to go there and be with them all. Whenever she was in Britain, she visited them if she possibly could, talking to them, playing with them and joining in with gusto whatever activity was on the go.

She visited and kept in touch for years with the boys from Buckley Hall Orphanage in Rochdale, and was a frequent and favourite visitor to children's wards in many hospitals throughout the country.

She adored her nieces and nephews, and eventually their children. 'Bless you both, and your mams for having lovely children', she wrote to her grown-up niece and her husband.

She laughed at herself when snapshots were taken, saying jokingly 'Mother and son', and often signed photographs with a message, 'to my son'.

She would have loved a child, especially a daughter, and there were many who tried to fill this place, but she wouldn't allow it. For one thing they were adults, or very nearly, and she had had no say in their upbringing. They were not flesh of her flesh, nor had they the experience of life as *her* child, either natural or adopted.

When she was touring the factories and camps in England during the war she planned to adopt two babies. She wanted

war orphans and young babies, not older children. It never
came to anything because when she thought deeply about the
implications, she knew she wouldn't be there with them all the
time, and she really did want to be the one to bring them up.

Her nieces and nephews were her young family. As an aunt
it didn't matter that she wasn't always there, but she felt very
strongly that as a mother it mattered very much.

Lillian Aza says she didn't think Gracie took all that much
interest in children. 'She never took any of the kids from the
orphanage under her wing. She could have done, educated them
and looked after them, but although she was always happy to
see them when they contacted her, and to go there when she
was in England, she never took up with any of them.'

Talking to Florence Desmond one day in the thirties, Gracie
said, 'You know, Florrie, it's a funny thing, if I have anything
I love, it's taken from me. If I had a child I think I'd be afraid -
even my dog got run over.' Later she said, 'I know I could have
adopted a baby, but at that time I was so involved in my career
that it would have meant leaving the child for another woman
to take care of. And I didn't believe in having a baby for someone
else to look after.'

She spent a lot of time with her nieces and nephews when
they were small, and Greentrees, the house she bought after
she and Archie parted, was often filled with the laughter and
noise of children. The garden was equipped with a swing, slide,
fairy cycles... and indoors were childrens books, puzzles, bricks:
everything a child could want. At Christmas time she dressed
up in a Santa Claus outfit, complete with flowing white beard,
and invited the neighbourhood children as well as her own
numerous nieces and nephews in to share the fun. She loved
and enjoyed children, but accepted they weren't for her.

When her youngest sister, Edie, was married at Telscombe
she bought nephew Tony a wedding outfit. It was a black velvet
affair with an Eton Collar and black leather pumps with silver
buckles. Tony refused to wear it, as he tells here.

'I'm not putting that cissy suit on.'

'Oh yes you are,' she yelled.

'Not,' I yelled back, my eyes filling with tears of rage, and ran off to find my gran or my mother - anyone in fact who might help me avoid wearing that awful get-up. Within minutes I had a pretty lively family row going, but to no avail. When Aunt Gracie made up her mind that was that! I wore the suit and scowled all through the wedding photographs.

It was the woman and not the artiste who wrote all the letters and cards. There was no need to do it for the sake of her career. She did it because she wanted to keep in touch with people, because of her very deep concern for individuals.

Sometimes, especially when she had been away, she would go to her office and work with her secretary on what she often referred to in her letters as 'this mountain of mail'. She kept faith with the people who wrote to her by answering them. When they were typed by someone else, Gracie always wrote a few extra words before signing them.

Margaret Hazell, who worked at Ealing Studios in the days when Gracie was making films there, recalls a later time when she helped Gracie to write her Christmas cards. Gracie was in London, staying at the Westbury Hotel. They worked through the alphabet in her book. Gracie writing the cards, Margaret addressing the envelopes, and Irena, her housekeeper from Capri, sticking on the stamps. At the end of the evening, very late, Margaret said, 'We've got to L.' Quick as lightning came Gracie's answer, 'And there's an 'ell of a lot still to do.'

But she always did them, personal cards signed by herself and often with a special message applicable only to that person. She did have printed cards too, but if she used these for friends or fans, she crossed out the printed words and wrote them in herself, so Mr and Mrs Alperovici became Gracie and Boris, and very often she left the space for Boris to write his name, so it was absolutely from them both. Sometimes the card was sent out before he had done this, the space for his name was empty, and you could picture her saying, 'There's a pile of cards there for you to sign, luv...' but before he did so they were whipped up and posted.

It was the woman not the star who invited Gertie Sammon into her dressing room at the London Palladium before her show because it was such a beastly night. 'It was a wintry night, and I was outside the stage door of the Palladium. Gracie came along, looked at me and said, "Come on in, luv, you look perished, Margaret's just brewing up." We all had a cup of tea and chatted. How many would have taken a young fan into the star dressing room and treated her like that? She was lovely.'

George Black, Palladium manager for so many years, said of her:

> Most stars, and especially the smaller ones, are a great trial to managers. They complain about lighting, scenery, the orchestra, and everything else. But not Gracie. When anything goes wrong she puts it right by making it part of her performance. Her brain acts like lightning. If all the lights went out she would sing in the dark as if nothing had happened. If all the scenery were moved off she would perform in front of the brick wall. Once, not at the Palladium, when a lights man missed a cue, I saw her deliberately pause in the middle of a song and wink at him. The stage manager might tick him off, but not Gracie.

I wonder if she was singing *to* him for a moment, knowing it might make him miss his cue? The little devil dancing in her laughing bright blue eyes, slightly to alter the words of a song she used to sing, *Laughing Irish Eyes*. It is quite possible.

One time when Bert Waller was accompanying her and she was singing to pensioners, she realised half way through *Swanee*, that it wasn't what they wanted to hear, and as she reached a high note she swung into *Walter, Walter, Lead Me To The Altar*, to their great delight and his amazement.

However, Bert Waller followed her, and after the programme he said, 'Look, lass, [Bert Waller also came from the north] if you ever do that again, send me a telegram first.'

Gracie replied, 'Bert, if you couldn't have done it, I wouldn't have done it either.' She admitted her accompanists needed to be mindreaders.

George Black wrote in an article for the *Sunday Chronicle* in 1935:

> Backstage staff, programme sellers, chorus girls, and all the other theatre people love her. She knows the stagedoor keeper's troubles, and just when the fireman's wife is expecting a baby, and the baby gets a birthday present. One day the manager of the Palladium came to me and said, 'Here's a pretty mess. Gracie Fields is coming into the Crazy Gang show next week, and the star dressing room is taken. If I turn anybody out there will be a big row, but what am I going to do with Gracie?' 'If I know Gracie,' I said, 'you needn't worry.'

His problem was solved before she arrived. Two members of the Crazy Gang went to the manager and said that they would turn out of dressing room number one to let Gracie have it. 'Give us a screen and we'll dress in the corridor,' they said.

But when Gracie arrived she would not hear of this arrangement. 'Put me in with the other girls, it will be like old times.'

Australian born Vola Young, who toured as 'Vola Vandere', recalled a time in Scotland when she was given the star dressing room by mistake. 'It was a luxurious suite,' she said, 'and when I had dressed for my part of the programme, I found Gracie Fields changing in the "prop" room, among all the dust and cobwebs. Earlier she had come into the suite, realised what had happened, borrowed something, but said nothing. Horrified, I said to her later, "You should have told me." And Gracie smiled and said, "You were settled in there. I didn't want to disturb you."'

In that Palladium 'Crazy Week' Gracie borrowed a pair of Jimmy Nervo's trousers and Bud Flanagan's battered straw hat and twice nightly joined in the fun with as much relish as any of the comics. She did everything, took part in any gag, and even stood against a board while the knife-throwing Carsons outlined her figure with daggers. Bud Flanagan found her in the theatre one afternoon when he had come to fix up a trick. Surprised, he asked her what she was doing there so early. 'I'm enjoying myself so much', she said, 'that the show can't start too soon for me.'

It was Gracie the woman, not the performer, who boarded the liner on which George Black was a passenger on a Mediterranean cruise in the late thirties:

> We called at Naples and Gracie came over from Capri to see me. She had a great welcome from the passengers, and a special luncheon was given in her honour. When the time came for her to leave she was asked if there was anything she wanted.
>
> 'If you don't mind,' she said, 'I'd like a nice piece of bacon. It's hard to get nice bacon in this country.'
>
> I shall never forget the picture she made as she sat in the boat which was to take her back to Capri. She was surrounded with flowers, but clasped in her arms was a large piece of bacon from the ship's pantry. Everybody on board crowded to the rails to wave farewell to her, and as the boat glided away Gracie began to sing. She sang song after song until gradually her voice died away in the distance.
>
> When a friend who had been with her asked afterwards, 'Gracie, did you have it in mind to sing to them?' she replied, 'No, I just felt like it. They were so kind to us.'

It was the woman who said, when confronted with a mass of letters on her return to Capri after a holiday, 'These b***** letters, I get more now than when I was working for me living', but she said it with a laugh, and she gathered them to her and took them off to the office to read and answer.

The late Bernard Braden had a lovely memory:

After a long recording session in 1949 she took me to lunch, and on our way back to the studio kept stopping in Bond Street to window shop. Dressed in a mink coat, with a matching fur hat, she looked remarkably genteel, and I overheard another well-dressed lady say to a friend, 'Isn't that Lady Churchill?'

At that moment Gracie glanced at her watch and realised it was time to get back to rehearsal. She stepped off the pavement with her arm raised towards an approaching taxi and, putting the fingers of her other hand to her mouth, produced a piercing whistle, followed by a shouted 'Oi!'. I really thought that the other two ladies were going to faint.'

Bernard had another story:

It was four years after the taxi episode. We met again in Edinburgh where I was playing to half empty houses in a theatre and she was filling the Usher Hall. We bumped into each other in the lobby of the hotel in which we were both staying, and agreed to have a late supper in the hotel restaurant that night.

At two in the morning she was recounting hilarious anecdotes to me and nine waiters because there were no other customers left. None of the waiters seemed anxious to go home, and Gracie realised that, if anyone was going to bring the soirée to an end, it had to be her. She had a good look round the room, eyed each of the waiters separately, then looked at me and said loudly, 'Well, as you haven't asked me to sleep with you, I'm going to my bed now...'

In November 1931, when Rochdale Football Club were in financial difficulties, not having the fare to go to their next match, she sent a telegram to the Mayor, 'Have just seen report in London *Daily Mail* re Football Club. Am quite willing to defray travelling expenses of club to Barrow and wish them luck.' The outcome was that the team went to Barrow, and

Gracie paid not only their expenses but also the players' salaries for that week, and a short while afterwards gave a concert in aid of club funds.

Sir Anton Dolin remembers a joint signing session with Gracie in Capri.

> I had been to lunch, and immediately afterwards someone came in to say there were hundreds of tourists down by the pool and several coaches with daytrippers, all hoping Gracie would be there.
>
> 'Come on luv,' she said, 'you're coming with me.' I protested a little. 'Nonsense, they'll love to meet you, come on.' And together we went down, and for an hour sat there signing autographs, talking to fans and smiling for their cameras. She was so natural and seemed to have the right word for them all.

Another time, when Sir Anton and the dancer John Gilpin were there for lunch, Gracie said, 'What would you like to drink?'

'Campari and soda, please.'

'You're a b***** nuisance,' she said. 'We haven't got any soda, and I'm not going all down to the restaurant for it. Choose something else.'

So they had Campari and orange juice. Gracie had some too. 'It's good', she said, 'best drink I've had in years.'

Some time later, when she was in London and Sir Anton enquired what she would like to drink, she replied unhesitatingly, and with a twinkle in her eye, 'Campari and orange, please.'

In 1932 there was a sixteen year old blind boy in her audience. His dream was simple: to shake hands with the star who so often brightened his dark hours on radio and gramophone.

He came to her dressing room, shook her hand and touched her face, and they talked together for a while. Gracie asked him if he would like to stay for the second house. Eagerly he told her he would, so she arranged for a chair to be placed for him behind the scenes where he could hear the programme through. Then she had a word with her pianist (yes, she did in this case because she planned to do it), and changed several of her songs completely, so he should hear something different the second time around. He never forgot that.

On a visit to Rochdale in 1964, to open a new hospital extension, Gracie demonstrated in public an emotional exuberance that was so natural it was a joy to see. With crowds watching, she was handed a velvet-covered box containing a silver key. She moved forward, there was a great burst of song from that outdoor audience, and, as their voices swelled towards the top, Gracie ran over to the barrier and conducted them. 'You sing it better than me now', she said, laughing and crying together, and a chorus of voices contradicted her, 'No one sings *Sally* like you Gracie. Come on, luv, sing it with us.'

She did, and before the emotion on both sides could turn the occasion maudlin, Gracie remembered the Mayor and official party and, holding up the box in her hand she said, 'I've got to go, loves. Nobody can get in because I've got the key.' She smiled her apologies to those she had kept waiting, 'It was such a magnificent welcome - I could *never* have ignored it', she told them.

Gracie had many magic moments of her own, funny, moving, sad, and she often regaled her friends with the funnier ones. Like the time she was singing to soldiers, and after her first song a very Scottish voice called out, '*The Holy City*, Gracie.'

I said, 'All right, luv, I'll sing it for you later on, but not right now.'

'I finished my next song and again it came. '*The Holy City*'

'I've promised you I'll sing it, but a little later on in the programme.'

'OK, Gracie.'

After the third song: '*The Holy City*' This time I didn't take any notice, but went right on to my next number. When I'd finished he yelled once more, '*The Holy City*'. This time some of the boys, feeling they'd had enough of these interruptions, bashed the poor lad on the head. Right there and then, long before I had intended to, I sang the song. I was afraid if I didn't do it straight away he'd be seeing the Holy City instead of hearing it.

One time when she was visiting a poor district of Birmingham, she accidently brushed against some washing on a line, and a woman shouted at her, "Ere, where are you going? You've dirtied my Albert's shirt an' I've used up all me soap.'

Before Gracie had time to apologise, the woman's neighbour said, 'Shurrup, that's Gracie Fields.'

'I don't care if it's Joan of Arc, she can't come 'ere dirtying my man's clothes,' was the cross reply.

Another story she used to tell against herself was of something that happened in the thirties in London.

I was very lonely, everything seemed so different to working on tour. This will show you how green I was in those days. I went into a teashop by myself and asked for a pot of tea.

'Indian or China - or would you prefer Orange Pekoe?' the rather pert waitress asked me.

'I don't know anything about oranges,' I said, 'but bring me a pot of tea.'

When it came there was a little bag inside the teapot, tied up with a piece of string. I didn't like the look of that so I chucked it out. Then I found I'd thrown away the tea.

Years later Gracie could be as sophisticated as anyone, but she still enjoyed telling these stories from the beginning of her career. In a way it kept her on an even keel with her people, that mass of humanity who adored her and refused to believe that she could ever change, or be less than perfect.

One story she relished from the other end of her career comes from a tour of Australia and New Zealand when she was sixty-seven. She and Marlene Dietrich were staying in the same hotel, and Gracie saw her on the stairs one morning. Later she said to her secretary, 'I've just seen Marlene Dietrich and she looks marvellous.' The little maid, who was also there, cleaning the room, looked across and said stoutly, 'Don't you worry, I clean her room as well as yours, and first thing in the morning she looks just as bad as you.'

One of her old landladies went to see her in *S.O.S* at the St James Theatre. She went round after the first act, before Gracie left for her Alhambra stint.

'You were very good, my dear,' she told her, 'and you look so *beautiful* on the stage. I never saw such a change in anyone.'

Another landlady story comes from writer Eric Braun, who is a great cyclist. He cycled to one of Gracie's concerts in Bournemouth and in 1963 and 1964 followed up her invitation to pedal to Capri to stay with her and Boris.

'I went for two never-to-be-forgotten holidays as their guest, and after the second trip received a mystery phone call. Asked who was speaking, an unmistakeable husky Lancashire voice said, "Tell him it's one of his old landladies!"'

From 1952 comes another true tale. A merry reveller on New Year's Eve boarded the packed Victoria to Brighton train at midnight and as he wandered through the carriages looking for a seat, greeted everyone cheerfully with 'A happy New Year to you all.'

The great British travelling public read their books or papers and maintained an aloof silence against this well-wined person. Then suddenly from one carriage where he gave his greeting came a reply, 'And a reet happy New Year to you an' all, luv.' It was Gracie, travelling back to Brighton after a show, who answered him.

Florence Desmond recalled working with Gracie in *Sally In Our Alley* in 1931. During the break for lunch most of the cast took off their shoes and put on a pair of slippers. They were

often standing from 6am to, sometimes, 11pm, but Gracie never
changed into slippers.

'She had a pair of clogs, very beautiful they were, tan leather
with rough studs round them. She told me they had been made
for her by a fan. One day I said to her, "Wouldn't you be more
comfortable in a pair of slippers?" "No, luv," was Gracie's reply,
"I'm more comfortable in clogs than anything else."'

In 1948 Val Parnell, then manager of the London Palladium,
said to Florence Desmond, who was closing the first half of the
bill that week, 'Gracie Fields is in the box. I want her to come
back to the Palladium but she won't risk it, she thinks the people
don't want her anymore.'

Florence said to her pianist, 'As soon as I've finished, while
I'm taking a bow, run as fast as you can to the orchestra pit and
ask them to be ready to play *Sally*.'

Then she said to the audience, 'There's somebody here tonight
that you know and love, and she's never stopped working for
this country. As a tribute I'd like to sing a verse of *Sally*.'

She did, and the spotlight found Gracie as she finished and
'the house went wild. They clapped and cheered, and Gracie
stood up while they all took up the second chorus, which she
sang with them. Afterwards Val Parnell brought her round to
my dressing room. I'll never forget it - tears were running down
her face as she said to me, "Florrie, you little bugger..."'

17. The Inner Woman

Gracie's mother died in 1953, and her father in 1956. Jenny was seventy-eight and Fred eighty-two. They were both very proud of all their children.

For Jenny, Gracie's achievements in the theatre were worth all the hardships of the earlier years. She was interested in achievement more than in money, although she was a sensible woman who never underestimated the value of the latter. She also relished the acclaim given to her eldest daughter, but the deepest satisfaction was in her own heart.

Fred, amazed at first by his daughter's fame, warned her not to 'get above yourself, lass, never get stuck up', then settled down to enjoy the comfort and privileges that came with her career.

They both travelled with her a great deal in the earlier days, sitting proudly in the audience at shows, launches and openings of fetes, and applauding heartily in public, saving their criticism for private hearings.

Jenny never lost her love for the theatre and stage folk, and Gracie took her onto the London Palladium stage on matinee afternoons, and they sang together.

On Jenny and Fred's golden wedding day she said, just before the end of her turn, 'Shall we ask them to come up?'. As always, Gracie made it a family occasion, a meeting of friends, a party - and, with an arm around each of them sang *Just A Song At Twilight*, to that audience's great delight.

Once Gracie began making money, she was generous to all her family. 'I'd rather they had it now while we can all enjoy it,' she said. 'Silly to wait until I'm dead.'

Jenny especially shared Gracie's love of children. Eventually she had many grandchildren of her own because Edith, Betty and Tommy all married and produced families.

Both Jenny and Fred were buried at Telscombe, in the little church where they had worshipped for so many years.

Gracie worried deeply about her family. After her mother died she more or less became head of the clan. The Stansfield family were very matriarchal. Gracie was afraid of their growing too far apart and felt she had to keep everyone together. Although she could not always be there with them, if they were in one place she could keep her eyes on them all more. With this in mind she had built three bungalows in the garden of her Peacehaven home, one for Edie, one for Betty and one for Tommy. It worked for a while, but eventually they all moved out because as their families grew, they needed to spread.

Years later Gracie wrote, 'What a lot of movers the Stansfield family are. Guess it's our mother's fault. When people ask me where we lived in Rochdale I usually answer, "every street" because I remember so many houses we lived in. Your mam [Edie] changes towns and Betty countries. I think I'm a bit more settled than most of us, I just move up the mountain for the winter' (to her other home – Canzone del Mare did not have central heating.)

Sometimes there were tensions and jealousies. In the early days Jenny concentrated all her efforts on Gracie's career and later, when they were all on the stage there was rivalry, especially between the sisters. Beneath it was a deep family love for each other, and this was the stronger emotion. 'We are all a very tight family, and when one is sick we all worry for each other,' she wrote to her niece.

All her life she loved and cared about her family. At different times she had them all over to Capri for holidays, her own generation, their children and their children's children. Even ex-wives and their new men, all were made welcome, but especially the children.

She loved to go to their concerts and open days at school if she was home, but it wasn't easy to do this because word usually got out that Gracie Fields was in the audience, and it became a celebrity occasion. This made her reticent because she could see what was happening and the effect it had on the others. She overshadowed them, and although on these occasions she tried not to (she *could* pull rank with the best of them if she thought it necessary or had a mind to), she could not help it because of her name. She could never be someone's auntie in the audience.

When a reporter talked to her about her accent she said, 'You're not going to report me in broad dialect, are you? I mean, I'm not a snob or anything, but I just speak with a natural accent. I call people luv of course, but that's just natural and friendly.' This was probably prompted when some of the older generation took things too much the other way. 'Eh, listen to our Grace talking all posh', was said so much that Gracie accentuated her accent when she went home, for the sake of peace and quiet.

She had a power over the rest of the family. They didn't fear her, but they wanted to please her and did exactly as she told them. When she was in hospital during that last illness, they telephoned and spoke to her and even suggested going over.

'No,' she told them, 'No, I'm perfectly all right and don't want a fuss.' So they didn't go.

She had a very strong personality. Her aura, magnetism, whatever you like to call it, was so compelling that sometimes it frightened her. 'It's a gift,' she said, 'a terrific gift. I don't ask for it, but since it's there I can't deny it.'

Her sister-in-law, Annette, said, 'If she asked Tom to do something, he would never *not* have done it.'

It helped to make her lonely. She realised people did extra things if she was there. 'I don't want them to feel they've got to run around after me,' she often said.

Gracie had a marvellous brain. She was quick at picking things up and absorbing them, from dance routines to problems. She was nervous about educational subjects though, because she had not had much formal schooling. She could do it but lacked confidence. On the stage, where she had been most of her life, she had the confidence of her ability, and, although often filled with nerves before a performance, she went ahead. It was what life had trained her to do.

She said that when she went to school she could not keep up with everything. She was moving around with the juvenile troupes, singing, dancing and never staying long enough in one place to have any continuity of schooling, and when she was back home she was only a halftimer.

'I *wanted* to learn', she said, 'I wanted to know everything. I wanted so hard, but I had nobody to help me at home. Mother, who was very ambitious, couldn't, and father wasn't all that interested in education.'

When she was slightly older, she read everything she could lay her hands on. 'I used to read Dickens in bed by the light of a candle,' she said. 'I couldn't get enough education. I had such a lot of catching up to do.'

The fact that she did catch up didn't compensate in her eyes, she still thought she was uneducated and often commented about it in a joking GF fashion.

When her nieces and nephews were doing homework, she always asked about their progress. She was keenly interested and listened, but then she would say, 'Well I don't understand what it's all about, you ask Boris, he knows these things.' It was lack of confidence, because she was an intelligent woman who absorbed details very fast. She was also keen for Boris to feel one of the family, and involving him in this way possibly helped, although he didn't really understand the British system of education as she did.

When one of her fans passed an exam in the Open University, she wrote on the back of a photograph of herself, 'Congratulations, you're a clever lad, you don't have to sing for your living like lass on't front, luv, Gracie.'

When she was made an honorary MA at Manchester University in 1939, she commented, 'I wonder what my old schoolmaster would say now.' A reporter asked him, and he said, 'I never thought little Gracie Stansfield would get a degree.' Because she was ill she could not attend the ceremony for her MA so had to have it sent to her.

She remained nervous about educational matters for most of her life. 'I've knocked about a bit,' she said, 'so I suppose I must have picked up some scraps of knowledge along the way.'

She wrote a good letter, always reaching the point quickly and clearly, and often humorously. 'We came back from America on this little rowboat', she wrote on the back of a postcard of the Queen Mary, and in a letter to May Snowden she told her about a song which was all the rage in the USA. 'It's called *White Christmas*, which is something no one who has always lived here has ever seen.'

Her words were vivid. In a card to Nell Whitwell she said, 'Thank you, Nell, for thy letter. You sound real lonely. Cheer up, luv, Gracie.' No waste there, and in dialect, which she often wrote to her Lancashire friends.

You could write part of Gracie's story through her letters, for, although they were often short, she said so much in them. 'I do, do, thank you...' And one where she mentioned a photograph she had enclosed, and forgot to enclose it, 'They take folks away when they get as bad as me, love', it said on the print which followed by the next post.

Touches of humour, a putting down of herself in a way, came through in many letters and cards. She never wanted people to think she was boasting about her achievements, yet she wanted to give them the photos and the joy she knew they derived from them.

'I'm a very lucky "Old Gal"', she wrote in one letter, 'I must say too, I feel embarrassed by all this devotion, but oh so grateful. You are such kind folks. God bless you and keep you well, and a big, big thank you. Love, Gracie.'

'Glamorous Gertie', she had written across one picture of herself in a beautiful evening gown.

She never entertained illusions about her voice. 'I'm pleased you and so very many enjoyed the Batley Variety Club BBC show. A great pity the BBC were unable to have taken it during the first three nights I was there, then my voice was real clean and clear. They had to come and do it the night before I finished my two hard weeks' work.'

To writer Naomi Jacob, whom she knew well through their work for ENSA, she wrote just after her marriage to Boris, 'You will be saying I know, what a B****** is that there GF. Well, after all the silly excitement and nonsense I'm now a respectable married so and so, and very, very happy indeed with a real fine fellow. I hope you will meet him one day, then you'll know what I'm a talking about.'

She always wanted to do the right thing. Deeply instilled in Gracie was a need to conform if she could, and again that other exuberant aspect of her nature, the other side of the coin that said, 'What the - hell, it's my life.'

She wrote hundreds of letters and cards every year. Her postbag, from the time she became famous, was huge. At the peak of her career her manager and his staff dealt with it, only giving her selected ones. There were many begging letters, and at first she believed them all to be genuine. The ones from widows who couldn't pay the rent, that was a favourite then, and so often when investigated, turned out to be from affluent young men or women who were simply scrounging. It was a sharp lesson to her not to be too trusting. As she grew older and did less professional work, she read and answered her mail herself.

Her love of colour and variety came to the fore in her choice of ink for her letters and cards. Sometimes it was blue, sometimes green or red, and always that distinctive bold writing. Often, for fun, she signed herself Uncle Charlie, Maggie Driffen, Fanny Adams, to people who knew her well and would get a laugh out of it.

She was always most concerned that her fans should not be out of pocket when they sent her anything, but they were only too happy to do so, and she never failed to say 'thank you' and sometimes gently chide them for 'wasting your hard earned cash on me.'

Gracie's address books travelled with her all round the world. She kept family, friends, and fans in separate compartments in her mind, but all received cards from her. She behaved naturally. In an interview once where this being 'one of the people' aspect of her character was mentioned, she said, 'Well I'm a homely girl. I guess I am one of the folks - I like everything matey. I like to think we're all one big family. They belong to me and I belong to them.' Which she did, but only to a certain point - beyond that point was a very, very private woman whom few people knew well.

Neva Hecker was intrigued by the contrast in Gracie's singing styles in her films. From *Walter, Walter, Lead Me To The Altar*, to the softest, sweetest ballad. 'It hardly seemed possible it could be the same woman', she said. She wrote to Gracie, who replied, and for a while they corresponded. Eventually they met, and Gracie offered her a job as her 'American secretary'.

Mary Barratt met her during the thirties. She was then working as a companion to someone in Lytham St Anne's. She and Gracie wrote to each other, and when Gracie was appearing in Blackpool they met for the first time. Gracie said she took an instant liking to this woman she already knew from her letters, and impulsively offered her a job. Mary's reply, 'I'd love to if you can wait for me. I can't leave the woman I'm working for until I'm sure she'll be all right', made Gracie more sure than ever that this was a good omen.

Mary came to work for Gracie, 'doing anything that needed doing. I typed letters, washed the car, did the cooking on cook's day off, did Gracie's hair, anything and everything over the years really.'

Also over the years a deep friendship grew. Mary met her husband, Leon Davey, when she was with ENSA during the war and it was Mary and Lillian (Aza) who organised and protected Gracie in her stage life, as much as anyone as volatile and impulsive as Gracie could be organised and protected.

Lillian's husband, Bert Aza, once told the BBC, 'I could *never* undertake to get Gracie to say anything which was written down.'

In another letter in 1948, when the BBC were hoping to 'talk her into doing two more live programmes', he wrote, 'Gracie is certainly coming to this country, but we will not know until she comes bouncing into the office, which will be within the next ten days I should think. I cannot get Gracie to make up her mind what she is going to do, and nothing will be settled until her arrival here.'

Looking at scripts for various radio programmes so often it says, 'Gracie - ad lib patter', or 'Gracie - ad lib intro to song', and a pencilled time.

After her visit to Britain, Sicily and Africa in the forties, Gracie was asked to talk to the Victory Committee in America. The idea was to recruit some of the film stars into going, even if they couldn't sing or dance, because the boys would like to see their movie favourites anyway. Someone wrote a script for Gracie to read. She tossed it aside, 'It was written by someone who hasn't been there,' she said, 'if I'm going to tell the story at all I'll tell it my own way.'

She didn't really like long-term commitments, conforming in this respect because of her work, but what she thoroughly enjoyed was doing things on the spur of the moment. There was excitement in that for her.

18. Fans and Friends

Gracie was fifty-four when she married Boris. She was rich: Monty left over £70,000 when he died, and when the estate was finally cleared up and the property sold it was in excess of £150,000. She had been earning steadily again since the war, and went on working because her voice was too good to waste. The people wanted her and what artiste doesn't feel a thrill over that? There was also her great sense of duty. It was a duty she loved and could not fully live without. She had to sing.

> As long as the ordinary folk want to hear me sing, and want me to make them laugh, it's my job to go on. I was born an ordinary little girl in a Rochdale street, and I had two sisters who were prettier than me. But God gave me a gift, and I can never forget that all my life I am under an obligation. While there are hospitals to be cheered up, and crowds who come in out of the rain and pay for a seat, it's not enough for me to decide that I've made enough money out of them and they can go to blazes.

These sentiments were absolutely genuine. Her career was a vocation for her, especially after her cancer operation in 1939. 'It was during that illness that I learned all those things that have carried me through my life since', she said.

She toured Canada, America and Great Britain, appearing on the first Independent Television (ITV) show in Scotland, and Boris went too. He wanted her to retire, and although she didn't do that, she did cut down on her work.

She was back in Britain for Queen Elizabeth's coronation in June 1953, and among the songs she sang on Henry Hall's 'Coronation Guest Night' were *The Coronation Waltz* and *In A Golden Coach*.

In 1956 she was ill again, not desperately so as before, but she needed an operation for gallstones. They were in the USA at the time, and Gracie was taken by ambulance to hospital in New York. She recovered well and took it easy for a while.

Britain saw much less of Gracie in a working capacity after she married Boris, but she did many tours - Canada, Greece, our troops in Germany - and everywhere she went she drew the crowds and filled the theatres.

In 1955 she won the Silvana Award on American television for her performance in a straight play, Barrie's *The Old Lady Shows Her Medals*, repeating her success in this play in Britain the following year. Barrie's story of the lonely old Scotswoman and the 'son' she longed for gave Gracie an opportunity for acting which she used fully. The reviews were good and in some cases sounded surprised.

'A New Gracie', said one. 'Armchair Theatre, produced by Denis Vance was another winner. Gracie Fields gave a moving, sensitive performance in J.M. Barrie's *The Old Lady Shows Her Medals*. Here was a Gracie never before seen on TV, an actress of deep perception, warmth, and human understanding, in the Barrie classic of the lonely spinster who longed for, and found, a son. She must have moved millions to tears.'

'Stripped of glamour, and dressed in a shawl, she played the lonely old Scots char who becomes a mother-on-probation to a soldier orphan. With a first class performance from Robert Browne as the soldier, she reminded us that there is much, much more to our Gracie than just a comic song', said another.

Neva Hecker, her American secretary, said, 'I wouldn't have said she was a great actress, but she acted from the heart and that was the important thing. I remember in *Paris Underground* [1946] there was a scene with Constance Bennett when she was let out of prison. Every time I saw that shot it made me cry. Lights, technicians, noise, it caught me every time because she did it for real.'

Gracie was in America with Boris, some time in the late 1950s, when they were locked in the dressing room. She always liked to be at a theatre with plenty of time to spare, but on this occasion they had every possible sort of delay and she rushed in, made up quickly, 'Right, I'm ready.'

They went to the door to discover it was locked, the catch had jammed. For a few minutes they both struggled to open it, but it was well and truly stuck, so they looked for other means of escape. There weren't any. Gracie shouted for help at the top of her enormously powerful voice. Help arrived quickly but could not get in, and the fire brigade were sent for. They knocked the door down, and Gracie, brushing the dust from her dress, raced on stage as they were finishing her opening music, singing it as she went on. (Her theme song in the USA was *All For One and One For All* which she sang there during the war.) It was an open air theatre and a windy evening. The breeze blew her flimsy scarf into her mouth, but she sang on, eventually managing to detach the scarf and do a bit of business with it in her hands instead of round her neck.

She had a tremendous following in America and went on a radio show when she was eighty, answering questions and singing snatches of songs with a vivacity which enchanted her audience, who seemed to appreciate her direct and blunt answers to their equally blunt questions.

Australia too always gave her a wonderful welcome, and she had many fans there. She wrote regularly to them, for although she was often unpredictable about attending parties, she kept up a flow of letters and cards to people all over the world, for years.

John McCallum says in his book, *Life With Googie*:

Gracie Fields was as generous as she was warm-hearted. She came to Australia twice for Williamsons and had the same tremendous response from audiences as she had in England. In Sydney over twenty thousand people filled the Sports Ground one night to hear her sing in a charity performance.

I shall never forget her first night in Adelaide. Crowds filled the street outside the South Australia Hotel after the performance chanting 'We want Gracie. We want Gracie'.

She went onto the veranda of the hotel and sang for them until after midnight. I can see her now, standing alone at the veranda rail, no piano, no microphone, and below her the street lights shining on thousands of upturned faces listening to her. There must have been ten thousand people in North Terrace that night, stretching from King William Street to the Railway Station. Adelaide had never seen anything like it - and didn't again until the Beatles came five years later.

It was a hot summer's night, and as the vocal gymnastics of *Sally In Our Alley* and other favourites spiralled up towards the Milky Way and carried easily over the heads of the people packing the steps of Parliament House opposite, they must have been heard across the gardens in Government House, and beyond, on the banks of the Torrens. The Beatles later stayed at the same hotel, but they didn't sing to the crowd outside from the veranda as Gracie did, with or without a microphone.

'Gracie was always a great professional.' Clifford Ashton, of Rochdale, who photographed her many times, said that in the early years when flash bulbs were so expensive, all the photographers lined up and when everything was set, one person was delegated to fire the flash. 'Gracie was a natural,' he said, 'whatever she was doing, when we were ready, she held the pose for a second or two to enable us to get our pictures.'

She was quite uninhibited as to how she posed, licking a cornet, eating an apple, pulling faces - 'It'll get a laugh', was her response to any query.

She was quick and impulsive and had a vivid sense of humour. Neva Hecker tells the story of Gracie walking down the street one day, when she was feeling particularly good, dancing and singing. She glanced at Neva, then said to her, 'All right, you can walk the other side if you like, you don't have to know me.'

'Gracie being Gracie' is what her fans called it. Ray Rastall returned a beautiful photograph to her once because the autograph was fading, requesting that she re-sign it. She did so and wrote, 'yesterday' against her signature, then enclosed a small, personal snapshot of herself as she was then and wrote 'today' against that.

In Florida, when she had laryngitis at rehearsal, to save her voice she whistled *Now Is The Hour* instead of singing it. 'Afterwards', she said, 'I overheard the pianist tell the rest of the band, "You may as well pack up, boys. I just heard the new act. She's a middle-aged whistler."'

She often made fun of her own status. On another occasion she was too early for a rehearsal and the only people about in the theatre were the stagehands. 'I've come for an audition', she said. A just long enough pause, then, 'Me name's Gracie Fields and I sing', with an extra emphasis on the 'g' at the end of the word.

On stage at a concert for the Royal Navy, she said, 'I'm forty-four, I have teeth that were made by a mechanic, I wear glasses, and my legs...eh lads, I'm glad I earn my money with my throat...'

Pianist Russ Conway played for Gracie several times.

I idolized her when I was small, and when Teddy Holmes recommended me to her for a concert, I was thrilled. It was in Malta just after the war, and she was singing to the troops. She flew out, and I was to follow in another plane, but fog or something hindered the take-off, and we were delayed for hours. We finally got off the ground, but I knew I shouldn't make it in time and I was terribly worried.

It was a mad dash from the airport to the theatre. Gracie was already on, singing unaccompanied. We waited until she had finished the number, then someone took me on stage and introduced us, in front of two thousand troops. I had never actually met her until then. She took it all in her stride.

'Hullo lad,' she said. 'Are you all right?' I was sweating. She smiled. Such a friendly, warm smile she had. 'We'll arrange for some beer and sandwiches for you in a minute,' she went on, steering me gently over to the piano.

I sat down and played for her, and it was a wonderful experience. I learnt more stagecraft by playing for two artistes than from anyone else in the business. One was Dorothy Squires, and the other - Gracie Fields.

She had many famous accompanists, including Isador Duncan, Ivor Newton, Vic Hammett, Jimmy Bailey, Robert Probst, Clive Lythgoe, Bert Waller, Ray MacAfee, and of course Harry Parr Davis. Harry was seventeen when he took a song to her and his brilliant career, cut short when he died at the age of forty, was just beginning. *Sing As We Go, Wish Me Luck As You Wave Me Goodbye, Pedro the Fisherman* (from *The Lisbon Story*, another musical Gracie turned down) are among his many song hits. He played for her for nine years, and became like one of the family.

Gracie didn't cling to her background. She was rich for a longer period than she was poor, but poverty usually leaves the deeper memory, and she admitted that she really did enjoy talking to people. 'You can't do that in a taxi.'

At certain times, in certain moods, she delighted in being recognised. When she was no longer appearing regularly on a stage it was gratifying when someone said, 'Excuse me, but aren't you Gracie Fields?'

'It's easy to encourage applause,' she often said, and she usually stopped it, of course, but if she *wanted* to be recognised, talk theatre or have a singsong, she only needed to break into *Sally* for it to happen. Some found it distasteful, while others thought it endearing. She liked being a housewife for some of the time. 'I'm either starring or charring', was a phrase she coined.

She enjoyed improvising, sometimes with hilarious results, but there was the other side of her which liked things to be done perfectly. Mary Whipp recalled watching her with admiration as she skinned, cut and sectioned a salmon expertly. 'We've got salmon for lunch and steak and kidney pud for dinner,' she said.

She told Cilla Black when she was there, 'I make the best Yorkshire pudding on the island. Well I'm the only one who makes Yorkshire pudding on Capri I think!'

While Gracie enjoyed elegant living, it was never at the price of comfort. Her homes were gracious, colourful and comfortable. She had two on Capri - Canzone del Mare at Marina Piccola and a smaller one in Anacapri.

Derek Warman waited thirty-five years to meet her. 'We corresponded,' he said, 'and I met her for the first time only five months before she passed on.' She was waiting for the bus to take her back to Anacapri, and she drew him a little map showing him how to find the house. 'I'll leave the gate open for you', she said, and sure enough, when he arrived at the appointed time the following day, the little brown gate was open in welcome. He had a friend with him, and after tea and talk with Gracie he asked if he might take a photograph of her.

'Wait a minute, let me put some lipstick on, got to look right', she said. The result was an exciting picture, so full of Gracie's character that it seems alive.

All her life Gracie seemed tough and vulnerable at the same time. 'You had to be tough to survive in our business', she said, 'but it didn't mean you never felt anything.'

'She was easily hurt,' Lillian Aza said. And Gracie told Mike Sunnucks of Maidstone, 'Being a star is like being placed on a tightrope. They cheer you, but there are always people waiting to shake both ends of the rope.'

Frank and Joy Foster met Gracie in the mid 1950s. We were in a taxi on our way back to the piazza when we heard her whistle from inside the gates of the Canzone del Mare. The driver stopped for her to get in, and she laughingly told us all that she had an appointment with her dentist.

Frank asked her why one of the dogs was limping, and she said, 'He jumped in the sea to follow me when I was swimming and must have hit his leg on a rock.'

Frank said he would look at the dog if she would like him to, and she said, in the broadest Lancashire, 'Ee, are you one of them there bonesetters?'

Frank, whose birthplace was Bolton, replied, 'Aye, I am that.' He put the dog's leg right and they all became friends.

Gracie kept most of her friends all her life. She entertained her fans when they visited Capri, trying to have only a few there for tea at a time. Some tried to become part of her family. 'But I can't allow this,' Gracie said. 'I don't like to be any more to one than to another.' She was kind to them all but firmly resisted any overtures into her private life unless she made them herself.

There were different kinds of fans. The tourists who came into the restaurant and swimming pool to see a celebrity, the fans she knew by name and sight who had waited outside stage doors and seldom missed a concert, and the ones who wrote to her. Together they ran into thousands.

Family and friends meant so much to her, and sometimes she was bossy with them. She liked to feel in control, liked to know where all her family were, and while the one side of her longed to get away from it all and not be answerable to anyone, the other was maternalistic, the Victorian matriarch. She would have been marvellous with a huge family, tending each one's special needs. In fact this is what she did on a large scale.

Her friendly, easygoing manner could deceive you into thinking you were one of the inner circle, but that was seldom true. The few who were knew what a privilege it was.

Her impulsiveness is well demonstrated in an incident that took place when she was appearing at Drury Lane back in the thirties. There was no publicity involved because no one ever knew of it, except the taxi drivers and the waiters at the Savoy. She was leaving Drury Lane one night after the show, on her own. It was pouring with rain, and in the Strand all the taxi drivers were huddled in their cabs.

'Haven't you got any customers?' she asked.

'No, Gracie. It's such a filthy night there's nothing doing at all.'

'Come on then, forget about it. Leave your cabs where they are and come with me. We'll all have some supper.'

(Gracie seldom ate much before a show, usually a cup of tea and piece of cake or a few biscuits, then a meal after she had finished work.) She took the cabmen across the road to the Savoy Hotel and treated them all to a slap-up meal. On her first night at a theatre anywhere in London after that, there was always a huge bouquet from 'your taxi drivers.'

The antithesis of this story is the one Arthur Askey tells about Gracie and Boris going into a hotel in Manchester after a show. The manager sent the waiter to the fish and chip shop for a meal because the cook had gone home and he had nothing to give them. Gracie saw the waiter return, and when the meal was served, on plates, she laughed and said, 'You could have left it in the paper, it would taste just as good.' This was the sort of remark that annoyed Boris, but in public Gracie shrugged it off. In public she was GF and coped. In private she withered, and didn't always answer back because she hated dissension so much.

Trumpeter and band leader Nat Gonella said:

> Gracie Fields started me on my career. I met her in 1925 when I was seventeen and leader of the orchestra which played for Archie Pitt's shows. Gracie always took such an interest in anyone connected with the show. She thought I had 'a lot of talent' and encouraged me to practise. She gave me a wind-up gramophone and six dance band records. Until then I had only known I wanted to play, but not which type of music, but when I listened to these records I knew I had to play like this. So really it was Gracie who put me on the road to success.

He also recalled her taking all the band out for the day on the Sunday. 'We were working in Plymouth, and she took us all over to an island for the day - there were fourteen of us. She hired bicycles and told us to go off and enjoy ourselves.'

Bernard Miles said:

> She was a wonderful artiste with a pure voice. People often spend years of time and vast amounts of money trying to

achieve half the sound she managed naturally. She gave me some excellent advice. She told me to work nearer the floats [footlights] so that if I leaned over I could shake hands with the band or take a shilling out of someone's pocket in the front row. She also told me to speak up 'and that doesn't mean to shout, but to tilt your head so you can be heard in the gallery.'

Deeply interested in talent and how other folk expressed themselves, she would often watch an unknown act from the wings. She watched with great concentration and encouraged those she found good, often suggesting them for a place on a bill where she was appearing.

Mona Newman saw her at a charity concert at the Phoenix Theatre, London just before the war:

She was the principal artiste on the bill. I was standing in the wings watching the various acts when someone dug me in the ribs with the remark, 'He's good, isn't he?'

We got talking, and Gracie chatted about herself, not in any way boasting. She said that her housekeeper had been coddling her, sending her to bed tiddly most nights to try and rid her of a cold in anticipation of this concert. Between talking she would suddenly do a high kick and then settle down beside me again. I found her a most warm, friendly individual, and not in the slightest degree aware of her own importance.

One of the artistes, not by any means a well known one, was complaining about being the next but last on the programme. Gracie, without hesitation, said, 'OK, luv, you take my place. I don't care where I go on.' She did go on after the interval, and the audience was loth to let her go.

She was above needing a special place on the bill to win the audience by then and she knew it.

19. Final Tours

Gracie gave many 'final tours', and every time the reporters asked, 'Is this a farewell? Are you retiring?' She even laughed about the number of them herself, but each time she said it, she fully intended it would be so.

After concerts in America in 1965, one paper reviewed her performance like this: 'Newspaper reports from America show that Gracie Fields achieved one of her biggest triumphs on her farewell performance in New York last week. Earlier she had announced her retirement from the world of entertainment.'

Gracie sang *Now Is The Hour for Me to Say Goodbye* as she left the stage forever and made her final bow to an audience of 8,000 at an outdoor stadium. She cajoled, enlivened and saddened her audience for an hour, but still they roared, 'One more, one more.'

'What's the matter, haven't you a home?' she shouted across the footlights.

The Metropolitan Opera of New York, which presents the summer concerts at the stadium, billed the programme 'Salute To Britain'. The crowd chose to turn it into a 'Salute to Gracie'. The New York critics warmly praised Gracie's performance. In the *New York Times* Harry Gilroy called it a triumph:

> She swept the audience along in a tumult of laughter and applause that suggests that Gracie Fields had better reconsider retiring. This time, however, Gracie is really in earnest about her retirement. Before leaving New York to fly back to her home on the Isle of Capri she said, 'Enough is enough. Now I just want to be with my husband and enjoy the rest of my life.'

But she said she could not bring herself to do a farewell tour of

Britain. In 1964 she did one for impresario Harold Fielding, which some sources said was to be her farewell to her homeland. It began on 6 September in Blackpool and finished on 4 October in Eastbourne.

'One of my first remarks to Miss Fields, as I called her years ago at my first meeting with her,' Harold Fielding said, 'was this, "what special arrangements do you want in the dressing room?"'

'I asked because at the time I was handling concert tours for people like Jeanette Macdonald, Grace Moore and Lily Pons, a few of the great ladies who came to me via America. Sometimes their demands were quite extraordinary, such as red eggs for breakfast, or a white drugget right from the point in the dressing room where the evening's gown was put on, extending all the way to the spot on the stage where she entertained the public.

'Gracie summed it all up very simply, "Just nothing, luv - I don't even need a mirror to brush me hair in."

'My wife and I found over the years that this was true, and matched with another quirk of dear Gracie which we soon mastered. The tour would start out with four or five travel cases. As we progressed from town to town, the cases mysteriously got less and less, until it was very soon down to just one case. Mary Davey, the wonderful lady who looked after her on tour here, let me into the secret. Almost every day Gracie would insist on diminishing the cases by posting parcels back to London.'

For the 1964 tour Harold Fielding gave a reception at his theatre, the Prince Charles, and Gracie, in tremendous form, even had the press singing *Hullo Dolly*.

Two days before the tour began she switched on the Blackpool Lights before a crowd estimated at over ten thousand, who cheered, applauded and pleaded with her to sing. 'It's always been an ambition of mine to switch on the Blackpool Lights', she confided.

Organist Reginald Dixon, often called 'Mr Blackpool' because
of all the years he had worked there, had played a selection of
Gracie's songs before she arrived, and then the people began to
chant, 'We want Gracie! we want Gracie!'

She came onto the platform wearing a short fur coat over a
black dress and accompanied by her husband, Boris, and the
Mayor of Blackpool. Thanking the crowd for the wonderful
reception, and in response to their demands for her to sing, she
said, 'I'll be glad to sing any song you want, but remember that
I've not been working in the theatre for five years and on Sunday
I start a concert tour so I dare not sing too much out of doors
in case I harm my throat for the tour. Just one song, please be
satisfied with that, and realise I'm sixty-six not thirty-six, even
though I may only feel thirty-six right now.'

She sang *Sally*, then, in spite of her words, could not resist
their applause and cheers and broke into *Volare*, substituting
words of her own to fit the occasion. Afterwards Gracie, Boris,
and the civic party toured the illuminations on a decorated tram
before going on to supper at the Imperial Hotel.

It brought back memories for eighty year old Mr William
Robinson who recalled the time he had presented her with a
sword once owned by the skipper of the *Alabama*, the first
great ocean raider of modern times, which was sunk in the
English Channel in 1864. On that occasion she had led a tour
of the illuminations for the Blackpool Disabled Men's
Association, and Mr Robinson had said, as he handed her the
sword at a ceremony in the Town Hall, 'A tribute from a
Yorkshire lad to a great Lancashire lass', and Gracie, her eyes
twinkling with laughter, had chased him round the Mayor's
Parlour with it, saying, 'It's the War of the Roses all over again.'

Two days after switching on the lights, she opened at the
Opera House, Blackpool, the first venue of her eleven concerts
in a four weeks tour.

Some of the critics in the papers were dubious, some were
scathing, a few were encouraging when it was known that Gracie
was going to embark on a concert tour of Great Britain at the
age of sixty-six and after a five year 'retirement'.

'It's the reporters who say it's a farewell tour, not me', she often said, 'I've never committed myself to retirement.' (She once told actress Florence Desmond, 'Always leave the door open in case you want - or need - to return.')

'A Comeback for Gracie Fields', one headline said. 'I've never been away', she answered. But she admitted that for five years she had 'semi-retired' in her Capri island home.

The reviews after each of those concerts were immensely satisfying to an artiste who never short-changed her audiences. Even the critics who had predicted a 'nostalgic success' admitted that this was Entertainment with a capital E.

What a comeback for Gracie. On the opening night of her concert tour she had yesterday two capacity audiences at the Opera House in frenzied applause and yelling for more. The silver haired star, dressed in a glittering seagreen twopiece and a bronze evening coat which she delicately placed on the piano ('nice and posh like Boris told me to'), reigned on stage supremely for the entire second half. One might have expected an evening of pure nostalgia. It wasn't. Because this was no famous has-been singing a swan-song. In front of us stood an utterly dynamic performer who swept her listeners from breathless silence to laughter at the tilt of a lilt.

She sang her 'S' songs (they all begin with S and have all been lucky) *September*, *Summertime in Venice*, *Scarlet Ribbons*, and of course *Sally*. With a green scarf as her only prop she embarked on her comic range, and went Irish, Scottish, and Rochdalish in her inimitable way. She was a scream, was our Gracie. In contrast she went into medleys, one from *The King and I*, one blending old and new songs. And you could have heard a pin drop during *Bless This House*...

Another said, 'Today the concert halls of Britain have been taken over by the pop groups. Everybody says that there is no audience for anything else. But our Gracie has proved them wrong. And last night four vanloads of flowers were sent by Gracie to Blackpool hospitals. "I suppose the youngsters will call me Mother Beatle", she said amid laughter.'

Another critic wrote, 'A stoutish, handsome woman drew the crowds in Blackpool last night. She captivated two capacity houses, each of 3,000, at the Opera House, with the voice of a mischievous angel and the humour of a tough-minded mill girl.'

Boris had not wanted her to do the tour. 'Sometimes it's hard for me to understand why she wants to leave the sunshine of Capri for the possible grey clouds of England', he said at the time. Perhaps because he had no country he could never feel the pull of home as Gracie did. Sunshine was no substitute for the love and approval of her own.

Gracie was excited and happy, yet realistic. 'It's not so much for the brass, I've never squandered my money, never even lived up to my income,' she said. 'I don't want to be forced to work when I'm old. I'm doing this tour now because I love my work and I love my audiences, and I miss the people. The old voice is working well enough, and I'm not singing every night.'

The impetus of the Blackpool welcome occurred everywhere she played. 'It's not just a northern hullo for one of their own', Gracie commented with relief.

In Torquay, after her two shows there, 'It's Graciemania', shouted the headlines.

Seafront traffic screeched to a halt when hundreds of people rushed towards the stage door of the Princess Theatre to shout their thanks to Gracie Fields. The area around the theatre was jammed, and people lined the road on both sides. Gracie drove along the seafront, the sunshine roof of her car down so she could stand and acknowledge their cheers and cries of 'thank you, Gracie.' And well she deserved their thanks, for she proved to them during the show that she had retained that old magic which for so many years had people laughing and crying at the slightest change of her mood.

Another critic wrote, 'The biggest surprise of all was her voice. It never wavered, and she struck the high notes as clearly and as definitely as of old.' In fact, as she was the first to admit, she had 'put everything down a key.'

In Portsmouth a young reviewer wrote:

As I took my seat high in the Portsmouth Guildhall last night I felt the perfect outsider, like a communist at a moral rearmament meeting, or a teetotaller at a stag party. The hall was packed, many not the sort you expect to find at Sunday night concerts. It was not only age which separated us, but excitement. I sat curiously detached. To me, like many young people, Gracie Fields was just a name. I had heard her singing on the radio, and once caught a glimpse of her on television, but my reactions at those times were uncharitable to put it mildly.

I knew of her great reputation, but the Gracie Fields cult was a mystery to me. It is no longer. After spending an evening in the company of the ever-young Gracie, you can count me in as one of her admirers. Gracie Fields had won me over.

She is a remarkable woman. Sixty-six, yet lively, energetic, versatile, and vital, with that spark which drives all the big show business names. Gracie ended with *Now Is The Hour*, which included the poignant line, 'while I'm away please remember me' - how could we forget her?

In 1964 Beatlemania was at its peak, and reporters were quick to ask Gracie her opinion of the Liverpool four, and indeed of the general trend in the music of the day.

'I like the Beatles,' she said. 'I've got some of their records, but I wish they would get their hair cut now they're accepted. They could be such ambassadors for England among the younger generation.'

And the Beatles replied, 'It's part of our image, we can't change that.'

Impresario, and organiser of that tour, Harold Fielding said:

Until the advent of Tommy Steele and the way he can go down a street and bus drivers and cab drivers alike will lean out and say, 'Hullo, Tommy', Gracie was the only artiste in the world I had found who would be besieged all the way down any street by the public, not being cheeky but being loving; who would hail her one after another with 'Hullo, Gracie'. I well remember standing on York Station one day and wondering why the train did not take off for our next stop, when suddenly I realised that the engine driver was down talking to Gracie.

But Harold Fielding's most poignant memory is of Bristol:

The Colston Hall where she was appearing was one of our happy hunting grounds, and it stood with a large facade of steps in front of it like St Paul's Cathedral. Around me in 1964 were many of the stars such as Johnnie 'Cry' Ray, for whose safety one sometimes worried, but Gracie got the biggest crowds of all, and that night at Bristol when she wanted to walk down the steps there was literally the whole two thousand audience standing there to greet her.

'Leave it to me, luv,' she whispered, and then to the crowd, 'If I sing *Sally* to you, will you then let me walk down quietly?' and just as if it was a miracle, and without any encouragement from the police, the whole crowd parted and left her a safe walkway down that myriad of steps.

The last concert of her tour was at the Congress Theatre in Eastbourne. Here it was the same story, all seats sold and an hour before her performance a queue hopefully waiting in case there were any cancellations. 'I'd have given a fortnight's holiday pay just to see her,' someone said, 'I was too late to get a ticket.'

Boris had only stayed for the Blackpool concerts. 'He had to fly back to look after the old joint', she laughingly told reporters. They telephoned each other every day, but Boris didn't want to be away from Italy for a month, especially on such a tour, when, as he said himself, she was Our Gracie, 'and I should like her to be my Gracie.'

She stayed for almost another week after that last show, visiting her family and friends at Peacehaven and Brighton, doing some Christmas shopping, taking in some of the London shows, then, on the following Saturday, she flew back to Italy and Boris. 'To do a different kind of knitting', she said. From the early days Gracie referred to her work as 'doing me knittin'.'

There were rumours that she was looking for a house in the Brighton area in spite of Boris's objections. The marriage was going through a bad patch at this time, but she desperately wanted to make it work.

It had been a strenuous tour, but she flourished in the warmth of her audiences' adoration and loved being back in harness. She did not want to be working all the time now, but she missed the theatre very much and would have liked to do selective tours. Boris wanted her to stay at home.

She sang to the tourists who came out to Capri in the summer. 'Give us a song, Gracie.'

'Right, what d'you want to hear?' And her voice rang out clear and true still.

They usually did come to Britain for some time during the winter months in a private capacity, often for Christmas, as in 1971. They stayed on for the New Year; then Boris had a heart attack and spent some weeks in hospital. In a letter to friends Gracie said, 'We expect him home tomorrow. We are getting older'er every year and trying to do as we did thirty years ago, so this has been a warning.'

Before that, in 1965, she followed her British tour with a return to Australia and New Zealand under the banner of J & N Tait (the concert division of J.C. Williamson Theatres Ltd).

This began in February in Sydney. Boris wasn't in Australia with her. He returned to Capri unwell, he was awaiting a hernia operation at the time, and they spent their thirteenth wedding anniversary apart.

The New Zealand concerts took her to both the North and the South Island. The tour finished in March at Dunedin in the South Island, and on 2 April, the day before she left for Capri, she gave a final concert in Melbourne, Australia. It was twenty years since her last concerts in that part of the world, when all the proceeds were given to war charities and funds for servicemen - a total of £67,000.

'I saw more in one day this trip than I did in three months in 1945', she said. 'I was so rushed last trip; Australia was army camps and hospitals, and wondering when I would get to bed.'

The reviews were good and affectionate. 'Gracie's art is ageless,' read one, 'whether singing a song, telling a story, or just being herself, the vital personality, irrespressible humour, and gift of mimicry which have made "Our Gracie" a household word for generations, shone through triumphantly to the end.'

'Gracie still a rich brew,' said another. 'In Brisbane in April 1945 she left her audiences cheering themselves hoarse. At the City Hall, twenty years later, the audience demanded encore after encore. With a verve and polish that any younger entertainer would envy, Miss Fields at 67 gave a stimulating two hour performance.'

'The shortest cut to a lynching in Brisbane last night would have been to stand up in the city hall and shout boo. If ever an artiste had an audience eating out of her hand it was Gracie Fields.'

Gracie read the reviews if she had time, but mostly she took her cue from her audience and her own instinct. She made it look so easy. That was part of her professionalism, Gracie always did her homework. She knew what her voice was capable of. 'Not *The Holy City* now, I know what I can't do, luv', and when pressed, 'Numbers like that need orchestration or a choir, and I don't think it would be fair on the audience.'

In between her shows she visited, as always, homes, hospitals, the young and the old. Quietly, without fuss. 'I'm Gracie Fields, can I come and have a chat?'

After her visit to the children's ward in Christchurch Hospital, she sent them a giant Easter egg. She chatted to the nuns at the Little Sisters of the Poor Home in Randwick after she had sung and talked to the patients there; and at a blind school in Sydney, when she wasn't getting any response from the children, she suddenly sat down on the floor with them and said, 'Do you know any of the Beatles' songs?'

'Yes,' they chorused.

'So do I,' and within minutes they were all singing, *She Loves You*, and half a dozen others, swaying and rocking with Gracie on the floor.

She went to Bondi Beach hoping to watch lifesavers in action, and when someone mentioned the Freshwater Surf Carnival, she was interested. Someone else suggested hiring a car and going along, but Gracie was already talking to the crew of the North Bondi boat who had a truck with their boat on a trailer. In a short while she had an invitation for her and her friends to ride in the back of the truck with them.

'It was great', she said when she arrived, 'they're a wonderful bunch.' She spent two hours at the Surf Carnival, 'The first I've ever seen,' she admitted, 'except on films.'

They asked her to attend the official tea. 'What will you drink?' they said.

'A cup of tea, please.'

More in fun than anything else, they said, 'Give us a song and you can have a cuppa', and to quote one person who was there, 'Cor lumme - if she didn't give 'em a song with the throttle right out.'

In 1968 Gracie returned to Britain for two weeks at Batley Variety Club in the West Riding of Yorkshire. The Club, built on the site of what had once been been part of a sewerage works, started in 1966. It was a dream come true for owner James Corrigan, former fairground barker and bingo operator.

It wasn't Gracie's first appearance in Batley. Fifty-two years previously she had passed that way in the review *It's A Bargain* and merited three lines in the *Batley News*, 'Particularly smart is Gracie Fields, a lady mimic whose impersonations of famous comedians of the day are very amusing.'

Now she was seventy years old, only a month away from her seventy-first birthday, and she had the audience standing to cheer. ('I don't often have a standing ovation in England', she said at the time.) James Corrigan, founder and proprietor of the Club said, 'She was fantastic, she lost forty years when she was on the stage.'

One reviewer wrote:

> There were quite a few sons and nephews in the audience, cajoled into the trip by a mother or aunt who had never crossed the threshold of a nightclub in her life before. You could pick them out in the audience. One of the 'pressed' men said on the way in, 'I'm only going to keep my mother company,' and, asked on the way out what he thought of the show said, 'Completely converted. I never thought she'd be like that - she was magnificent. I hope she comes again.'

On her first night she wore a silver cape lined with shocking pink, a white dress embroidered with silver, and carried a flimsy, but in her hands, extremely versatile white headscarf.

She watched the scampi and chips being served and commented to her audience, 'I know I was born over a fish and chip shop, but I never expected to sing in one.'

'I'm doing it for the lolly', she joked with the press when they interviewed her. 'I plan to see all my folk right for cash before I go.' But when one reporter persisted in that line of questioning, asking how much money she was giving to her family, Gracie told him very sharply to mind his own business about that and stick to getting a story about the show.

When it was learned that Gracie was earning £10,000 for her fortnight at Batley, MP Tom Swain tabled a question in the House of Commons asking if she would be allowed to take all her earnings out of the country, and whether this salary for two weeks work was taxable at normal rates.

Gracie split her two weeks at Batley with a week's rest in the middle, so she could be 'on form' for each, and she made a typical Gracie gesture by going on an hour earlier than the usual 'star spot' so her fans from Rochdale, thirty miles away, could see her and get back home in reasonable time. 'Anyway I think ten thirty is quite late enough for me,' she said.

Her outstanding success at Batley amazed many of the younger generation, and gained her hundreds more fans among them. At a time when young people were very much in evidence in the entertainment business ('and some of them are very, very good', she said), Gracie drew headlines like 'Gracie Fields is wowing the youngsters in the clubs.' 'Even the young ones fall under Gracie's magic spell.'

After announcing *Little Old Lady*, she said, 'I used to sing that for my mother, now I sing it for myself!' As before, she mixed the bag, old ones for her audience and because it was expected, the newer ones for herself, but also for 'the customers', as she called them. 'It's good to keep up to date, and there are some brilliant songs being written now. I like to give them an airing too.'

'She gave us quite a few modern numbers in a way that was a lesson to some of our microphone-hugging younger performers,' wrote one reviewer. 'Her *Those Were The Days* left no doubt that show business of years ago really were the days. Judging by her repose, breath control, and brilliant technique they're just not making artistes like her any more.'

After Batley it was Christmas in Britain, then back to Capri. Gracie enjoyed her home and over the years had made it beautiful. When she first went there she took with her many bargains she had purchased in the Caledonian and Portobello Road Markets, and gradually she and Boris added paintings, china and glass from all parts of the world. Built around a tree outside is a table consisting of tiles painted by local artists with scenes from the Sistine Chapel in Rome.

The wide terrace which overlooks the swimming pool has been the setting for hundreds of photographs, as indeed has the pool itself. Gracie was a tremendous swimmer and she enjoyed diving too.

'I stopped diving when I was eighty though, because it worried Boris so much.' She seldom stayed in the water for long, but she swam every day, usually going in early before the crowds were about. 'Otherwise I feel like a performing seal.'

When she was seventy-eight she fell six feet onto a concrete terrace. 'A loose railing, but I made a perfect fall, just cracked two ribs instead of my head, I managed to pull it forward during the fall. Also I had the roller curlers in my hair, all covered nice and sexy with a silk scarf, so only got a small cut and that was soon OK. Now the X-ray pictures show I'm just as good as new. Still I'm being a bit lazy and letting 'em all wait on me, I haven't yet started moving the furniture around, but I soon will', she wrote home to her family.

Because the ambulance could not get down the steep road, firemen carried her on a stretcher to the vehicle, where she joked with them about the damage she might have done.

She had a quiet courage that sometimes hid the depth of her wounds from the unaware. In 1964 she went on for a show after a wound in her head, caused by the removal of a cyst, had been stitched. She styled her hair in a 'bang' to hide the plaster and did her full show.

When she had shingles in 1977 she bore the pain stoically. 'I think she was about the most uncomplaining person imaginable,' Hazel Provost, who wintered in Capri that year to help look after her, said. 'Just got to grin and bear it,' was Gracie's comment when the pain was extra bad, and later, with recurring attacks, 'Past forty, shingles is harder to lose than before, and I'm well past that.'

Age didn't bother her, and sometimes she reminded others that she 'wasn't twenty-one any more.' At eighty she was receiving genuine offers of work. 'People want me to do a concert to keep their theatres open,' she said, 'but they must realise my age - they'll have to have younger, newer talent.'

She had a vitality which belied her years. Her features, always strong, became gentler as she grew older. In youth she was in turn dark haired, golden haired and auburn. In maturity she was grey, silver and eventually white.

In 1972 Bill Grime asked Gracie if he could have a photograph of her sitting in a chair in front of the scroll and casket she received when she was given the Freedom of Rochdale in 1938. He wanted it for a lecture about the town, which he was doing in the autumn. On 6 October Gracie wrote, enclosing some beautiful snapshots of herself and showing the casket and scroll behind her.

Dear Bill and Edna Grime,
Bet you've been thinking GF's let us down. Not being a Master photographer [among his many other accomplishments Bill was] I got into quite a mess, forgetting my camera needed a battery to work from, so wasted two twenty reels of film until I found out the trouble.

At last I've got enclosed photographs for you. I may have a better'er one in the reel I've in my camera right now, but it's funny how long it seems to take to shoot 20 photographs. Anyway this will have to do, hope it's OK.

She went to so much bother to get *exactly* the snap he wanted for his lecture, yet was dismissive about it. She always maintained her interest in Rochdale and what was happening there, signing the petition to keep open the Memorial Gardens opposite the Town Hall and keenly appreciative when she was informed about various town activities.

In October 1970 she opened the Vitool factory on a site opposite her birthplace. Handed a hammer to put up the plaque, she gave an impromptu rendering of *If I Had A Hammer*, before climbing a chair to do the job. There were never any half measures for Gracie. If she was to bang a nail in, she did, pausing long enough to hold a pose for the cameras before she got on with the job in hand.

Hilda Harris recalled an evening at a concert in Birmingham Town Hall, 'My seat was level with the platform on her left. In the middle of a song she spotted me, and moved to within inches. The spotlight followed her. I was getting hot under the collar, wondering what trick she was up to, then she winked, and moved away.'

Gracie's irrepressible fun shone through every performance, yet no matter how she made her audiences laugh and cry, when she came offstage she was her ordinary self again immediately. The unwinding came later. On stage she was Gracie Fields, the artiste, there to entertain the folk. She had the talent, 'God gave it to me', and she kept it fresh.

Gracie had an old 'banger' which she drove all over the island of Capri. When it finally gave up, she travelled by bus or taxi, as she said, 'in style'. She could have afforded a new car, but the old banger suited the island's hilly territory, and it suited her lifestyle there too. It was 'right' and she was happy and comfortable with it. She swore at it sometimes when it was being difficult, but she raced about the island in it, and it afforded her as much pleasure as any of the posh cars she was used to being driven in on official dates.

She also loved walking, and strode out with her dogs. Always Gracie had dogs about her, much loved animals who accompanied her as often as possible over the years. She was a dog rather than a cat person. She also loved birds, and for a time bred canaries in Santa Monica. This became difficult when she was travelling so much and had to rely on other people to look after them, and she gave it up.

In her seventies, she climbed to the top of the crag overlooking her home with the speed of a woman many years younger. 'There are 365 walks on Capri,' she was fond of telling her visitors, 'one for each day of the year.'

She was extremely knowledgeable about the island's history, and about her own property, telling the story of the house's origins to any interested party. Wherever she went in the world, especially in her later years when she could spend longer in a country and the pace of her work was more spaced out, she found out about 'the things that make it tick.'

'Mostly the people,' she said, 'but there are other factors too, industry, natural elements, but more than anything else the people determine a country's character,'

When rheumatism caught her quite badly, she still walked. Her advice to Norman Empire, one of her correspondents who was in the grip of it, was contained in a viewcard of Capri sent in 1974. 'Sorry you're being troubled with arthritis, it's a rotten ailment. Touch wood, I got rid of rheumatism - old ladies' and gents' complaint - I had it very badly four years ago, and the Good Lord took it away. I try to do a lot of walking.'

When she had visitors for tea, she used to go down to the restaurant, returning up all the steps, which were fairly steep, and balancing a huge gateau on her hand. She knew this created a minor sensation and she loved it.

When, in the early days of their relationship, Boris swore at reporters, then apologised to her, she said to him, 'Swear away, luv, after being in the theatre all my life it's like home from home. I do it myself.'

The islanders accepted her as one of them. She often helped them in difficulties. During the war she bought underwear in the USA and sent it home to England to be eventually taken and distributed to the Italians who couldn't afford any.

On one occasion, chatting to a young teenage lad who was terribly shy and self-conscious about a large, abnormal growth on his face, Gracie suggested he could have treatment to remove it, but he explained it was impossible locally, and he obviously couldn't afford specialist treatment. Discreetly she made enquiries, and in a short time he had a successful operation, never knowing the cost of all that was involved.

She did so many kindly acts in this manner, quietly, tactfully, pleased to be able to help in a practical way.

20. Indian Summer

In 1978 Gracie returned to Rochdale for the last time. She went to open a theatre named after her, and, as she remarked in a broadcast in America a few weeks later, 'While I was there they had me opening the market and one or two other things as well.'

At first she thought a group of students were running the theatre, and she agreed to give a concert for the opening. 'They are calling it the Gracie Fields Theatre, so naturally they want me to be there for the opening', she wrote.

The visit turned into a royal return. Bands played, brass was polished, the red carpet and flags were out. Over two thousand people waited to see her when she arrived to unveil a statue in the new shopping centre. Before that the town band played songs from her repertoire, and the crowd sang them. As ever, she stopped to hold a baby and talk to the people, especially the older ones on this occasion. For two days Rochdale feted its famous daughter.

Gracie visited Broadfield School and watched a pageant put on in her honour. When the children did a mime about various incidents of her childhood, she mouthed the words with them and afterwards went across and acted and danced for them, showing how she had rattled her box following the maypole and singing all those years ago. In the hall she went down amongst the children and sat crosslegged on the floor with Boris and chatted to them.

At eighty Gracie still had that charisma that could turn a bunch of children who could not be expected to be wildly enthusiastic about her into a cheering audience.

'Gracie Fields to me was not really someone important. I thought she was just an old person who used to be a singer. This is what I thought BEFORE I saw her. She was great, I hope she comes again', wrote one child later. Another wrote, 'What had started as a fairly good morning turned into a <u>fantastic</u> morning', and a little girl called Wendy submitted, 'We should all be proud to have gone home and said, "Gracie Fields came to our school today." And our friends might say, "So what!" BUT THEY'LL NEVER KNOW WHAT THEY MISSED. She was wonderful.'

From the school she went on to a luncheon in the town hall, but the highlight of her visit was the concert on the second evening. The morning of the day of the concert she said, 'It has been a wonderful visit so far, and I hope and pray my voice lasts out so I give the performance I have come to give, and everybody is still speaking to me afterwards.' She did - and they were. She sang seventeen songs, finishing with *Volare*.

The Gracie Fields Theatre seats 670 people. Its stage is 90 feet wide and 33.5 feet deep. It has six microphone positions and a film projection facility. Council-owned and run, it is part of the Oulder Hill Complex and is three miles from the centre of Rochdale. During term time and daytime it is a school hall - in the evening a theatre. It cost £800,000 to build. The architects were the Greenhaigh and Williams Partnership. It is modern, with sharp corners and angles from the outside, but Gracie, for the evening she was there, did what she had done before, what she used to tell people to imagine - she turned it into everyone's front room with a piano and a group of friends (who overflowed into a hall outside, to which the concert was relayed).

Gracie said to her audience at the end of the concert, 'Tonight has been one of the most wonderful, fabulous moments of my life. It's like a dream. Thank you for making it come true. At eighty it's wonderful having a theatre named after you, as long as I don't have to come back tomorrow and clean it.'

And for many in that audience who knew her when she did in fact help her mumma scrub the stage at the Rochdale Hippodrome, and for others who knew she had done so in her youth, it proved yet again how close to her roots Gracie was.

The reviews the following day were vigorous. 'She was bathed in spotlights and showered with flowers (was there a living bloom left in Rochdale that didn't end up at her feet?)' asked Jack Tinker of the *Daily Mail*.

'The Grand Lady of Rochdale, 80 year old Gracie Fields, sang her heart out at a concert in her home town on Saturday night', wrote Ann Morrow of the *Daily Telegraph*.

'The hankies came out and the tears flowed as amazing Gracie launched into *Sally* with a voice which belied her 80 years', wrote David Thomas of the *Manchester Evening News*.

Before she left Britain, Gracie attended a Variety Artistes' Luncheon in Manchester where she was given a golden disc from Warwick Records for her contribution to the growth of the record industry, and a silver heart for her work for handicapped children. Rochdale MP Cyril Smith was there.

> The luncheon was in aid of a new kidney unit for Booth Hall Children's Hospital, and as we were moving from her room to join the assembled company she pressed a cheque into my hand for £500, and said quietly, 'Put that in the fund.' Then we went down to meet the other guests and the Press, and she bubbled over with excitement at the idea of being given a 'prize' for her contribution to the world's entertainment.

Gertie Sammon, who had been one of the crowd during the visit and watched Gracie open the market, also went to the railway station in the hope of seeing Gracie and Boris off. She bought a platform ticket, and, because the rheumatics in her knees were playing up pretty badly, was using her stick that day. She walked along the platform, and then she saw them, and smiled at Gracie through the window.

> Gracie got up and came to the door. I told her I just wanted to thank her for all the joy which had helped me through life, and to wish her and Boris a safe journey home. Gracie looked down at my walking stick, 'You shouldn't have come on those bad legs, my love, but thank you for coming to see us off.' She shook my hand. 'God bless you', she said, then the guard was closing the doors and she went back to her carriage and Boris, but she waved and smiled as the train pulled out.

This was the real Gracie - no publicity, no photographers, the simple human warmth of one person for another. You can't turn that kind of feeling on and off. She could have sat on that train and not come along to the door to talk, there was no photographer to record that kindly gesture, but it happened, and it is one of many such incidents throughout the years.

Back in Capri there was an enormous mail waiting to be answered. 'Often when she was supposed to be resting for an hour during the afternoon, the door would suddenly open and there she'd be, having just remembered something or other, or someone special that should take priority in being answered', Hazel Provost said. 'While I was sorting the mail, sometimes the door would re-open three or four times. She often complained that she couldn't sleep as her brain was jumping all over the place. In the end she used to get up and put the kettle on.' She had a passion for tea. In all her homes there were always lots of kettles, teapots, mugs and cups.

In November of that year, 1978, came the excitement, and it still was exciting to her, of an appearance at her tenth 'Royal Variety Show'. She practised each day from the moment she knew, keeping her voice 'easy'. 'I don't want to sound like an old lady.'

All the papers mentioned her the following day, with headlines reading, 'Gracie steals the Royal Show', 'Pride of our Alley surprise of the evening.' Afterwards she was among the artistes presented to the Queen Mother.

She was very proud of her Dameship, which came in the New Year honours. 'Dame Gracie - fancy that!' she signed a letter soon after, and on the back, 'I hope my friends will still think of me as "Our Gracie."' Then, that double edge again, the silly after the serious, 'As long as they don't call Boris "Buttons!"'

She sent hundreds of photographs to her fans and friends, many with a personal message on the back, and on these, her 'Dameship snaps', she wrote, sometimes in blue, sometimes in red and sometimes in green, 'The New Dame, Old Gracie'.

In April she went back to Capri with Boris and answered all the post that was waiting there. Derek Warman, who visited her soon after, says he will never forget the stack of letters in neat rows which covered the table and which she was working her way through.

Throughout the years her fans wrote whether she was working or not, and she was meticulous in answering them. 'I'm glued indoors until I get this mountain of mail answered. Took me two days just opening the envelopes.'

'Who wants to be a celebrity - Mama Mia, not this old gal, yet I simply must answer the dear folks who spend their money buying fab birthday and Christmas cards', she wrote to her family in 1972.

After a *Stars on Sunday* series:

So many more new fans write, they send me crazy yet I can't think of having a secretary now, they are more trouble than help, especially if they don't have a clue how to answer people, so this old lady gets it done eventually. It's not fair, you do a job folks enjoy, then have to pay for it thanking folks for the letters they send. Why don't they leave their addresses out, but they nearly all ask some silly question, so I've got to answer 'em, blow them all.

She *did* answer them, and she *did* appreciate them. 'They put me where I am and I love 'em all', she wrote later, 'Just that now and then I go on strike like everyone else.'

When she was talking of selling The Haven she said:

At eighty I can't think of a better place than we have here. I'm not rushing things, after all a woman is always changing her mind. When I'm home I enjoy it very much, but if I was always around I'm afraid I'd be worried with invitations to keep on with my old job and with this continuous shingles it's quite impossible. They give me hell sometimes.

Five years before she had written:

> So many callers and no servants, excepting our old Maria
> who shouts at us every day. She battles along, and when I say
> battle I mean battle, shouts at all of us, Boris and me too, but
> she's such a worker. Still no other person seems to be able to
> work with her except the old cook. I believe she calls us all
> sorts of terrible names - as I don't understand the lingo it
> doesn't bother me.

> I've so many wonderful cards and letters this year. They do
> give me a lot of hours at this machine, besides cost of stamps
> and cards, and I really dislike writing at any time.

Her orders for Capri postcards must have been enormous, and
although she had lived there for so long she always maintained
her knowledge of Italian was minimal. 'I can talk to the children,
I can sing it and I know enough not to get rooked', she said.

When she was working she had employed secretaries of course,
but there would not have been enough work for a full time one
now, even if she could have found one that suited.

In July 1979 Gracie fell ill. All her life she was prone to
bronchitis, but this time she was taken to a Naples hospital
with bronchial pneumonia. She was there for six weeks, and
when she returned home, looking very frail, she set about
answering the further piles of mail on her table. 'The Good
Lord isn't ready for this old gal yet, so slowly each day I'm
getting stronger', she wrote to her friends.

Hazel Provost, who went out to help look after her, and to
keep the pile of letters to a reasonable level, said, 'She seemed
to recover well enough to enjoy the company of her gorgeous
little great nephew Guy from Australia, and was soon looking
after the flowers once more, and occasionally we would go "up
to the big city" as she often called the town of Capri, to "see
what was new", but she tired much more easily.'

Her great nephew, Guy (Michael Stansfield's son, and her
brother Tom's grandson), was seven then, and each afternoon

he and Gracie spent time together. The rapport she had with people, big or little, old or young, never left her.

On Thursday 20 September, one week before Gracie died, she, Boris and Hazel had lunch in Anacapri. Hazel said, 'I remember the flowers on the table and the waiters fussing around - she seemed very happy and she enjoyed the meal.'

On Thursday 27 September she woke, commented on what a lovely day it was and said she would go for a little walk after breakfast. She never went for that walk. She had a heart attack and died.

Gracie was buried in Capri, after a service in the garden of Canzone del Mare. The six pall-bearers, dressed in white teeshirts and black trousers, and who worked in the restaurant, attended the coffin. They paused for a poignant moment on the terrace to salute the view she had loved. Island taxis and five of Capri's buses took the mourners to the cemetery at Anacapri.

It had been a wonderful last year. The Rochdale concert, the Dameship, and the knowledge that so many folk cared. When she died, the flag on Rochdale Town Hall, as on many other buildings, was flown at half-mast, and a photograph of Gracie, taken by Clifford Ashton on her last visit in 1978, was hung in the reception hall of the new municipal offices.

The manager of a bingo hall decided not to announce the news because he said so many elderly people who loved her were there, and the shock to many of them might be too heartbreaking.

One lady, whom a radio reporter told of Gracie's death, passed out in the street in the centre of Rochdale and was taken to a chemist's shop to recover.

This sorrow was reflected in hundreds of hearts and homes throughout the country that day when the news broke. A young reporter from the *Sunday Post* was sitting on a bus in Glasgow at lunchtime on Thursday 27th September. He was beside a pensioner and says he could not help but notice she was distressed. When he asked her if there was anything wrong, she said, with tears in her eyes, 'Oh son, I've just heard Gracie Fields has died.'

She was much more than a star, more than a public figure in people's lives: to so many she was a real friend, someone who cared how they were making out, someone who was very much a part of their lives. A week after she died quite a lot of people received their final, treasured postcard from her.

A few weeks afterwards there were memorial services, one in Peacehaven, one in Rochdale and one in London.

The Rochdale service took place on 20th October at the parish church where her parents had married and she and her sisters and brother were christened. The vicar, the Reverend Canon Hoyle, said, 'Friends, we meet together in this parish church to worship God, Father, Son and Holy Spirit, and to give thanks for the life and the work of Gracie Fields. We remember especially the tremendous pleasure she has given to so many people of so many generations in our own land and beyond the shores, and her immense zest and love for people.'

The Mayor of Rochdale read the first lesson, Miss Violet Carson (Ena Sharples from Coronation Street) read the second lesson, and the Reverend Canon David Clegg of St Margaret's, Prestwich, and chaplain to the Actors' Church Union, gave the address. Over five hundred people crowded into the church, family, local dignitaries, actors, actresses and ordinary folk.

The London service was held in St Martin's in the Fields on 15th November. It was a beautiful service, simple, dignified, very moving. There were large daisies (which she loved) in varying shades of pink either side of the altar, and a full congregation. The Reverend Austin Williams conducted the service, Michael Parkinson read the lesson, Roy Hudd gave the address, and Elizabeth Harwood sang *Ave Maria*.

Afterwards, on the steps of St Martin's, with the first drops of rain beginning to fall, the congregation mingled. This was the atmosphere, a getting together of friends on this sad occasion.

The Peacehaven service took place in the village church where Jenny and Fred Stansfield are buried. Annette Stansfield, Gracie's sister-in-law, said:

> You saw what Gracie really meant to the people at that service. They trudged over the downs, and it wasn't an easy journey for many of them. It was an autumnal morning, very chilly; people came on horseback, on foot, in cars, and the service was relayed into the village. It was beautiful.
>
> We had a telephone call from a lady called Beatrice Hockley who was in her nineties. She wanted to come very badly, but there was no transport, so Tom went for her. He brought her to the church, and during the service we asked her to get up and say something about Gracie. She had no idea we were going to do this. She had brought a little picture of Gracie with her, and she propped it up in front of the pew and said, 'I'm a widow, and I was ever so lonely, and I've written to Gracie and she's always written back.' We had never heard of her until she rang up, and she was only one of hundreds.

At that service the veterans of Dunkirk, who had kept in touch with Gracie for so many years, asked if they might come and form a guard of honour, and if they could bring a poppy wreath for Gracie and put it on her mother and father's grave, which they did.

There were tributes on radio and television here and abroad. American radio put out a two hour show about her life, and national and local newspapers printed articles and memories. In January 1980 a limited edition of a china memorial plate was made. In white, green and gold, it shows Gracie in full song at her 1978 Rochdale concert when she was eighty years old.

A Memorial Appeal was launched in Rochdale which raised over £10,000, with money contributed from fans all over the country, and including £1,000 from Bielefeld, Rochdale's twin town in Germany. The money was spent on new equipment for the Moorland Children's Home and on a pathway being constructed leading to the home (it had been a rough track before) which is now called 'The Gracie Fields Way'.

Many people would like to see a statue of Gracie in the Memorial Gardens, but the face of Rochdale, as of most of our towns and villages, has changed tremendously during the last thirty years, and many of the folk who live there now know Gracie only as a name and not as a person.

In their wills, Gracie and Boris left everything to each other, and then on to Gracie's family. During her lifetime Gracie had earned and given away millions of pounds, much of it to hospitals and good causes. She took care of everybody she wanted to before she died, made her own personal bequests to people and said (in the will) that anyone who contested or attacked it would be bequeathed one dollar only.

Until the last few months of her life on earth Gracie had seemed nothing like her age. At eighty she was still singing to the tourists who came to Capri. The restaurant had been in other hands (Jenny and Giorgio Iacono's) since 1977.

Tommy Keen went to Capri every year. He became such a fan that Gracie used to suggest that people who wanted her records should write to him. 'I've sent her records and music all round the world,' he said.

Ray Rastall, champion cocktail maker (he has won numerous cups and trophies) named a cocktail after her: *Our Gracie - my personal tribute to a great Artiste and Lady.* Ingredients are gin, Cointreau, grapefruit and orange juice.

Boris stayed on in Capri after Gracie died, visiting his wife's grave each day when he was well enough. They had set up a 'trophy room' in the Anacapri villa to show certificates and awards Gracie earned during her career. In the last years of her life she did 'get things together a bit', and left a bequest to Rochdale Museum of the casket containing the Freedom of Rochdale scroll, theatre posters, programmes and song sheets of some of the numbers forever associated with her.

After Boris died in 1986, all this, along with her bush hat with the badges of some of the regiments she entertained during the war, went north, and Debbie Walker and her team at

Rochdale Museum set up a brilliant exhibition showing various aspects of Gracie's life.

It was opened by comedian Roy Hudd, who said in the foreword to my first biography of Dame Gracie (published in 1983), 'She was the greatest female artiste we have ever produced. She touched my heart when she sang love songs and my funny bone when she sang comic ones. She was, before the word had even been invented, a superstar.'

21. Our Gracie

Of her three husbands the longest period was with Boris (twenty-seven years), but it wasn't all sweetness and light. He had a white hot temper and this was often in evidence. Many people thought she was afraid of Boris, and at one period this was possibly true. He ruled the roost, and for the sake of peace and quiet Gracie conformed. Not always of course, but most of the time.

She would have liked to have come back to England to live, but kept Capri on too, and she could have afforded to do this.

Boris, however, did not wish to leave Capri, even for a few months each year. Her idea was the spring and autumn in England, and the winter and summer (when everyone came out to see her and have a holiday at the same time) in Capri.

In the early days of their marriage Gracie would have done a lot more work if Boris had been more co-operative about it. She was then still singing at top level, and had the vitality to tackle doing something she loved. She thrived on the receptions she received from her audiences. In many ways her greatest love affair was with them, and that lasted for ever. Not even Boris could stifle the depth of feeling between Gracie Fields and her subjects. He tried, but eventually acknowledged he had to share her.

Their marriage survived several crises, really deep ones, but out of it all a true love for each other grew, and in those last years it was Boris who looked after Gracie.

Her first marriage to Archie Pitt was a disaster on the personal level for them both. Archie was so much more worldly wise than Gracie at that stage in their lives, and in any case there was no love on either side. He thought she would be able to cope with the situation, and maybe when they married she thought so too, but she couldn't. She was totally out of her depth.

Archie did marry Annie Lipman after the divorce, but eleven months later he died from cancer of the liver. He wasn't a ruthless man, but he was a complex one, and Gracie, although she often said she was a simple lass, was as complicated as most of us are, given various circumstances. The only thing she and Archie had in common was show business and when Gracie became the nation's darling even that link went. She had discovered the love she needed, a passionate, adoring love from her audiences, which both fulfilled and sometimes frightened her by its intensity.

Although she didn't marry John Flanagan, he was another important love in her life. Before him there had only been a brief light romance with the brother of a friend, and that when she was very young and more in love with the idea of love than with the person. John was her first real true love, and she never forgot him. Had they married it might not have worked, but it gave her a few years of happiness and a certain amount of anguish too. Maybe she even idealised him in her mind to a certain extent after he died in 1976.

Monty Banks was her husband, lover, child, and friend all rolled into one. He gambled, flirted, drank, worked and played hard, but he loved her. They understood each other. Their years together brought happiness and heartache, and if he had lived it is possible they would have adopted a child, or children.

They were comfortable with each other, and both did what they could to improve conditions for people. Monty's tenant farmers were all provided with the latest agricultural implements, and a new house with bathroom and central heating. Gracie understood this aspect of his character so well, this need to help his own.

He brought genuine fun and laughter back to her life. In a working environment he was completely professional, as she was, but in his private life he was often very irresponsible and in a way this tied in with her impulsiveness. His tragic early death left a gap in her defences as well as in her heart.

Gracie Fields was a star through the 1930s, 40s, 50s, 60s and 70s - five decades, and although she did much less during the last two, the mention of her name, or one of her songs, recalls memories for thousands who saw her and for many more who heard her on record, radio or television.

In the 1950s when long playing records first came in, there was an assessment of the bestsellers in the first three months. The result was interesting - Harry Roy sold 20,000 copies, Stanley Holloway, 25,000, and Gracie 30,000.

She never made a film of her life, it was suggested many times, but Gracie herself vetoed it. In 1956 when she was fifty-eight years old, they talked of doing so.

'No,' she said, 'I'm not that doddery yet. They want me to sit in a rocking chair and say, "Now let me see, lass, what was I doing back in 1910?" That's not for me. I hate going backwards, I like going forward. That's what keeps me young.'

Fifteen years later when the subject resurfaced she said, 'I'm not superstitious, luv, if I have to go, well I'll have to go, that's all there is to it, but doing a life story is tantamount to saying you've had it - that you're going to drop down dead any minute, and I'm not ready to say or do that yet.'

Various actresses did go to Capri to meet her from time to time, the idea behind the meeting being that of a life story. She had her own ideas on who should play her, first choice being Maggie Smith. She also wanted to do the singing herself, or use her own recordings. Nothing came of it during her lifetime, although it was still being talked about just a few weeks before her death, when John Taylor took details of the project from her agent, Lillian Aza, to Capri.

Being Gracie Fields cost Grace Stansfield much of her private life during the first few of the famous years, when she was recognised and mobbed almost everywhere. She learned to cope with this in her usual twofold way, with dignity and fun.

She was an interpreter of moods. There were so many Gracies, elegant, sentimental, realistic, vulnerable, romantic, funny, blunt, serious. She reflected all of them through her songs, and in doing so transmuted them into golden magic.

The essence of Gracie was in her voice, all the feeling inside came out this way. She often sang the verse too, 'The lyricist took the trouble to write a verse and it's part of the song, it complements the chorus, or it should do', she used to say.

Gracie was in her natural element when she was singing. Anywhere, from a stage to a street, a mountain top to a mine, as long as she could sing, she could communicate fully. For some it's dancing, painting, writing, talking... Gracie came across to people through her voice. 'Come on, folks, I want to tell you something', she'd say, and go straight into a song.

Gracie didn't build a wall around herself, she spun a shell. It was very thin, like fine eggshell, but it was there. It was a protection. A protection from what? Intrusion, invasion of her privacy? So much of her seemed to be public property, but there was a cut off point. She needed her protective shell.

Gracie gave generously in every way - money, time and talent. She was often naive, but never stupid. She hated fuss, bigotry and pompousness, and admired loyalty, kindness and hard work. She enjoyed people of any creed or colour, and she judged them by what they were, or what she thought they were.

As with most of us, sometimes she was caught - in her position it was easy to be conned, and it did make her withdraw into herself over the years; but it never stopped her from the giving which was as natural to her as breathing. Her heart was infinitely generous, and she left a legacy of kindness which stretches throughout the world.

The magic she created embraced everyone willing to receive it. It was almost touchable, and never remote. There was so much rich talent contained in one personality, and it spilled over into every branch of theatre. Many actresses are brilliant in their own field, she explored and conquered a wide and varied area.

In 1934 in the *West Lancashire Gazette* a Mr Gregson wrote
that Gracie Fields could lead a revolution if she wanted.

> Thank heaven she harbours no such insane desire. All the
> same if I were the organiser of any political party I should at
> once move heaven and earth to bind her to my machine. Her
> personal appeal is more powerful than that of any political
> spellbinder I know, and she arouses more real enthusiasm
> and commands more genuine affection and loyalty than any
> statesman. Never in my life have I witnessed such amazing
> demonstrations of the *power* of one individual over massed
> humanity.

It *was* a kind of magnetism which happens to only a few.
Combined with her talents, ambition, and the dreams of her
mother, it manifested itself for the good of the people.

The depths and the richness, the quality of her voice need to
be recorded. Print is a poor substitute, but it is better than
nothing. The records and tapes will fade, break or wear thin.
The way she was as a person too, the glory of Gracie cannot be
captured within the pages of a book, but if a glimpse of what
she was can be gleaned from her story...

She was about all of humanity, the fun and the sorrow. She
depicted it for us with her songs, but more than that in the
colours of her voice because, as the *Times* said in its obituary of
her:

> The excellence of her singing at one time seemed a menace to
> her performance, for the sentimental ditties on which she
> lavished so much artistry were quite unworthy of her talent.
> Early in her career she had an entrancing trick of indicating
> her real opinion of these tearful ballads by introducing into
> the middle of her song some ludicrous trick of voice, or by
> absentmindedly scratching her back between high notes.

As an artiste she was supreme and reached millions of people.
She touched their lives, but, never content to be a figure alone

on the stage, she followed her own advice, which she once gave to Lord Miles; she reached down into her audience with her inner being, and she touched hearts with vast multitudes of them.

She was idolised and spurned during her career, and, to quote from Rudyard Kipling's poem, *If*:

> If you can meet with triumph and disaster,
> And treat those two impostors just the same...

She did. There is much more in that verse which fits, but I'll simply mention one line more, 'Or walk with Kings nor lose the common touch.' Gracie did that all her life. She never lost the common touch, and she managed it all without patronising and without sycophancy - simply by being her natural self.

Although enrapturing her audience en masse, she made each one love her individually too. It was a very personal feeling as well as the excitement of being part of this experience. For seeing Gracie on stage, being in the theatre with her, was a magical, uplifting experience.

During the course of research I am often asked, 'Was "Our Gracie" a myth? Someone created by Archie Pitt and continued by the publicity barons?'

No. It was sometimes an embarrassment to her, for there were many, many other aspects in her character, but she did embody the traits of Our Gracie. Written down it sounds sentimental, in the flesh it wasn't, it was real and true. In any case Gracie was a very sentimental person, keeping treasured letters and notes in folders, and re-reading many times things she loved. She was also a very down to earth person, outspoken and often stubborn.

When she was going to marry Boris Alperovici, Lillian Aza and Mary Davey asked her to wait a while, to be sure she was doing the right thing, but she would *not* listen to them. She always 'cut the cackle' and went right to the heart of the matter over anything she was involved in. Straight there in the most direct manner.

She often said something which reporters took to be true and printed, with headlines of course, then she would say it was nonsense. They had to decide when she meant it and when she was spoofing. Quite often she *had* meant it when she said it, and it was hard to retract once it was published, so she resorted to saying 'Sheer rubbish.'

Apart from this, she was good to journalists, appreciating that they were doing a job even as she was. Sometimes she delighted in being tactless, especially if she didn't like the person.

In the early days she mostly did as she was told by whoever was in charge. In that era people did. Gracie couldn't afford not to, because from quite a young woman she became the breadwinner of the family. If she hadn't made it on the stage her father, Fred, would possibly have continued working at Robinsons until he retired.

In Gracie's formative years her mother's influence was the dominant one, but her father's wit and stamina were very much in evidence too, and she always acknowledged her parents' sacrifices for her career.

'Basically I'm lazy, if it had been left to me I might have worked in the mill all me life, if I'd managed to keep my job that is.' Being lazy was a flight of fancy on her part, for she worked hard most of her life. She enjoyed 'singing for me supper' as she often called it.

In 1970 she gave a moving performance when she recorded the Frank Sinatra classic, *My Way*, and in 1975, when she was seventy-seven years old she sang a Shirley Bassey number, *Never, Never, Never*, with the passion of a young woman. She recorded her signature tune, *Sally*, thirteen times, between 1931 and 1975. These are original recordings, there are of course, many re-issues.

Her life spanned five reigns, from Queen Victoria to Queen Elizabeth II. She met three Royal generations personally, King George V and Queen Mary, King George VI and Queen Elizabeth, and Queen Elizabeth II and Prince Philip.

The Duke of Windsor, when he was Prince of Wales, attended several of Gracie's concerts, often accompanied by the then

Mrs Wallis Simpson, who later became the Duchess of Windsor. Gracie was a favourite with several members of the Royal Family, especially the Queen Mother. The admiration was mutual for Gracie revered her and was delighted when she learned the 'Queen Mum' was officiating when she received her DBE.

She was amazed as well as thrilled when, in 1956, the Queen postponed her appearance on the balcony until Gracie's programme on television was over. 'I was so touched and I felt very humble indeed', she said when she was told.

Sir Anton Dolin always took Gracie white tuber roses, and after she died he kept one by her photograph. Several years before, they had been talking of death and she expressed the wish that she should die before Boris.

'I don't want to be left alone again.' Then she said, half joking and half serious, 'I'll have to marry you, Anton. We'd be all right together, how d'you fancy the idea?' Beneath the jokey lightheartedness was a very real fear.

Madame Tetrazzini, who all those years before had tried to persuade her into opera, would go to see only one performer when she came to Britain - Gracie Fields.

Gracie had a tremendous amount of natural energy and stamina - she had to have stamina to undertake the often gruelling tours she did, and in her younger days she thrived on them. Later she felt the effects - during the 1947 Working Parties she was often far from well.

She always wanted to be doing something, although in the latter years she did relax more. 'I drove myself hard in the early days,' she said, 'almost burnt myself out once or twice. I thought of my work as a hard job. I loved it but it was strenuous.'

Over her work Gracie was a perfectionist. She made it look easy, tossing off remarks at interviews about 'trying out the old voice, one or two notes, yes, it's still there luv, we'll have a go.' In fact she was ever conscious of the trust her audiences had in her, and always made sure her voice was to concert standard. For herself too she wanted the very best she was capable of. She was relentless in her pursuit of doing a good job.

When she talked about retiring, which she did frequently, she used to say, 'Sometimes I don't know if I could do it - retire. I know I'm a restless sort of lass. Yet if I don't, there's the danger of looking like an old crock. I think maybe it's better if I pack it in.' That usually meant that the next time someone wanted her to do a tour she refused three times instead of one before she agreed. This was something apart from Boris's desire for her permanent retirement when she was still at her peak.

Gracie loved the theatre and knew it so well. She felt at home in the environment, and, like her mother before her, when she was in London or America she went to see as many shows as she could. Her work was tremendously important to her wellbeing.

She said that when she was badly nervous she went right back to the kind of singing her mother taught her when she was a child. As loud as possible. She used this approach in other ways than singing too. She was in control if it was anything to do with the theatre, but when she was nervous in other situations she resorted to the loudness. 'I couldn't help it, it's just the way it came out in me I suppose.'

Her talent was an all-round one. It had its heart in the music hall, but, because she was born too late for the peak of that era, she reached an even larger public. Through records, radio, television and films, millions of people saw and heard Gracie Fields.

The best of Gracie the artiste was in the theatre. There you caught the magic of the love affair between performer and audience. In the theatre Gracie gave her heart completely while she was on stage, and the thousands who watched and listened gave theirs. She turned a huge theatre into everyone's front room, and she lit up that room as two people do for each other, and a very few people can do for hundreds and thousands of others. 'God gave me the wonderful gift of providing laughter', she said.

That unique quality she had - that was as much at home being serious or comic - blended with the more private side of Gracie that knew about people.

Gracie the woman, or Grace, as many of her friends called her, was her other self. Between the two were the gamut of images she created, the many-faceted diamond that gave off sparks of colour and fire, that could be unpredictable and unfathomable, laughing and loving, practical and proper, noisy and nervous, innocent and inspired.

As long ago as February 1933, R.H. Naylor, the well-known astrologer, wrote:

> Speaking as a student of human nature I must confess that Gracie Fields fascinates me. In both her face and her horoscope there are unmistakable signs of unquenchable ambition, of a will that brooks no opposition.
>
> At birth the sun was placed in the sign of Capricorn, a group of stars which is symbolised by an animal climbing to the mountain top; then one remembers that she is born with the moon in Leo, and Jupiter in Libra. Leo stands for a royal generosity, an indomitable pride.
>
> Jupiter's position in Libra adds a fierce sense of justice, but emphasises the prodigal generosity of Gracie's nature. Who, either among audiences or personal friends can resist such a battery of magnetic qualities?
>
> The older Gracie becomes the more Gracie will be a law unto herself. I am grateful to Gracie Fields, for her horoscope sheds light on a question that has long puzzled me. You see a sense of humour and a willingness to be funny at the expense of 'refinement' is as rare among women as nuts in May.
>
> Miss Fields has yet to experience her greatest successes. About 1935 the sun in her progressed horoscope reaches the conjunction of Venus. This means money; it means still more fame; above all it means happiness. Somehow or other, the vivid, lovable, and strenuous thing which is the soul of Gracie

Fields will for a time find peace and content. But, mark you, only Gracie Fields will know about it!

Miss Fields strikes a bad patch about 1941 or 1942, but centres of propitious periods are marked as for (roughly) 1944 and 1949.

1935 was the year she signed the contract for £50,000 a film, met Monty Banks, toured South Africa and was blossoming rapidly from a rather naive woman who did what others, 'the bosses', told her into a kind of maturity that could cope graciously with any situation, yet please herself. And of course the early forties brought the 'patch' mentioned when there was trouble over her marrying and leaving Britain with Monty Banks. She did also become very much more 'a law unto herself as she grew older'.

John Clennell, in 1934, wrote a column for the *Telegraph*, called 'Faces of Destiny', and in August he featured Gracie Fields.

Her high wide forehead indicates intellect, reason, judgement, and intuition. Her high forehead centre shows that she is sympathetic, kind and benevolent, shrewd and farseeing.

She is capable of understanding and penetrating the character and motives of others. Her first impressions are best. She has a youthful spirit and knows how to put people at ease in her company. She is organised on a high key of mental action, is susceptable to surrounding influences, and is capable of keen enjoyment and suffering.

Exceedingly active, she dislikes a sedentary life. She is outspoken, frank, and candid. The full outer corners of her forehead denote a remarkable disposition and capacity to make fun, to joke, to perceive absurdities and the ludicrous. Wonderful gifts to make other folk laugh.

It is interesting how much of this proved true during Gracie's lifetime. Both were written in the early 1930s.

If Gracie hadn't gone on the stage, she would probably still have been involved with the welfare of others, because it was so much a part of her nature. She cared about humanity and did what she could to help when it came to her ears that help was needed - not just with money, although she gave plenty of that over the years, some with publicity, much without. Gracie gave her presence, her time and herself; for when she was there, every ounce of her was concentrating, she gave wholeheartedly. It sapped her, and, as was mentioned earlier, it very often exhausted the recipients, but it exhilarated them too, the full force of Gracie's dynamic personality cannot be denied.

Actor Roddy McDowall said, 'Being with Gracie was like having an inoculation, or a shot of oxygen about living, a good punch in the shoulder. She lived, everything that landed on her plate she took, and dealt with.'

Often very noisy, yet she loved tranquillity, and throughout all the jealousies within a family and among fans, which arose as they do almost everywhere there are people, she strove to maintain a state of unity. More than anything else, she wanted everyone to live in peace together.

'Wendell Wilkie wrote a book called *One World*', she said in 1946 after her years of entertaining troops all over the globe, 'and if I ever get round to writing about my travels I think I'll call it "One Folk." A smile you know is the same in any language and among every nationality.'

The public's perception of her was of a jolly, carefree comedienne with a wonderful operatic voice, and a warmth that reached out to them all. She was everyone's sister, best friend and girl next door. The inner circle knew the serious Gracie was at least fifty per cent of the person.

Of all the different mediums in which Gracie worked, she loved the theatre best. She hated filming at one time, although she grew to enjoy it more when Monty was directing her. Radio and television she took in her stride, especially if there was an audience, although as she grew older she admitted she liked it less.

'Television is for young people', she said. 'It's cruel on artistes who are getting on in years a bit - not just the close-ups but the whole business, getting dressed up, made up, the lot. I'd rather be with an audience than have a man pointing a black box at me.'

Apart from microphones in the theatre, which she didn't like for herself, Gracie was all for progress. In the summer of 1929 when the Variety Artistes Federation appealed to the public to boycott music halls which were currently being wired for sound so they could feature the 'talkies', Gracie took the opposite view.

'You might as well try to stop the sun from shining as try to stop the "talkies",' she said. 'The public will naturally want to see them - why shouldn't they? But good shows will always survive the "talkies". Remember when cinemas first became popular. Everyone thought that silent films would kill the theatrical profession then, but they didn't. We must always be prepared for new ideas and new machinery to come along.'

When she was banned (along with others) from radio because theatrical management thought it would stop people coming to the shows, she condemned it as shortsighted. 'You have to go with the times. I'm sure wireless won't stop people going to the theatre, it will simply be an added medium to work in.' She was proved right of course, and the ban was soon lifted.

Gracie was happy to sing for people anywhere, in a taxi, on a bus, outside in the street if the mood took her and them. She enjoyed singing for the sheer joy of it, but that didn't make it easy to have the career she had.

'Every time a song went over well I thought, good - that was all right, but how do I top it? Always it was a constant worry to keep up.'

She never gave less than the best she was capable of, and she refused to do three shows a night as time went on, because 'I couldn't do justice to them.'

Her delicious humour often involved sending herself up. The words she wrote to *Volare* always received a clap as well as a laugh when she sang them, for no one begrudged her the rewards of her labour because she somehow made it seem that she took each of them with her to the top.

> For a beautiful home by the sea,
> You've all helped to build it for me,
> ['True, it's true' - laughing with her audience]
> Without you where would I be?
> Most certainly not in Capri - Thank you.

Gracie touched many lives, and in the telling of her story, the facts and figures of her life, one is left with enormous joy because she lived. She drew from her audiences as they drew from her, mentally she always joined hands with them so that the stage and the auditorium became a huge circle singing together. She inspired loyalty to the utmost degree, kept up with the modern world and retained all that seemed best to her of the old.

Nobody could mix the fun and the seriousness so well, in neither did she ever lose the essence. The fun was no less funny for being underlined by the solemn, and the serious lost nothing by the merriment which had gone before, or would come after. Each was a perfect cameo which joined together to make a whole, each another link in the chain that swung out above all else to people to grasp and to continue.

In assessing Gracie Fields the artiste, one has the achievements to go on; in assessing Gracie Fields the woman, we have the testimonial of the people, the mass of humanity who loved her and whom she loved above all else. Queen Elizabeth, the Queen Mother, said, 'I admired Dame Gracie very much.' Countless other fans and friends said, 'We loved Our Gracie...'

Shows and Revues

REVUES

1915	Yes, I Think So
1916	It's A Bargain
1918	Mr Tower of London
1925	By Request
1928	Topsy & Eva (stand-in)
1929	The Show's The Thing
1931	Walk This Way

ROYAL VARIETY SHOWS

1st March	1928	London Coliseum
11th May	1931	London Palladium
15th November	1937	London Palladium
3rd November	1947	London Palladium
13th November	1950	London Palladium
29th October	1951	Victoria Palace
3rd November	1952	London Palladium
4th November	1956	London Palladium (cancelled due to Suez crisis)
18th November	1957	London Palladium
2nd November	1964	London Palladium
13th November	1978	London Palladium

Filmography

1931 *Sally In Our Alley*
Directed by Maurice Elvey. Cast included Ian Hunter, Florence Desmond, Fred Groves, Gibb McLaughlin, Ben Field.

1932 *Looking On The Bright Side*
Directed by Basil Dean. Cast included Richard Dolman, Julien Rose, Wyn Richmond, Toni De Lungo, Betty Shale, Bettina Montahners, Viola Compton.

1933 *This Week Of Grace*
Directed by Julius Hagen. Cast included Henry Kendall, John Stuart, Helen Haye, Marjorie Brooks, Frank Pettingell, Minnie Rayner, Douglas Wakefield, Nina Boucicault, Vivien Foster, Lawrence Hanray.

1934 *Sing As We Go*
Directed by Basil Dean. Cast included John Loder, Dorothy Hyson, Stanley Holloway, Frank Pettingell, Lawrence Grossmith, Morris Harvey, Arthur Sinclair, Marie O'Neill, Ben Field, Olive Sloane, Margaret Yarde, Evelyn Roberts, Norman Walker, Richard Grey, Margery Pickard, James R. Gregson, Florence Gregson. The script was by J. B. Priestley.

1934 *Love, Life And Laughter*
Directed by Maurice Elvey. Cast included John Loder, Veronica Brady, Norah Howard, Allan Aynesworth, Esme Percy, Ivor Barnard, Bromley Davenport, Esme Church, Eric Maturin, Fred Duprez, Robb Wilton, Horace Kenney.

1935 *Look Up And Laugh*
Directed by Basil Dean. Cast included Robb Wilton, Harry Tate, Tommy Fields, Vivien Leigh. The script was by J. B. Priestley.

1936 *Queen Of Hearts*
Directed by Monty Banks. Cast included John Loder, Enid Stamp-Taylor.

1937 *The Show Goes On*
Directed by Basil Dean. Cast included Owen Nares, John Stuart, Arthur Sinclair, Horace Hodges, Cyril Richards.

1937 *We're Going To Be Rich* (In USA called *He Was Her Man*)
Directed by Monty Banks. Cast included Victor McLaglen, Brian Donlevy, Coral Browne, Ted Smith, Gus McNaughton, Charles Carson, Syd Crossley, Hal Gordon, Robert Nainby, Charles Harrison, Tom Payne, Don McCorkindale, Joe Mott, Alex Davies.

1938 *Keep Smiling*
Directed by Monty Banks. Cast included Roger Livesey, Mary
Maguire, Peter Coke, Edward Rigby, Jack Donahue, Mike
Johnson, Eddie Gray, Nina Rosini, Tommy Fields.

1939 *Shipyard Sally*
Directed by Monty Banks. Cast included Sydney Howard,
Bromley Davenport, Oliver Wakefield.

1943 *Stage Door Canteen*
Directed by Frank Borzage. Cast included brief appearance of
many stars and top-line orchestras. Gracie sang 'The Lord's Prayer'
and 'The Machine Gun Song'.

1943 *Holy Matrimony*
Directed by John Stahl (from the book *Buried Alive* by Arnold
Bennett). Cast included Monty Woolley, Laird Cregar, Una
O'Connor.

1945 *Mollie And Me*
Directed by Lewis Seiler. Cast included Monty Woolley, Roddy
MacDowall, Reginald Gardiner, Clifford Brooke, Aminta Dyne,
Edith Barratt, Queenie Leonard, Patrick O'Moore, Natalie
Schafer, Doris Lloyd, Lewis L. Russell, Ethel Griffies, Eric Wilton,
Jean Del Val.

1946 *Madame Pimpernel* (In USA called *Paris Underground*)
Directed by Gregory Ratoff. Produced by Constance Bennett.
Cast included Constance Bennett, George Rigaud, Kurt Kreuger,
Leslie Vincent, Charles Andre, Eily Maylon, Adrienne
d'Ambricourt, Richard Ryan, Gregory Gaye, Andre Charlot,
Harry Hays Morgan, Roland Varno, Dina Symrnova, Otto
Reichow, Fred Gierman, Eric von Morhardt.

Index